W9-DGI-352

Dilemmas of the Welfare Mix

The New Structure of Welfare
in an Era of Privatization

NONPROFIT AND CIVIL SOCIETY STUDIES
An International Multidisciplinary Series

Series Editor: Helmut K. Anheier
> *London School of Economics and Political Science*
> *London, United Kingdom*

CIVIL SOCIETY AND THE PROFESSIONS IN EASTERN EUROPE
Social Change and Organizational Innovation in Poland
S. Wojciech Sokolowski

DILEMMAS OF THE WELFARE MIX
The New Structure of Welfare in an Era of Privatization
Edited by Ugo Ascoli and Costanzo Ranci

MEASURING THE IMPACT OF THE NONPROFIT SECTOR
Edited by Patrice Flynn and Virginia A. Hodgkinson

NEIGHBORHOOD SELF-MANAGEMENT
Experiments in Civil Society
Hillel Schmid

PRIVATE FUNDS, PUBLIC PURPOSE
Philanthropic Foundations in International Perspective
Edited by Helmut K. Anheier and Stefan Toepler

WORKFORCE TRANSITIONS FROM THE PROFIT TO THE NONPROFIT SECTOR
Tobie S. Stein

Dilemmas of the Welfare Mix

The New Structure of Welfare
in an Era of Privatization

Edited by

UGO ASCOLI

University of Ancona
Ancona, Italy

and

COSTANZO RANCI

Polytechnic of Milan
Milan, Italy

KLUWER ACADEMIC / PLENUM PUBLISHERS
NEW YORK, BOSTON, DORDRECHT, LONDON, MOSCOW

ISBN 0-306-46779-8

©2002 Kluwer Academic/Plenum Publishers, New York
233 Spring Street, New York, New York 10013

http://www.kluweronline.com

10 9 8 7 6 5 4 3 2 1

A C.I.P. record for this book is available from the Library of Congress.

Printed in the United States of America

Contributors

Edith Archambault, Université de Paris 1 – Sorbonne, Matisse, Maison des Sciences Economiques, 106 Bd de l'Hopital, 75647 Paris Cedex 13, France

Ugo Ascoli, Universita di Ancona, Facolta di economia, Piazzale Martelli, 8, 60121 Ancona, Italy

Judith Boumendil, Université de Paris 1 – Sorbonne, Matisse, Maison des Sciences Economiques, 106 Bd de l'Hopital, 75647 Paris Cedex 13, France

Magne Eikås, Høgskulen i Sogn og Fjordane, Avdeling for Samfunnsfag, 6851 Sogndal, Norway

Adalbert Evers, Justus-Liebig-Universität Giessen FB 9, Bismarckstr. 37, D 35390 Giessen, Germany

Guida Obrador, CRID-Diputació de Barcelona, Salvador Mundi, 6, 08017 Barcelona, Spain

Emmanuele Pavolini, Istituto di Studi Storici, Sociologici e Linguistici, Facolta di Economia, Universita degli Studi di Ancona, Piazzale Martelli, n. 8, 60121 Ancona, Italy

Costanzo Ranci, Politecnico di Milano, DIAP, Via Bonardi 3, 20133 Milano, Italy

Sebastián Sarasa, Universitat Pompeu Fabra, Dpt. Ciencies Politiques I Socials, Ramon Trias Fargas, 25, 08005 Barcelona, Spain

Per Selle, Norwegian Research Center in Organization and Management, Rosenbergsqt. 39, 5015 Bergen, Norway

Christoph Strünck, Department for Political Sciences at the Heinrich Heine Universität, Düsseldorf, Universitätsstr. 1, D 40225 Düsseldorf

Marilyn Taylor, Health and Social Policy Research Centre, University of Brighton, Falmer, BNI 9PH, United Kingdom

Preface

This book is the result of collective research, which lasted several years and was conducted by scholars from six different European countries. When we first met to discuss this project, our main aim was to collect studies and develop a common framework for considerations on the deep transformations characterizing welfare policies, due to fiscal problems which emerged in the early 1990s. It seemed clear to us, at that time, that terms such as 'privatization', 'commercialization', 'contract culture' and 'new managerialism' were only partially adequate to picture what was happening, and that it was necessary to develop a type of analysis able to frame together empirical research with a deeper conceptual and theoretical insight.

The scholars engaged in the present research have agreed to participate in a quite complex project, aimed, at the same time, at an empirical analysis conducted on a national basis, at a theoretical study able to foster a common conceptual framework and at a collective effort for an ex post reexamination of the consistency and the strength of theoretical frameworks used in the research.

The book is not, therefore, just a presentation of national case studies. It is, instead, the result of a common reflection by all contributors and editors, even if the final responsibility for the aggregate outcome and the general (not single-country-based) chapters belongs to the editors.

As it happens usually in comparative studies, this one too needed quite a significant amount of financial resources. We must thank FiVol (Italian Foundation for Volunteering) for covering all expenses related to group meetings, which have involved up to 12 people. Two seminars, held in Rome in two different years, were organized to prepare the common framework of analysis. In the first seminar, the theoretical and general setting for the national case studies was discussed. In the second one, there was a primary presentation and a debate of drafts of single countries' chapters and discussion on how to develop a comparative cross-national analysis.

Due to the amount of data collected and the complexity of issues arising from them, it has been particularly difficult to shape the final version of this book. We thank Helmut Anheier for his interest in the overall approach followed by this research and for suggesting Plenum as a potential publisher for the present work.

Preliminary versions of different chapters and the main results of the whole study have been presented at international conferences organized by ISTR (International Society of Third Sector Research) and by ARNOVA

(American Research on Nonprofit Organization and Voluntary Action). We would like to thank all those who have given us useful comments, and, in particular, Diane Kaplan-Vinokur (University of Michigan), whose suggestions have been quite accurate and detailed.

Many different people have helped to make this book possible, and the contributors and the editors thank all of them. Among others we would like to acknowledge three people who have worked at FiVol—Renato Frisanco, Cesare Graziani and Luciano Tavazza—who have believed in this project and have facilitated it very much, making the two meetings in Rome quite pleasant and well organized, in the best tradition of Italian hospitality.

MILAN, November 2001
U.A. and C.R.

Contents

Dilemmas of the Welfare Mix

The New Structure of Welfare in an Era of Privatization

Chapter 1

The Context of New Social Policies in Europe

UGO ASCOLI AND COSTANZO RANCI*,[1]

1.1. INTRODUCTION

The last ten years have seen the diffusion of new social risks accompanied by profound demographic transformations and changes in the structure of employment in almost all the countries of the European Union. The crisis of the Fordist organization of work, the lengthening of average life expectancy and the increased instability of the family have all contributed in increasing social inequalities. At the same time a large part of the population of Europe is now exposed to social risk previously rare or confined to specific geographical regions or areas of society: homelessness, intolerance, new social pathologies determined by social isolation and the need for care are appearing. Furthermore, the increase in the demand for care is pervading social groups that until recently were used to satisfy this demand through public welfare provision; today they see access to the providence of welfare reduced as a consequence of rationing policies pursued by the governments of many European countries.

This new pattern of risks is hardly met by the current structure of European welfare systems. The social risks basically addressed by traditional welfare states, in both universalistic and occupational versions, are connected with very low incomes or the impossibility of maintaining a permanent job.

---

* UGO ASCOLI • Universita di Ancona, Facolta di economia, Piazzale Martelli, 8, 60121 Ancona, Italy. COSTANZO RANCI • Politecnico di Milano, DIAP, Via Bonardi 3, 20133 Milano, Italy.

What is emerging today, however, are insecure working careers on the one hand and, on the other, needs that can be satisfied more through care services rather than by cash benefits. Furthermore, these needs are no longer affecting only marginalized populations, but they increasingly concern the middle classes and are, therefore, becoming much more widespread.

Insurance programmes provided by welfare states are increasingly less capable of meeting these social needs effectively and this situation explains why attention has turned more and more, in recent years, to social services. Admittedly, they absorb a much smaller part of total welfare spending than government insurance and minimum income schemes; however, as welfare policies shift towards the provision of care services, social services are destined to assume a central role. In the words of a well-known welfare expert, 'social services have become increasingly more important ingredients in the make-up of the welfare state and it will be necessary to reorient research in this direction' (Alber, 1995, p. 132).

The growth of demand for social services, nevertheless, places a large part of government (both central and local) in a paradoxical situation: while on the one hand welfare policies have become increasingly more necessary to fight new social risks, on the other hand it seems impossible for them to expand further if they maintain their current organizational structure. The growth of demand is set against a background of difficulties to further expand and develop state welfare programmes. The fiscal and political limitations that are causing welfare policies to flounder, are not only putting insurance schemes and minimum income schemes under pressure, but they are also a serious obstacle to any attempt to widen government financial and management responsibility in the social services field.

Much of the public debate on the future destiny of social welfare policies has remained trapped within this paradox for a long time. The state's inability to expand its financial responsibility has long made it impossible for the growing demand for caring services to be satisfied. On the other hand, the public demand for a significant reduction in public welfare expenditure seemed to necessarily imply forgoing the development of social policies capable of tackling the new social risks with relative success. Since public debate took the current organizational structure achieved by national welfare systems for granted and as unalterable, it consequently became polarized between those who supported a policy of reducing the welfare state and those who sought to maintain it at existing levels.

The social services field has, nevertheless, seen the development of a complex of policies that have sought to modify the regulatory and organizational structure of the system of services. While at one time the considerable weight exercised historically by private institutions in this field (by the Church or labour unions—according to the country) acted as a brake on the modernization of these policies, more recently it seems to have constituted a valuable resource for a general reorganization of the system.

The most significant developments are as follows:

(a) a devolutionary process of financial and planning decentralization has been set in motion favouring local administrations, with the intention of providing more specialized service adapted to local requirements and of improving flexibility and efficiency in local decision making;

(b) management techniques and procedures typical of the private sector (based on the New Public Management approach) were introduced to social services; a revision of the incentives system was also started to guarantee more efficient performance (e.g. introduction of budget constraints, reduction of guaranteed benefits, procedures for monitoring performance, evaluating results, etc.);

(c) rationing methods have been accompanied by measures aimed at increasing private sector (non-profit and for-profit) activity destined to the production of welfare services: tax allowances for clients of private services and more generous tax incentives for donations, with new tax concessions for non-profit organizations, have been granted through legislative change at the state level;

(d) a clearer distinction between funding and service delivery has been pursued, with public authorities taking responsibility for finance and regulation, delegating actual service provision to private and/or non-profit organizations through contracting procedures.

The political meaning of these developments is not always uniform. In general, all the developments cited above could be implemented independently of whether public welfare expenditure is cut. Nevertheless, in reality many measures that have been adopted in various countries with the purpose of making savings in public expenditure do not involve too sharp a reduction in the level of service provision. In some sectors these measures have even allowed an increase in total provision while the state has actually withdrawn from its financial responsibilities. Elsewhere, however, the same measures have legitimized a more decisive policy of welfare expenditure cuts and have thus been strongly opposed by the stauncher defenders of the welfare state.

One of the main difficulties in assessing the political impact of these measures is the fact that they are often accompanied by great ideological uproar (both for and against). For example, in many countries the introduction of personal tax deductions for the purchase of private social services was considered an attack on the universalistic conception of welfare, even though this measure does not necessarily involve any reduction in the level of existing coverage of needs on the part of public welfare. The transition from the state's finance of private providers by means of grants to finance by contracts has often been considered an attempt to cut expenditure by transferring political responsibility for cuts to private providers. Nevertheless, the use of contracts to regulate state finance of services provided by private organizations indicates more, not less, government regulation.

Our main intention is to explore the impact that this set of measures has had on the organizational and institutional structure of the social services systems found today in Western European countries. Generally speaking, this wide range of policy and legislative changes is aimed at obtaining a significant reduction in the scale or scope of state intervention. The developments mentioned in points (a) and (b) above, are aimed at a reorganization of the public system based on the introduction of market mechanisms in the management of public organizations. Measures contained in points (c) and (d) entail a direct and intense involvement of private and non-profit organizations in welfare policies. The term that is generally used to summarize and describe the latter set of measures is 'privatization'. It in fact refers to policies aimed at increasing the proportion of functions performed by the private or the third sector, for which the state has responsibility.

The passage towards privatization, which began at the beginning of the 1980s, constitutes a turning point that is not yet adequately explained. It has aroused both positive and negative reactions in different national contexts. For a long period, privatization was identified with free market politics and economics aimed at a substantial reduction of state commitment to universal welfare policies. In this sense privatization was considered as an attempt to constitute a social care market, with the idea that a return to market forces and competition would result in more efficient and effective services. With the passage of time, however, privatization came to take on a more complex meaning that could not be reduced to the mere transfer of responsibility for management from the state to the private or the third sector. It required, not so much, a simple contraction of state commitment as a restructuring of its role. The introduction of competition into the field of social services necessitated the creation of a system of regulation to safeguard against the failures of the market. Furthermore, the transfer of state responsibility to private organizations substantially changed the latter in a direction which, on the one hand, is desirable (when it implies greater effectiveness and planning capacity) and, on the other hand, is worrisome (when it threatens the organization's original identity and mission, and compromises its flexibility and independence to act).

It can be said that, in the course of a decade, the ideological character of privatization policies has attenuated very considerably, and they are no longer identified with anti-state policies. Today these policies give life to new institutional and organizational forms that can be compared neither to those typical of the free market nor to those of a system dominated by the state. At the same time, they undoubtedly constitute one of the strategic areas to assess and predict the structure that mature welfare systems will assume in the future. They go beyond the idea of welfare policies aimed at the progressive extension of direct state responsibility for the provision of services to those in need. Once the echoes of the ideological battle that accompanied the first development have died down, privatization can be considered as one possible solution to the paradox mentioned at the beginning. In this context, privatization is based on the possibility of developing a *system with a plurality of supply*, capable of using a wide range of professional and financial resources and of developing diversified forms of service provision appropriate to the specific nature of the problems to be tackled.

Privatization, as considered here, thus constitutes the signal for a new organizational structure of welfare systems and also for the development of new forms of coordination between the various actors in the systems. It constitutes a very wide field not only of opportunities, but also of risks and dilemmas; there is great uncertainty over the consequences of this process on the equity and quality of the delivery system. In any case, privatization must be seen not only in relation to its advantages in terms of the efficiency, but also in relation to its impact on equality. While there may be substantial economic and organizational advantages to the development of privatization, it may also involve new forms of social and political exclusion.

Our purpose is to consider the theoretical thinking and empirical research aimed at describing the privatization process and its impact on the structure of welfare systems. First, we present two forms of privatization that have occurred in Europe in the last decade. Then, we discuss the meaning of privatization, and the impact that it can have on the welfare states according to mainstream literature. Finally, we present the main dilemmas that the privatization process leaves unsolved for future research and policy making.

1.2. TWO FORMS OF PRIVATIZATION

Privatization policies are far from constituting a uniform and harmonious strategy. In a strict sense, they mean a transfer of responsibility for the supply of a service from a public authority to the private sector. Nevertheless, the meaning of the effects of this transfer may vary greatly.

First, in the field of welfare policies, privatization does not always and necessarily imply a reduction in public expenditure. When it includes a transfer of state agencies into private hands or the reduction of state programmes and the withdrawal of public authorities from specific responsibilities, privatization does actually involve a contraction in public spending. In other cases, however, it involves a change in the means employed to implement policies without it necessarily determining a reduction in public spending.

In recent years, various measures have emerged in European welfare policies in the general direction of increasing privatization of the systems of social provision. The main measures are as follows:

(a) the reduction of some public programmes, accompanied by an increase in the private provision of the same services;
(b) the shift of ownership of some service from public or semi-public agencies to private auspices;
(c) the development of policies involving public funding of private services;
(d) the introduction of deregulation that has allowed private agencies to enter fields previously dominated by state monopolies.

The great plurality of strategies and operational instruments adopted can be reduced by focusing on two main models of privatization that reflect, considerably, different approaches and political philosophies. While the actual strategies adopted in different European countries are generally based on a combination of the two approaches, it is clear that the public debate and the policy proposals regarding the privatization of social services are essentially focused on the models described below.

The first model considers privatization as a process of reorientation of the demand for services (*demand-driven privatization*). It is essentially based on forgoing any further expansion of state activity and on the simultaneous adoption of measures aimed at increasing private demand for social services. Basic to this model is the idea that, with appropriate support and incentives, the demand for social services can be redirected towards private supply, thus contributing to the growth of a 'genuine' market of private services. The introduction of vouchers and the concession of tax allowances for the purchase of private services go precisely in the direction of devising innovative forms of public support for private demand. Furthermore, the development of insurance schemes to supplement state insurance is based on the idea that part of the services currently distributed directly by the state can be allocated more efficiently and effectively by free market mechanisms.

According to its supporters, this model of privatization overcomes most of the limitations connected with a traditional system of 'welfare mix' based on the distinction between funding (state responsibility) and provision (coming, to a considerable degree, from private providers). According to this approach, the passage towards open competition for the provision of services aimed at private demand would in fact prevent the efforts to contain public welfare expenditure from an overall reduction in service provision (or in the lowering of quality standards) (Le Grand and Robinson, 1984).

It is, nevertheless, well known that the opening of new private care markets would not in itself be sufficient to compensate for the reduction (or lack) of growth in state provision. The greatest perplexity concerns the possible negative effects of this strategy on redistribution. The passage from a 'partnership regime' (Salamon, 1987), in which private provision is funded by public money, to a system based on the capacity of private providers (whether non-profit or for-profit) to collect a substantial amount of their funding requirement directly on the free market, would in fact seem to involve a progressive abandonment of services aimed at the disadvantaged in favour of the affluents in the society. The US case offers some indications in this respect: as Salamon (1993) shows, the primary objective of the search for alternatives to public funding has pushed most non-profit organizations to abandon service provision aimed at the most disadvantaged and the poorest groups, in favour of services addressed to clients with greater purchasing power.

A second consequence is that *demand-driven privatization* would introduce profound changes in the supply system. Specifically, it seems to make profound changes in the behaviour patterns of the majority of existing private suppliers, which are non-profit organizations. A policy of demand-driven privatization does in fact require the removal of regulatory and financial constraints that bar the entry of for-profit organizations to the social services markets. The concession of tax benefits to non-profit organizations may also be questioned in this respect as they create a situation of unfair competition with regard to for-profit organizations.

The *progressive commercialization* to which non-profit organizations would be driven by the opening of a private care market could also easily repress their vocation to work with the socially underprivileged. The US experience does in fact show that the increase in revenues from the sale of services by many non-profit organizations coincided with management acquiring greater control over both paid and voluntary staff and adopting vast internal restructuring programmes aiding efficiency and standardization of procedures.

Public services, on the other hand, once confined to the delivery of basic services to a large proportion of the marginalized population, risk playing a declining role in serving the underprivileged, both in terms of funding and of professional staffing.

Therefore, the demand driven model of privatization assumes a profound change in the organizational structure of current welfare systems, a reduction (or at least a freeze) on current levels of state provision, and also the entrance of large number of profit-seeking providers into the field of social services. The ideological assumption that justifies this organizational revolution regards the virtues attributed to the capacity of individuals to choose, once placed in a position of being able to freely discriminate between a plurality of private providers.

The second model of privatization assumes that the state maintains most of its current financial responsibility and aims at modifying the current mix of regulatory tools. Privatization in this sense only concerns the supply function of services and does not assume any growth in private demand for social services. This is, therefore, a *supply-driven privatization*, where the purpose is to privatize most of the service delivery functions and at the same time to introduce the mechanisms of competition into the procedures governing the transfer of funds from the state to private providers. The idea of these policies is that it is possible, by privatizing the supply of services, to obtain a distinct improvement in the efficient and effective implementation of welfare policies. For this improvement to take place, there must be a transfer of management responsibility from public agencies to private providers and a general pluralization of the supply system, to the point where it also includes profit-seeking providers.

All the measures aimed at expanding the degree of contracting out of state services and at supporting the growth of private suppliers financed by public programmes, therefore, fall within this approach. The passage from grants to a contracting system probably constitutes the most evident signal of this type of policy. Other measures aimed at multiplying private supply include the concession of tax benefits to non-profit organizations that provide services in the public interest, the use of tenders for awarding service contracts, and the experimentation of innovative forms of public–private partnership in the creation of new welfare policies and programmes.

It is a model which certainly does not break the continuity with the traditional structure of welfare policies in Europe, which in many countries is historically based on a regime of partnership between state and private providers. The innovation offered by supply-driven privatization lies in its attempt to transform the interdependence between state and private providers, often based on trust relationships, into exchange relationships in which the state takes the role of purchaser of services provided by private suppliers. The introduction of mechanisms of competition in the financial relationships between the state and private suppliers should, from the newpoint of the policy makers that support this strategy, overcome the rigidities and categorical constraints and the lack of innovation that characterize public supply, without necessarily implying a withdrawal of the state.

Nevertheless, the adoption of this model also gives rise to perplexities. First, it does not release additional finance other than that provided by the state. During severe budget constraints, the improvement in efficiency that the privatization of supply would seem to guarantee could be insufficient to meet the increased demand for social services. Even the capacity of private providers (non-profit organizations, above all) to raise extra funding in the form of donations and voluntary labour seems insufficient to sustain a significant increase in the volume of services provided to the public. Supply-driven privatization would, therefore, seem to risk appearing more as a rationalization of existing services rather than a capable way of expanding the system of supply.

Like the first, the second model also determines a profound change in the supply system. It exposes a large proportion of private providers to a process of commercialization, which risks inhibiting—rather than encouraging—their flexibility and capacity for innovation. The introduction of market mechanisms does, in fact, seem to reward organizations that demonstrate more capability in efficient and professional management of contracted services rather than those experimenting with new forms of services. In the future, this policy could consequently result in the paradox of supporting private suppliers which gradually lose most of the characteristics for which they were originally selected in preference to direct public provision (Evers, 1995).

On the other hand, the risks of bureaucratization could be greatly reduced if the state establishes 'soft' quality requirements for the services purchased that allow private providers to remain sufficiently independent. It is on this capacity that supply-driven privatization is basically founded. Only a state capable of developing regulation which is more enabling than binding, would in fact allow a gradual transfer of state responsibility to private hands without compromising welfare rights guaranteed until now by the state fulfilling the dual functions of finance and provision.

The difference between demand- and supply-driven privatization allows us to grasp the considerable differences that lie behind the policy orientations towards privatization. The theoretical and ideological concepts at the basis of the two models are, in fact, very distinct from each other. The first model—the demand model—sees the main advantage of privatization in its conferring on individual economic empowerment that the paternalism of state dominated welfare systems has hardly acknowledged. This model is based on the values of the free market, pluralism and consumerism. The second model—the supply model—bases privatization on recognition of the existence of private resources that can be fully used in the public interest as long as they are firmly set in a transparent system based on the rules of competition. The values here are those of subsidiarity and collective responsibility for the common good.

The role of state regulation appears to be different for the two models. In the first model the fundamental role of the state is to safeguard the individual's right to choose, as well as to stimulate and support private demand for services. Government intervention is concentrated on bolstering the purchasing power of individuals (through tax allowances), on the issuing of vouchers for those without sufficient purchasing power, on informing the public and encouraging the right of choice, and on implementing regulation aimed at preventing unfair competition between suppliers.

In the second model, the state funds service providers directly and can, therefore, still exercise substantial regulatory power over them. The direct responsibility of public administrations for funding does, in fact, legitimate the definition of binding standards regarding the content and quality of services to a greater extent than is possible in the first model. The very selection of private providers to be funded also occurs on the basis of more rigorous criteria and can be changed from time to time if results are unsatisfactory. It is clear then that with this model the state maintains a strong function of control and accountability with regard to the effectiveness of the services funded.

Finally, there is a difference between the two models in the role attributed to private providers. The first model, demand-driven privatization, rewards the capacity of providers to attract new clients and to adapt to the evolution of private demand. It is, therefore, a system which seems to encourage innovation, even if it exposes it to adverse selection phenomena and consequently to the tendency of providers to abandon clients which require costly care. However the second model, supply-driven privatization, rewards the capacity of providers to take on collective responsibilities and to share the objectives of public policies with the state. Nevertheless, it exposes them to direct financial dependence on public administrations and favours the development of favouritism in relationships with public officials.

As has already been said, there is today the growth of a mingling of measures inspired by both models. For example, the idea of 'quasi market', as proposed by Le Grand (1990), refers to a mixed system in which the idea of making funding of private sector providers dependent on the choice of private individuals, coexists with the aim of maintaining direct state control by means of forms of accreditation. Different ongoing experiences in European countries today are based on managed competition models with different combinations of measures oriented towards both demand- and supply-driven privatization. The two models of privatization do, in effect, constitute different but not necessarily contradictory prospects for the development of welfare policies. The first model aims more at developing a 'private market' for services, while the second aims at the creation of a 'public market' for social services. The second only privatizes the supply of services while the first also privatizes part of the funding.

At a practical level, systems that combine elements of both approaches are often constructed with 'welfare mixes' that give more emphasis to one model or the other according to the dominant values of the policy makers in different countries. One may predict that in the course of time intermingling between the two models will cause a new, more complex regulation to emerge that leads to the construction of more articulated social service systems than those existing today.

There, nevertheless, remain important points of contact between the two models. Both involve a reduction in direct management responsibility for service provision by the state, as well as the introduction of mechanisms of competition alongside state regulation. Both models, therefore, not only involve the simple transfer of delivery responsibility from the state to the private sector, but also considerable changes in the forms of coordination between service providers, users and the third party (the state, donors, etc.). They involve the passage from a state dominated welfare system to one in which state regulation coexists with regulation based on the principles of economic competition.

1.3. THE MEANING OF PRIVATIZATION

Undoubtedly the main reason used to justify promoting widespread privatization in welfare policies is because of the gains in economic efficiency that it seems to offer. One of the reasons for introducing privatization concerns the usefulness of basing the provision of services on full recognition of the property rights of the suppliers. Privatization in terms of ownership would, in fact, prevent a series of inefficiencies that inevitably afflict public agencies: the tendencies of managers of public agencies to maximize their budgets to increase their influence, the absence of any close link between salaries and profits, the very many possibilities of 'moral hazard' behaviour emerging on the part of the employees. The transfer of the ownership of the agencies that deliver services into private hands would allow more careful attention to be paid to the rules of the economic game and a more sensitive response to the demands of customers.

However, most of the advantages attributed to privatization in the social services field depend on the explicit creation of a service market, rather than merely on the private nature of the providers. The transfer of management responsibility from public to private providers is in fact considered useful, to the extent that it allows the laws of market competition to be used to ration and distribute the benefits of welfare (Walker, 1984). If the change in the ownership status of the suppliers results in the maintenance of a monopoly or oligopoly of the supply, this would not allow optimum conditions of competition to be achieved. The greatest challenge of privatization, therefore, concerns the creation of a new mechanism for coordinating supply and demand based on the laws of economic competition.

Privatization, therefore, implies a certain commercialization of social services (Savas, 1987). In this perspective, whether private suppliers of services are subject to a non-profit distribution constraint or not is of little importance. However, according to Hansmann (1987), it is the presence of non-profit organizations that prevents markets characterized by information asymmetries (like the field of social services) from being dominated by opportunistic behaviour and the consequent loss of efficiency. The special reliability of non-profit organizations would thus constitute a condition for markets exposed to information asymmetries to establish competitive mechanisms with guarantees of efficiency. The inclusion of non-profit organizations in the social services field (or even with privileged or exclusive access to the field), therefore, constitutes only a precondition for the development of a competitive services market: it is the model of coordination between supply and demand that is the decisive condition enabling gains in efficiency.

Privatization introduces new regulation in a structure of relationships between the state and private suppliers, which until now has been strongly characterized by authoritarian state regulation, neo-corporative arrangement or mutual accommodation. These three models are rooted, in Europe, in cultures and networks of relationships between the public and third sector that have been firmly established over the course of time and have crystallized into specific institutional structures. It is in fact these institutional structures that are in crisis as a result of the massive attempt to introduce the rules of economic competition to a field of policies that was previously almost entirely lacking in them.

What is going into crisis is, firstly, the 'welfare mix' model dominated by the strong regulatory power of the state over private and non-profit organizations that provide services. This model was defined by Wolch as a 'shadow state' and was particularly well developed in Great Britain (until the changes introduced by the Thatcher governments), in Scandinavian countries, and in some countries in continental Europe (e.g. France). According to Wolch, the shadow state is a 'set of auxiliary agencies, constituted separately from the state, but retaining those functions characteristic of a state sub-apparatus' (Wolch, 1990, p. 41), whose involvement in welfare policies leads to 'an extended and increasingly diversified pattern of state intervention' (ibid., p. 218). The formal transfer of functions from the state to non-profit organizations does not reduce but rather extends the influence and control of public administrations over non-profit organizations, which basically constitute 'public agents'.

In the 'shadow state' model, private organizations and the third sector are generously supported by public funding. State financial support is also accompanied by strong state regulation that is aimed at influencing the content of the services provided by private suppliers in order to make them consistent with public policy goals. This contractual arrangement has, nevertheless, progressively subjected private providers to economic dependence on the state, and to internal bureaucratization of their activities. By gradually assuming the role of a public agency, non-profit providers have also lost part of their traditional virtues, such as flexibility, independence, voluntarism and rootedness in the community (Smith and Lipsky, 1993). Therefore, the introduction of market mechanisms was considered, as the best way of restoring efficiency and overcoming the immobility typical of organizations that are too bureaucratic.

Privatization has also put under pressure the neo-corporative structure of welfare policies developed in many continental European countries (e.g. Germany and the Netherlands). Although the development of a mixed regime based on subsidiarity has led to a certain fragmentation of state authority, it has, in the course of time, increased the hierarchical structure of non-profit organizations, most of which are affiliated with peak associations increasingly involved in public decision making processes.

The concept of the 'government of private interests' has been explicitly proposed as a way to designate the segmented, mutual relationship between the state and 'intermediate' associations (Streek and Schmitter, 1985). According to this model, this relationship has been shaped mainly by *concertations* concerning particular, fragmented issues in which no party consistently holds a dominant position. As Streek and Schmitter explain, 'the attribution of public status to private groups involves much more than just their right to be consulted by the government on legislation..., it means also sharing the state's authority to make and enforce binding decisions' (Streek and Schmitter, 1985, p. 20).

The introduction of competition has put neo-corporative agreements under pressure, paving the way for greater attention to efficiency and for the rise of more contractual relationships between state and non-profit suppliers. The greatest limit of subsidiarity emerges as the fact that the state financial support of non-profit suppliers (consisting mainly of non-profit organizations) has left ample space for the creation of particularist links and the survival of strong organizational inertias. The idea that greater competition might restore greater transparency and dynamism to the mixed welfare system has thus become widespread, at the price of reducing the social consensus and joint participation of public and non-profit actors.

Finally, privatization has also created tension in the mutual accommodation model, which characterizes welfare policies in the countries of Southern Europe (Italy, Spain, Portugal and Greece). This model is based on sustained state financial support, but without a corresponding equally strong authoritarian or concerted regulatory capacity. The system is consequently heavily exposed to particularist interests and political patronage.

In this context the introduction of market mechanisms has led to the narrowing of the long-lasting margins for discretion from which both private providers and public officials that control the levels of public sector finance have benefited. Privatization has, therefore, resulted in an increase in state regulation and transparency as well as in reducing space for particularism and political patronage.

In general, then, the meaning of privatization basically consists of introducing a new mechanism of coordination between the state and private or non-profit providers—based on market regulation—and in combining it with previous forms of regulation. The new models of welfare emerging from this introduction of market mechanisms are 'mixed', not just because they involve both public and private or non-profit actors, but also because they include different forms of regulation and coordination between these actors. The main new feature of privatization lies in the pluralization and diversification of the regulatory models and not in the involvement of private or non-profit actors, which were traditionally present in the welfare policies of the majority of European countries (Paci, 1987). Considered from this aspect, there is no doubt that privatization does not simply involve a shift to a more efficient organization of the system from an economic viewpoint; it also constitutes a form of restructuring of the supply system that changes the direction in which welfare policies are developing. According to Starr (1989), privatization is an integrated attempt to redefine the relationship of the state with the market and civil society. It is, therefore, an eminently political process, which redistributes rights and power, modifies policy networks and the institutional context in which welfare policy is made, and influences the ways in which welfare needs are defined. Starting with the transformation of the supply structure, privatization radically changes the strategies and objectives of welfare policies, modifies the political and social interests represented in policy making, the form of policy making itself and the criteria for including in or excluding citizens from the benefits provided by these policies.

What effect these processes of innovation have had on the institutional structure of welfare policies and on forms of policy making remains largely unknown. The very few studies so far available do in fact lead to contradictory and ambiguous conclusions. There are scholars who point to the growing reliance on private or non-profit providers as an instrument used to limit welfare spending, to reduce 'social citizenship' and to ration services (Smith and Lipsky, 1993). Thus, privatization's political meaning is not to increase efficiency but rather to make it possible to advocate policies for rationing services. In the same perspective, Seibel (1989) insists on the considerable advantages to be gained by elected politicians from delegating responsibility for public policies to private or non-profit actors and from the consequent depoliticization of the decision making processes involved in welfare policies.

Nevertheless, according to others there is a 'soft' version of privatization that involves the transfer of responsibility not so much towards profit making firms but towards non-profit organizations, more willing to take account of considerations concerning the quality of the services they provide (Salamon, 1993). Privatization is also seen as an alternative strategy to reducing welfare expenditure; it makes systems more competitive while the amount of resources employed remains unchanged, making budget cuts less necessary (Le Grand, 1990). Finally, it favours the mobilization of private resources and a diversified supply of services. According to Kramer et al. (1995), for example, in various European countries, privatization has made it possible to maintain, if not to increase, the existing level of social services provision over the last decade.

Nevertheless, these interpretations do not fully grasp the fundamental change introduced by privatization. This does not consist of reducing public spending, nor on the contrary of maintaining the level of coverage of needs guaranteed in the past. Privatization in fact lends itself to different political uses and, has served various functions; it has been adopted, in the policies of different national and political situations, both to reduce and to expand, or at least to maintain welfare levels. What makes it a fundamental new phase for the future of welfare does not concern so much the level of services but rather their mixed and plural structure.

According to a widespread opinion, the main reason why privatization has been judged so positively by policy makers is to be sought in the failures that characterize state social service provision. At the basis of this failure, as Weisbrod (1988) explains, is the incapacity of the state to satisfy marginal demand for welfare. Other theories, insist on the inefficiency and rigidity of state bureaucracy, or on the categorical constraints binding its behaviour. Any explanation which bases the success of privatization on the failures of state regulation, however, appears weak. More specifically, it is based on two assumptions, both of which are questionable.

The first is that the choice of regulatory model from those available is made by policy makers on the sole basis of economic advantage. According to failure theories, the main reason for adopting privatization policies in many European countries would be that they guarantee more effective and efficient service provision than is possible with other regulatory models. There is no doubt that the introduction of competition to social service supply systems has been greatly determined by economic imperatives. It would, nevertheless, be reductive to assume that privatization is simply an adaptation to changed environmental conditions that required a less expensive structure for the supply system. The choices and decision making processes that gave shape to these policies occurred within a certain configuration of alternatives, expected consequences and preferences, which were strongly influenced by the institutional and cultural context in which the major political actors acted. These policies were chosen because they were considered not only less costly, but also more appropriate, more legitimate and consistent with the ideological and cultural orientations of the policy makers.

The second assumption is even more substantial and concerns the theoretical model adopted to explain the passage from one model of regulation to another. According to the failure theory, it is assumed that the failure of a regulatory principle necessarily involves the adoption of a new and more efficient model. The passage from one model to another is, thus, reduced to the choice of the most efficient means.

In reality, the different regulatory models available to policy makers are not exclusive means of varying efficiency and effectiveness according to the problem to be solved and to the institutional setting of the problem. Each regulatory model does, in fact, assume a specific form of coordination between the parties who implement it, according to which only certain types of relationship and organization take on a specific meaning. Therefore, the passage from one model of regulation to another implies a more general change in the structure of relationships between public, private and non-profit actors that involves institutional, political and cultural changes.

Therefore, changes in the form of regulation must be explained in terms of the transformation processes that concern the network of political actors and also their cultural and ideological orientations. What is needed is the formulation of new hypotheses about the causes that determine the passage from the previous models to a model based on a combination of state and market regulation.

One obvious characteristic of this passage is that it coincides with the building of an appropriate institutional setting. Contrary to what is assumed by economic liberalism, privatization in the social services field coincides with a process of new institutionalization. Market regulation does not in fact constitute, unless in an illusory manner, a mechanism for automatic regulation of the system. It requires appropriate institutional and political intervention far from the prescriptions of economic liberalism.

It is sufficient here to recall the most significant forms of regulatory intervention. First of all, the introduction of competition between the state, private or non-profit suppliers and individuals has required the rewriting of laws and the creation of new institutions to guarantee the operation of private or non-profit suppliers. Measures aimed at regulating the new contractual relationships between the state and private or nonprofit suppliers have been adopted and new independent controlling bodies have been established. In some countries such as Italy, governments have even designed and provided for new forms of private institutions and new forms of regulation for these institutions. Secondly, a large number of economic measures have been adopted which aim at striking a new balance in the economic importance of different sectors and their capacity to supply services. Also, tax concessions, for example, have been introduced for private suppliers; special government funds have been set up to stimulate the start up and establishment of new private or non-profit providers. Finally, private or non-profit providers have been assigned new and substantial public responsibilities, to the point where a certain confusion of roles has emerged; private or non-profit suppliers have often been involved not only in the provision of services but also in joint planning processes. This has involved the growth of a decision making area occupied by both political and private or non-profit actors, in which the boundaries between the sectors are increasingly more uncertain and difficult to define.

Taken as a whole, these processes define the physiognomy of a new welfare policy environment, in which a new configuration of relationships between the state, private and non-profit suppliers is taking shape. The term 'welfare mix' can be introduced precisely to describe this new institutional situation, which constitutes the most significant result of the privatization policies pursued in Europe in recent years.

1.4. THE DILEMMAS OF THE 'WELFARE MIX'

The 'construction' of a mixed system of welfare is compelling political actors to tackle a number of problems. They are characterized by differing degrees of intensity depending on the context and are closely connected with the strengths and weaknesses of the public and private parties involved. The third sector certainly represents one of the crucial elements in the new situation: the transformations underway among its various components appear, therefore, to be of great importance. The processes of institution building brought about by privatization do in fact assume the existence of a third sector in which entrepreneurship and professionalism becomes increasingly stronger. The question remains open as to whether this process will give rise to heightened organizational isomorphism and hybridization of the characteristics of non-profit organizations.

In the context of social services, the interaction between public actors and the third sector constitutes the cornerstone of the new construction. Therefore, it is of fundamental importance to invest in research in the interorganizational processes underway, in order to decipher the behaviour of the actors in the various contexts and begin to get a glimpse of the new form of welfare mix that is taking on shape.

> Two contrasting theoretical perspectives have emerged: the dominant one emphasises the rapid institutionalization of the third sector as the

primary partner of government in the provision of human services, the promotion of culture and the arts, and as an advocate and core component of civil society. The other, less well known view is sceptical about the usefulness of a sectoral model based on corporate form because it overlooks the blurring of boundaries, interdependence and interpenetration among organizations which have absorbed many of the major features of their sectoral counterparts. Bureaucratization, professionalism and marketization have also contributed to the growth of a pervasive institutional isomorphism, and the growth of mixed hybrid organizations that have both public and private characteristics. (...) In any case, new analytical perspectives are needed if social policy questions are to be reformulated in the context of a mixed economy where sectoral lines have changed and may have less significance. (Kramer, 1998).

The new forms of regulation and the new configuration of relationships between the state and 'for-profit/non-profit' service providers have to face up to a series of problems for which there is a wide range of possible solutions. We have identified them as 'the dilemmas of the welfare mix'.

Delegation or sharing of responsibility: This represents the most general dilemma. There can be a total transfer of responsibility to the private/third sector, from the planning level to that of actual service provision, or there may be shared responsibility between partners; the latter may in turn be limited to the final relationship with users or extend to policy making in a sort of co-planning process. This latter arrangement would allow sharing of the most important choices and practices to be widened to the entire community albeit with respect for only particular responsibilities.

Which interaction: cooperation or competition? Interaction between the public and private/third sectors may occur within a matrix that is above all *cooperative*, in which the common goal of providing services with a high standard of quality is pursued by establishing a dialogue and continuous interchange, once a mutually determined framework is shared; alternatively, the relationship may be based on mechanisms designed to regulate *competition* between private/third sector organizations, as exemplified by tenders for contracts or similar types of competitions.

Both these models seem to have their good and bad points; in the cooperative system, the public sector can choose with which organizations it wishes to work, but this arrangement lends itself to the degeneration of relationships that may drift into particularism and favouritism; in the competitive system, however, while there may be greater guarantees of transparency and honesty, there may be greater difficulty encountered in setting up shared political goals.

Organizational efficiency or quality of the service: When the new structure of welfare policies is imagined, there is an increased evaluation of managerial aspects that must characterize how the services are run. In that case organizational performance should be measured essentially on the basis of the resources employed, the time spent, and the quantity of services delivered. There is, nevertheless, another side to the coin, that concerns the quality of services: will the processes of social exclusion be fought against effectively? Will the well-being of members of society and the degree of social inclusion increase? Will the new services, though more *efficient*, be able to deal with the challenges and risks of post-industrial society *effectively*?

Stability of cooperative relationships or the chance to innovate: There is no doubt that the welfare system is trying to find a new equilibrium and, therefore, both the public and the third sectors are searching for stability in their ways and methods of cooperating: forces that push in that direction will, therefore, be powerful. This rebalancing may, nevertheless, involve increasing bureaucracy in their relationships. Consequently a tendency may arise to inhibit certain capacities of the third sector to innovate under the weight of a cumbersome system of accountability. There is no doubt that in a context of the growing use of state resources by the private/third sector, this dilemma appears to be extremely pervasive.

Central or marginal role of the volunteering: In many western countries, it is observed that the increasing involvement of non-profit organizations in service provision has coincided with an increase in their specialization and a strong tendency to acquire professional skills. These phenomena would inevitably produce a phenomenon of 'devoluntarization': volunteers would be progressively excluded from direct involvement in the provision of services in favour of highly professional paid workers. Volunteers would, therefore, only play important roles in the collection of funds, in advocacy and by participating in the governance of organizations. There is, nevertheless, also the possibility of volunteers achieving a new 'centrality': in some cases the quality of provision may be enriched considerably by having volunteers assist paid professional workers. This would make it possible to combine specialist knowledge and social skills in order to provide more effective care of individuals. Such an ambitious goal requires long and difficult organizational changes and implies questioning firmly established professional cultures and behaviour patterns.

Identity or service provision: We are faced here with another general dilemma; up to what point can a non-profit organization, committed to the provision of a service, maintain its original identity and mission. What is at stake here is the delicate balance between loyalty to organization's values and the demands of running a 'public' service: growth in size, specialization and professionalism may take up time and attention and result in a strong tendency to conform to the dominant models of corporate management. In this case many of the specific properties of non-profit organizations would be lost.

Those who use the services—customers or citizens to be involved: If a market is to be set up consisting exclusively of 'customers' with the right to choose and, therefore, to sanction the success or failure of enterprises, then it appears indispensable to give individuals the opportunity to choose which service is most appropriate to their needs. If, however, the objective is to involve the community in the actual planning of services and, therefore, to have consumers participate in the 'production' of local response to needs, then it becomes of strategic importance to build an 'appropriate organizational context' that promotes dialogue, participation and joint planning (e.g. including consumers as members).

Conservation or disappearance of a public sector role in the delivery of services: According to some views, the public sector should withdraw completely from direct service provision (specially with regard to personal care services) and restrict itself to funding and monitoring. For many aspects, however, it is important for government to maintain a direct role, especially where experience and professionalism, and therefore valuable human resource assets, have accumulated and may be lost. The presence of a service provider employed in the public sector can be of great use for the purpose of creating intense forms of cooperation with the private/third sector. It would certainly facilitate the exchange of information and knowledge, without which no innovative practices can be constructed.

Uniform or diversified services: The introduction of new forms of contractual regulation could induce greater standardization of services provided by the third sector as a consequence of the requirement to remain within accepted limits. One of the fundamental motives behind the activity of these organizations would in this case disappear: they would lose their ability to respond to the needs of the community focusing very strongly on the specific situations and needs of individuals. On the other hand, these characteristics must be reconciled with those typical of a public service, tending to the universalistic, and capable of guaranteeing equal services to all citizens.

1.5. THE CONSEQUENCES OF PRIVATIZATION

In industrialized countries, the attention of policy makers and academics has now focused on the new structures of social policies that are needed to tackle major challenges of the end of the century: ageing populations, the growing instability and variation in families, insecurity in the labour market, rapid obsolescence of abilities and professional skills, massive and unstoppable immigration from the 'South' of the world, pollution, and the spread of hardship from traditional areas of need to 'normal' areas of society. Now that any idea that the 'old state' might be able to deal with social problems by itself has been abandoned, a new 'motor' is being engineered, at least in many European countries, that know how to combine efficiency in management with effective results. This effort is based on intense cooperation between its four main components, the public sector, the commercial private sector, the third sector, and the family and relatives networks.

This search for a new way to 'fine tune' welfare policies is apparent in all fields of welfare policies, from pensions to health. However, there is one very significant difference. Almost all European pension systems provide a guaranteed base level of state pension, to which at least one higher level can be added coming from the private sector. A similar situation is found in many health systems, which, however, appear to be characterized by greater organizational complexity as well as a greater presence of private organizations at all levels. In social services, on the other hand, the entire policy may rest on a single 'public–private' pillar. This makes the task of finding a new structure much more intricate, given the extremely varied set of risk and need situations where, at the same time, the fragmentation of action and the lack of structured policies are very great.

In any case, whichever political philosophy prevails in a determined context, we are faced with a new generation of welfare policies which, as it has been shown, is based on new institution building processes since the privatization of welfare systems is constructed socially and politically as well as culturally. New regulations, new tax policies and new market rules and institutions are being encouraged, giving increased prominence to incentives and 'enabling' policies. What are the goals that welfare policies will be able to pursue *after the demise of welfare state*? Will the ability to fight many of the forms of social exclusion increase or will the gap between the 'guaranteed' and the 'non-guaranteed' be made even wider? (Billis, 1998). There are many who fear that third sector organizations will become 'state agencies' or that as they will have increasingly to compete with each other, they will end up neglecting the weakest social groups; this would be even more serious during the current crisis negating the universalistic paradigm.

There also seems to be a widespread fear that the massive involvement of third sector organizations in service provision will put the important roles they play in client advocacy and promoting civic values at risk and, therefore, damage the democratic infrastructure (Alexander et al., 1998). Others emphasize that the only way to put a brake on 'welfare destructuring' is in any case to 'return to policies that activate local communities ... by means of a system which must involve service providers, public and private sector, for-profit and nonprofit, working side by side and overcoming the traditional opposition between the different spheres' (David, 1998). Many questions remain over the redistribution effects of the processes underway: those who have attempted comparisons between third and private service provision have found that alongside many similarities, on average the former provides better quality service and more user satisfaction (Schmid, 1997). We are, however, very far from possessing any fully satisfactory empirical evidence.

Strong perplexities are manifested over the possibility of the third sector actually being able to play an increased role in service provision; in the US, for example, very serious questions are raised as to whether non-profit organizations possess the organizational resources to face up effectively to the great stresses they are being subjected to by the 'devolution revolution' that is invading that country (Harris, 1998).

Finally, the study of privatization processes in social services allows two lines of analysis, which have rarely met until now to be brought firmly together: research into welfare systems and the analysis of the third sector. This perspective seems to be of fundamental importance in the beginning to understand the 'post welfare state era'.

1.6. METHODOLOGY

Studies of the third sector in recent decades have shown that its dimensions are certainly significant in industrialized countries (even in non Anglo-Saxon countries) and that it has a considerable impact on economic systems and on welfare systems in particular. They have also very clearly shown that the most useful paradigm for analysing relationships between the public and the third sectors is without any doubt that of interdependence: intense interaction between the state and the non-profit sectors has always characterized many spheres of welfare policies from health to social services (Kramer, 1981, 1992; Gidron et al., 1992; Kuhnle and Selle, 1992). Knowledge of these facts, however, has hardly spread among students of welfare, who often remain prisoners of an 'economic-structural' or 'politico-institutional' analysis based on identifying only the traditional actors of policy making. Furthermore, comparative analyses are based mostly on the 'hard' data of welfare spending: no welfare state model after Titmuss has so far made any mention of the third sector.

What is necessary now is a long-term reconstruction of individual national cases with a 'sociological approach', performed from a 'socio-cultural' viewpoint and aimed at widening the field of investigation to include a more social dimension centred on orientations, values and collective identities present in various ways and to varying degrees in the social fabric, but capable of impacting, at par with economic and political factors, on the choices of the welfare state. This would move, once and for all, away from the concept of welfare state towards that of welfare systems.

We will thus come to find ourselves in a 'wider theoretical space obviously crowded by a greater variety of actors; alongside the state and the political and administrative élites, not only will there be political parties and large trade unions but also professional bodies, voluntary bodies, insurance companies, social movements, informal self-help groups, new emerging classes, the nuclear family and relative networks and, last but not least, the consumer citizens with their preferences for well-being' (Paci, 1989, p. 17).

This work is intended to fall within this line of study. The welfare system is placed at the centre of the discussion, with special attention afforded to the social services. We sought to reconstruct a certain number of national cases starting at the 'roots' of the welfare state and then to focus the discussion on the set of relationships running between the public and private/third sectors in the shaping of new policies. The analysis looks at the relationships not only in qualitative, but also in inter-organizational, institutional and political terms. Attention is given to expenditure data and to easily 'measurable' factors as well as to the actors, placing those of the third sector at the centre of the scene, and in particular to actors that have their own orientations, identity and values that may at times even come into conflict with public policy goals.

The criteria by which the countries were selected are tied to the recent attempt to identify different 'welfare families' (Leibfried, 1992; Esping-Andersen, 1990) and 'welfare mix' families in Europe. It seemed reasonable, on the basis of the working hypothesis, to have, on the one hand, at least one country for each grouping and on the other to remain within the two most significant cases both for Southern Europe and for continental Europe, since these are the aggregations most in question. In this book therefore, Spain and Italy constitute the 'Southern European' family, France and Germany the 'continental European' family, Great Britain the 'Anglo-Saxon' family and Norway the 'Scandinavian' family. It will be interesting to see whether this proposed interpretation of European welfare systems stands up to the thrust of the analyses and discussion contained in the national case studies that follow.

One preoccupation common to the group was to avoid a mere collection of data and to guarantee effective comparability of the results. To do this a common conceptual scheme was drawn up, which required much work and a precise methodology. Work began at a seminar organized in Rome in January 1997. Preliminary reports on the relationships between the state and the third sector for each individual country were taken as the starting point for discussions. The reports had been prepared on the basis of a scheme developed in the months preceding the seminar. Problem areas and common conceptual approaches were identified and a common scheme for the presentation of the national case studies was drawn up on the basis of this. A first draft of the national case study papers was then produced and these were discussed at a second seminar held in Rome in June 1998.[2] The results of this work are presented in this book. After chapter two focused on the mixed economy of social care, six chapters, each containing a national case study, follow and the last chapter contains the general conclusions. It is up to our readers to judge whether this publication succeeds in making a modest contribution to the discussion and debate in progress on the new social policies of welfare mix.

Notes

1. Ugo Ascoli wrote part 4 through 6 and Costanzo Ranci wrote part 1 through 3 of this chapter.
2. This methodology together with the publication of this book was assisted by the financial support of the FIVOL to whom we owe our sincere thanks. We also owe our deepest gratitude to the individual staff at the FIVOL who assisted us in many administrative ways.

Chapter 2

The Mixed Economy of Social Care in Europe

Costanzo Ranci*

2.1. THE MIXED ECONOMY OF SOCIAL CARE

Most of the problems that Continental Western European welfare systems are currently facing derive from the lack of public programmes of social care. Responsibility for care is mostly unloaded onto families, that fulfil this responsibility either by 'self-servicing' or purchasing services on the private market. However, the new risk profiles that emerge in contemporary societies make it increasingly more difficult for families to satisfy their care needs by themselves.

Various causes have contributed to the poor development of social care policies in most European countries (with the exception of Scandinavian countries and the partial exceptions of France and Belgium). The idea that has generally prevailed to date in European countries is that care is performed more effectively if it is done directly by families, with the help of a few purchased private services and state assistance to address special needs. According to various authors, the lack of state social care services signals a gender bias in welfare policies towards the male bread-winner at the expense of services aimed at strengthening the autonomy of women (Anttonen and Sipilä, 1996; Daly and Lewis, 1998). The development of 'in kind' social services is seen as a necessary condition for emancipating women from domestic duties and their gaining access to permanent work[1] (Esping-Andersen, 1999).

One of the more interesting acquisitions in the recent debate on the future of social services in Western Europe is the rediscovery of the crucial role that

*Costanzo Ranci • Politecnico di Milano, DIAP, Via Bonardi 3, 20133 Milano, Italy.

family plays in 'welfare regimes' (Esping-Andersen, 1990). While attention has shifted from social insurance and income support schemes towards provision of social services, it is obviously clear that the role of the family cannot be ignored, not only as a beneficiary—but also as direct provider—of welfare services. The current level of development of social policies in different countries reflects not only the degree of state commitment to meeting social care needs, but also the degree of responsibility for care provision placed on families. Sainsbury (1994) identifies two social policy models, that differ according to the approach taken towards families: an 'individual model' where entitlements are awarded to individuals and therefore also to women independently of their husband; a 'breadwinner model' in which entitlements are awarded on an employment basis and therefore above all to men.

In countries where a 'breadwinner model' prevails, most social services are provided by families with very little commitment and resources from public authorities. Only in some of these countries, social policies have been financially assisting at those families providing care allowances, or by reconciling family care duties with the working careers of women (e.g. through work-leaves). In countries where the welfare system has developed along individualistic lines, welfare policies are aimed more at reducing family responsibility by transferring part of the responsibility for care to the state.

The growing attention paid to the caregiving role of the family has solicited more sophisticated concepts to describe welfare policies. Esping-Andersen (1999) pointed out that welfare regimes are a consequence not just of state and market combinations and interactions, but that the family also combines and interacts with these sectors. As a result, welfare state intervention has been examined in terms not only of the direct benefits it gives families, but also of the consequences it has on care activity, and on the composition and organization of the family.

Despite the general agreement that it is now obsolete to think about welfare provision solely in terms of either public or private sectors, most of the discussion on the relationship between public policies and the family has nevertheless fallen into a dualistic scheme of interpretation. Public welfare policies have in fact been considered, both in the feminist (Lewis, 1993) and comparative (Esping-Andersen, 1999) literature, as being aimed at freeing women from family care duties. In other words, they have been assessed on the grade of 'de-familialization' of caring duties, to suggest the idea of a sort of zero-sum game between the family and the welfare state: the greater the state commitment to social care provision, the smaller the family care load on women (and vice versa). Policies aimed at maintaining interdependence between the family and the welfare state (e.g. by the concession of tax benefits to families with a dependent elderly person or with several dependent children) are in this context liquidated as timid, since they only allow a modest reduction of family responsibility and indeed also often run the risk of trapping women within the domestic walls.

Naturally, there is no doubt that increased state provision of in-kind services will in any case translate into a lightening of the care load on families.[2] The data available clearly shows that in countries where there is greater state provision of care services for the elderly and pre-school children (Scandinavian countries and Belgium and France for children only), there is also a higher percentage of working mothers (Anttonen and Sipilä, 1996, p. 95) and a smaller proportion of elderly persons living with their children (Esping-Andersen, 1999); while the opposite occurs for countries where there is less state provision of these services (which is especially found in Southern European countries according to Anttonen and Sipilä's data).

Nevertheless, an increase in state provision of care services does not seem easy to obtain, if one considers the limits on the growth of state welfare spending, the cultural resistance found in many European countries to reduce family responsibility for care services, and the organizational difficulties connected with the provision of highly personalized services. Squeezed between the two rigid alternatives of support to families and more state service provision, social policies seem destined to remain a minor component of most European welfare systems.

It is possible, nevertheless, to add another relevant component to this picture. The social care field is in fact characterized by a mixed economy in which roles are played not only by the state, the market and the family, but also by the crucial contribution of the third (or non-profit) sector. The national cases analysed in this book show the importance of third sector organizations in the provision of care services. Table 2.1 uses available data to present the market share of third sector organizations in social care, compared with state and private enterprises. Although there are considerable differences between sectors, it is clear that the provision of care services by third sector organizations in Continental and Southern Europe is definitely greater than state provision, while it plays a complementary role in the UK and in Norway.

The data for Germany and France is the most complete: recent studies show that in these countries the third sector accounts for 60 per cent of all persons employed in social services, constituting therefore the main sector.[3] The data for Southern European countries is unfortunately incomplete. Nevertheless, available data suggests that the third sector dominates in the provision of residential care services (where they provide 81 per cent of places in residential care in Italy and 56 per cent of places for the handicapped and 31 per cent for the elderly in Spain). It should be remembered that community-based services in these countries have not been developed to any great extent, and that still today, residential services remain the cornerstone of social services systems. In the UK, the third sector is important in child care,

Table 2.1. Market Shares of the Third Sector, State and Market in the Provision of Social Services

Market Share	UK	Norway	France	Germany	Spain	Italy
Residential homes						
Elderly			28% third sector 59% state 13% private sector	68% third sector 15% state 18% private sector	31% third sector 30% state 40% private sector	
Handicapped			85% third sector 11% state 4% private sector	84% third sector 7% state 9% private sector	56% third sector 26% state 17% private sector	
Other clients			*Adults* 81% third sector 17% state 2% private sector	*Childs* 73% third sector 18% state 9% private sector		
All kinds of users	14% third sector 40% state 46% private sector					81% third sector 19% state 0% private sector
Child care (including pre-school nursery, homes for problem children)	*Full time services* 18% third sector 33% state 49% private sector *Part and full-time services* 82% third sector 6% state 12% private sector	*Full time services* 32% third sector 68% state 0% private sector	70% third sector 26% state 3% private sector	62% third sector 37% state 1% private sector		

Other services	Handicapped *(all services)* 40% third sector 60% state 0% private sector	Handicapped *(home care)* 90% third sector 8% state 2% private sector
	Alcoholics *(all services)* 63% third sector 37% state 0% private sector	Elderly *(day centres)* 37% third sector 54% state 8% private sector
All social services	55% third sector 41% state 4% private sector	61% third sector 22% state 17% private sector

Note: UK: number of beds in residential homes and number of child care places, 1990, Kendall and Knapp (1996); Norway: number of employees, 1985, NOU (1988); France: number of employees, 1994, SESI (1997a and 1997b); Germany: number of employees, 1990, Anheier (1997); Spain: number of places (for Catalonia only), 1996, Department of Social Welfare, 1996; Italy: number of residential places, 1988, National Institute of Statistics, 1993.

while in the residential care field, the 1990 reform favoured a huge increase in the supply of services by commercial enterprise, which considerably reduced the third sector's presence in a few years. In Norway, a large percentage of services in a few specific sectors such as child care, services for the handicapped, and for alcoholics are provided by non-profit organizations.

On the whole, the third sector occupies an important position in providing social care, both in traditional welfare policy areas (residential care) and in more recently developed areas, such as community-based services and home care. While in Southern European countries the importance of the third sector is still concentrated in residential care, in other European countries there has been considerable expansion in innovative fields: it is sufficient to consider that the large majority of child care services in major European countries (France, Germany, UK) are provided by non-profit organizations and that even in a country characterised by a strong state commitment to child care—like Norway—a good third of the services are provided by the third sector.

By focusing on the contribution of the third sector, we can see more clearly the mixed economy character of the social care field. At least four different types of actors operate in this field: the state, for-profit organizations, non-profit organizations and the family. In many countries, and above all in the child care and handicapped service sectors, the main provider (apart from self-servicing families) is the third sector. Without the presence of these organizations, national social services systems would be almost completely non-existent in Italy and Spain, more than halved in France and Germany, and considerably reduced in the UK and in Norway. The third sector also appears considerably larger in size than the private market sector (apart from the case of Great Britain, which was affected by a profound reform of the system in 1990 which opened up space to heavy commercialization of residential services). Thus, despite the scarce attention the third sector has received in the policy debate on social care, it constitutes the main official channel for the distribution of social care services in Europe.[4] Any rethinking of European social care policies cannot afford to ignore the role and potential of the third sector.[5]

At least three factors can be identified to explain why non-profit organizations constitute a fundamental component of national social care systems in Western Europe. Firstly, the field of social care is characterized by very little standardization compared to other welfare fields (e.g. health). The very personalized nature of the services provided makes it extremely difficult to set quality standards on a uniform and agreed-upon basis. Aspects such as the ability to create a trust relationship with the beneficiaries, individual and administrative flexibility, openness to change and attention to clients' requirements become crucial factors in measuring quality. Thus, services provided by organizations with little professionalism, but based on voluntarism and on moral and religious commitment, can be easily considered legitimate.

A second factor concerns the social characteristics of the beneficiaries of social care. These services are in many countries mostly targeted at low socio-economic classes and at beneficiaries with very low incomes. This aspect explains the limited extent of services provided by private for-profit organizations. Furthermore, clients of social care services show little independence and ability to make choices and frequently need to be accompanied and supported in their decision process. Non-profits have been seen as more trustworthy and benevolent than for-profits (Weisbrod, 1988) and less likely to render harm or indifference to social care needs.

This difficulty in defining the quality of social care services and the low income level and inability to make choices of most of the beneficiaries have hindered the development of a private sector supply because of resulting problems of information asymmetry and moral hazard. The market failure to which social services are exposed explains, according to Hansmann (1980), the spread in this field of organizations subject to a non-profit distribution constraint.

There is, however, a further reason for the development of the third sector in the social care field. It is a field in which state action started to develop much later than in the traditional fields of income security and pensions. In the 'golden era' of Western European welfare state expansion (the 1960s and 1970s), social care was considered a marginal field, still subject to a logic—that of means testing—foreign to the universalism on which the progressive extension of contributory schemes and national health services was based. Limited state intervention thus encouraged and legitimated the action of religious congregations and philanthropic organizations, particularly those with humanitarian and religious motives, to help the most deprived and socially excluded groups in the population. The traditional presence of these bodies has long been a substitute for direct state provision. Thus, in reality it constitutes one of the main pillars of the system, and one that is difficult to replace.

There are then many causes—historical, economical, organizational—that explain the considerable diffusion of non-profit organizations providing social care. A consequence of this mixed system—as is shown below—is that the expansion of social care policies has been characterized by overlap of function and close interdependence between sectors. These widespread practices of 'shared governance' have wide margins for innovation, but also for amateurism, traditionalism and institutional inertia.

2.2. DIFFERENT PATTERNS OF THE WELFARE MIX IN SOCIAL CARE

As may be easily deduced from Table 2.1, there are considerable differences in the contours of the welfare mix that have become established in the countries considered in this book. These differences reflect not only the variety of different national welfare models, but also the specific nature of the relationships and roles that have been formed in the social care field between the activities of the state, the family and the third sector. We may speak of different *models of social service provision* and also explore the relationships between these models and the more well-known typologies proposed for classifying different welfare systems or 'regimes'.

The current literature on the welfare state and the third sector has proposed numerous criteria for classifying welfare systems. However, most of the models proposed present two limitation for our particular purposes. Firstly, they do not consider the presence or absence of the third sector as a determining criterion for classification. Secondly, they are not limited to exclusive consideration of the social services field.

To illustrate this first limitation: Anttonen and Sipilä (1996) identify five social care service regimes: (a) the Scandinavian model, characterized by widespread provision and by a high participation of women's labour in the field; (b) the Southern European model, characterized by very limited provision of public services, by the predominance of service supply from the informal or illegal market and by a modest proportion of women employed; (c) the British model, characterized by means tested programmes; (d) a subsidiarity model, typical of Central European countries, in which the dominating role of the family in social care provision is accompanied by both extensive presence of religious and political organizations and by the support of state funding; and (e) a Franco-Belgian model, characterized by an extensive network of child care services which makes it possible to keep a large proportion of mothers with small children employed.

Anttonen and Sipilä's classification, like other similar models, does not assign any importance to the organization of service provision; rather, it focuses on the relative degree of responsibility for social care covered by the state or left on the family.[6]

With regard to the second limitation of current models, the literature on the third sector has proposed other typologies, which, however, do not focus on any specific welfare field. One of the most well-known is proposed by Gidron et al. (1992), which categorizes national cases on the basis of the distinction between the role of the major fund provider and that of the major supplier of services.[7] Another typology is proposed by Kuhnle and Selle (1992), which considers the nature of the relationship between the state and the third sector by distinguishing the dimensions of operational and financial dependence and of nearness/distance in terms of communication and contact.[8]

Another model has recently been proposed by Salamon and Anheier (1998), in the context of a wider theory which seeks to explain the existence of the third sector in terms of 'social origins', or the embeddedness of the third sector within a specific economic and social structure.[9] This theory distinguishes four models of third sector regimes on the basis of the size of the sector and the extent of government spending on social welfare: (a) *a liberal model*, characterized by a large third sector coinciding with a low level of welfare expenditure (typical of Great Britain and the United States); (b) *a statist model* characterized by little state commitment, limited size of the third sector and the prevalence of care by the family (the example given is Japan); (c) *a social democratic model* with a high level of state welfare spending and limited extent of the third sector (typical of Scandinavian countries and of Italy); and finally, (d) *a corporatist model* characterized by high levels of government spending on welfare and a strong third sector (typical of Germany and France). This variety of regimes would also explain, according to the authors, the existence of different funding models: the liberal model with the relative predominance of voluntary and private con- tributions; the social democratic model together with the corporatist model with the predominance of government funding; the statist model with a predominance of funding coming from fees.

Although there are doubts over the classification of some national cases[10] and the choice of variables as criteria,[11] the theory of social origins undoubtedly constitutes an important contribution to the understanding of the relationships between the development of welfare systems and the role of the third sector. It points to the existence of a specific connection between the welfare state model that has become established in different countries and the degree of expansion—as well as the internal characteristics—of the third sector.

By applying the same approach to the social care field, it can be seen whether there is any correlation between the size of the third sector in a country and the degree of expansion of public policies in the social services field.

One first step in this direction is to look at the organizational model of social services provision. If we follow the indications of Gidron et al. (1992), then we consider not only the role that the third sector plays in service provision, but also the main source of its funding: to what extent it depends on the state or on other sources for funding.

The first criterion, concerning the relative 'weight' of the sector with respect to the market share of the state and private providers in the provision of social care, shows the degree to which the total provision of social care depends on the third sector. As can be seen from Table 2.2, the contribution of the third sector to total social care provision varies greatly not only from country to country, but also from sector to sector.

The second criterion shows to what extent the third sector depends on state funding. This depends not only on the degree of financial independence enjoyed by non-profit organizations, but also on the level of financial commitment made by the state to spending on social care. The comparative study by Salamon and Anheier (1999) shows that non-profit organizations operating in

Table 2.2. Data on the Characteristics of the Supply and Funding Systems for the Provision of Social Services in the Six Countries Considered

	UK	Norway	France	Germany	Spain	Italy
Market shares						
Residential care (to elderly and disabled)	14% third sector 40% state 46% private sector	—	28% third sector 59% state 13% private sector	68% third sector 15% state 18% private sector	34% third sector 28% state 38% private sector	81% third sector 19% state 0% private sector
Child care	82% third sector 6% state 12% private sector	32% third sector 68% state 0% private sector	70% third sector 26% state 3% private sector	62% third sector 37% state 1% private sector	(only handicapped)	—
All services	—	—	55% third sector 41% state 4% private sector	61% third sector 22% state 17% private sector	80% third sector 16% state 4% private sector	—
Funding of the third sector[a]	40% state 30% private giving 30% market	Mostly state	58% state 6% private giving 36% market	65% state 5% private giving 30% market	49% state 20% private giving 31% market	57% state 7% private giving 36% market
Welfare provision						
Welfare state services[b]	2% child care 9% home care	12% child care 16% home care	20% child care 7% home care	3% child care 2% home care	3% child care 2% home care	5% child care 1% home care
Family welfare provision[c]	16% aged living with children 35% unemployed youth living with parents	11% aged living with children — unemployed youth living with parents	20% aged living with children 42% unemployed youth living with parents	14% aged living with children 11% unemployed youth living with parents	37% aged living with children 63% unemployed youth living with parents	39% aged living with children 81% unemployed youth living with parents
Women in labour force[d]	53%	71%	57%	58%	41%	46%

[a] from Salamon et al., 1999
[b] from Anttonen and Sipilä, 1996, Table 1
[c] from Esping-Andersen, 1999, Table 4.3
[d] from Anttonen and Sipilä, 1996, Table 3

the social care field are funded heavily by the state. On average, 45 per cent of their income comes from the public sector. This percentage is exceeded only by non-profit organizations operating in the health care field—55 per cent—and in the education field—47 per cent. The data in Table 2.2 shows that, with one single exception, the countries considered in this study receive more than 50 per cent of their funding from the state: *state funding constitutes, therefore, the main source of finance for non-profit organizations operating in the social care field.*

A typology (given in Table 2.3) can be reconstructed from the data in Table 2.2 that contains four models of social care provision.[12] Some of these models represent national cases and others the situation found in a particular field of services within a given country.

The first model, a *subsidiarity model*, sees the state providing generous funding (covering costs almost completely) to third sector services, which represent the main provider of social care. The state performs the functions of funding and control, providing only a small proportion of services; the strong independence between state and third sector leaves only a residual space for the development of private enterprise provision. Of the countries considered in this study, Germany is emblematic of this model: the third sector accounts for more than 60 per cent of employment in the social services field and is particularly strong in the residential field (where it provides 68 per cent of the supply); this role is supported by strong state funding (which covers 65 per cent of the provision); income from the sale of services and from donations accounts for only a small proportion of funding.

The second model emphasizes the *dominance of the third sector*. It is characterized by the dominating presence of the third sector in the provision of social services, with a corresponding more limited financial commitment from the state than found with the first model; the state meets costs only partially. The countries where this model is found—like France and the UK in child care, Italy for residential services, and Spain for services for the handicapped— reflect the historical presence of non-profit organizations in the social care field, often of religious origin, and a more limited state commitment which

Table 2.3. Models of the Organization of Social Care Provision

Role of the Third Sector in the Provision of Social Care	Degree of State Funding	
	Total (over 60%)	Partial (under 60%)
Dominant (over 50%)	*Subsidiarity model* Germany	*Third- sector dominant model* Italy, Spain (handicap), France (child care), UK (child care)
Complementary (less than 50%)	*State dominant model* Norway, France (resid.)	*Market dominant model* UK (resid.), Spain (resid.)

translates into more limited direct state provision (in Italy the public sector provides less than one-fifth of all places in residential institutions; in France the state provides directly 26 per cent of child care services and in the UK, 6 per cent; in Spain direct state provision for the handicapped accounts for 16 per cent of the total) and only partial funding of third sector provision (in Italy the state provides 57 per cent of total third sector income, in France it provides 56 per cent of the total, while in Spain, 49 per cent). In this model too, the strong presence of the third sector leaves little space for private enterprise (virtually non-existent in Italy, while it accounts for only 3 per cent of child care provision in France, 12 per cent in the UK and 4 per cent in Spain).

The third model is characterized by the *dominance of the state*. Social services are mainly provided by the state, which allows only a residual role for non-profit organizations. Third sector organizations are of some importance only in specific sectors, and in any case, they are almost completely dependent on the state for funding. In the national cases the most representative of this model is Norway, where the third sector only plays a role, and in any case not a major one, in specific sectors (like child care, where the services provided by the third sector account for a third of total provision). The case of France is similar in the residential services field; total state provision accounts for 59 per cent of places, and the costs of non-profit residential service provision (accounting for 28 per cent of places) are covered almost entirely by the state.

Finally, the fourth model may be considered as a *market dominated*, since alongside direct state and third sector provision a considerable proportion of services are provided by private enterprise organizations. In some fields, such as residential services in the UK and Spain, the proportion of services provided by for-profit organizations is dominant. Furthermore, state funding in this situation is quite limited; in fact, a considerable amount of the expenditure of third sector organizations is covered by private giving and by service fees. We find in this case not only a substantial presence of organizations operating on market principles, but also considerable commercialization of the services provided by non-profit organizations. For these two reasons the model is different from the others due to a greater commodification of the services and the more residual nature of state intervention, both in terms of direct service provision and of funding of private or nonprofit providers.

2.3. MODES OF COORDINATION BETWEEN THE STATE AND THE THIRD SECTOR WITH RESPECT TO THE LEVEL OF SOCIAL CARE PROVISION

The typology given in Table 2.3 does not clearly identify distinct national models. The situations generated in specific fields are in fact different, and they place some countries—like France, Spain and the UK—halfway between different models. Nevertheless, we can still observe whether the differences in the sectoral organization of social care provision coincide with differences in the general level of social services provision in the countries considered. We wonder if the modes of organizing the provision of social care give rise to varying levels of covering the social care needs of the population.

Table 2.4 gives the main results of this analysis, which compares the models of organizing social care provision on the basis of indicators of the overall level of state provision of services, of the social care needs that are met by the family, and finally of the degree to which the family is retrieved from responsibility for social care services (shown by the percentage of women in employment[13]). The data, where possible, shows percentages for specific sectors.

It emerges clearly from the data that where the third sector in social services provision dominates, there is also a generally low level of direct state provision of services and strong expectation that families will provide social care for their members.

This situation is typical of Italy and Spain (but also in the UK, in the child care field): therein public social care provision is generally residual and means tested (Ferrera, 1996), thus leaving ample space to the third sector, which is supported only partially by state funding. In this model the third sector plays a role of substitute for state provision and enjoys a certain financial and regulatory independence (Ascoli, 1987; Barbetta, 1997). The outcome is *a dual type social services system* in which the fragmentation of initiatives, the plurality of the supply, and a general scarcity of professional and financial resources prevail (Pasquinelli, 1993). It would be wrong, however, to conclude that the only distinguishing feature of this model is its strong familism. The analysis performed shows that in the countries where this model is found, third sector

Table 2.4. Models of Social Care Provision

	Third-sector Dominant Model	Subsidiarity Model	State Dominant Model	Market Dominant Model
Welfare state provision	*Low* 3–5% child care 1% home care	*Low/high* 3–20% child care 2–7% home care	*High* 12% child care 16% home care	*Low* 2% child care 9% home care
Family welfare provision	*High* 37–39% aged living with children	*Low-medium* 14–20% aged living with children	*Low* 11% aged living with children	*Low* 16% aged living with children
Women in labour force	*Low* 41–46%	*Medium* 57–58%	*High* 71%	*Medium* 53%

social services provision is much greater than direct state provision. Thus, it allows the general level of welfare provision in these countries to come closer to that of countries with a more developed tradition of public welfare policies. The principal features of this model, do not consist so much of the limited size of the overall provision; rather, this model is characterized by the fragmentation of services, the lack of coordination between state intervention and third sector action, and the strong influence exercised by particularist interests in policy decision making processes and in state funding procedures.[14]

At the extreme opposite to the third sector dominant model we find the state dominant model. In this case, the residual role of the third sector is largely due to massive, direct state provision, which pushes the overall level of social provision up, and thereby encourages female employment and general removal of responsibility for care from the family. This is the Scandinavian model, strongly distinguished by the high level of professionalism in care provision and the assumption of responsibility by the state for direct provision of services. To this well-established picture (Esping-Andersen, 1999), the analysis given here adds the observation of the complementary role of the third sector, which operates in this context as a 'public agent'. This conceptualization does not mean that non-profit organizations in these countries constitute a mere extension of state bureaucracy; on the contrary, they have in fact enjoyed considerable operational autonomy, even though they are generously supported by state funding (see the chapter on Norway). Integration between the two sectors has occurred above all in cultural terms, through strong agreement on policy objectives and recognition of the eminently public aims of voluntary action. There is also a certain separation between the funding function, performed entirely by the state, and the provision of services, which in certain fields is delegated, to a significant extent, to the third sector.

The subsidiarity model is located halfway between the two models already described. It is characterized by a low level of direct state provision of social care, even if this is higher than the level found in the third sector dominant model. This situation is accompanied by the placing of considerable responsibility for care on the family, but to a lesser extent than is found with the third sector dominant model. The presence of considerable financial commitment from the state and abundant third sector provision allows an intermediate balance between direct provision of services and care performed by the family. The concept of subsidiarity, on the other hand, actually conjures up the idea of a 'mixed' system, based on cooperation between all the components, of society (Anheier, 1992). This intermediate position is also reflected in the regulatory model, which affords considerable autonomy of initiative to non-profit organizations; but at the same time, it involves them in wider decision making processes through which their work is coordinated with state programmes. In this subsidiarity model, non-profit organizations, coordinated in a few vertical, very compact internal structures, have thus acquired a privileged public status. This status has allowed them the right to participate in policy making and to obtain state funding through channels protected from the possible presence of competing providers (Offe, 1981). The sizeable state funding and the tradition of joint decision making also make the overall supply system less fragmented and dispersed than is found in third sector dominant models (Seibel, 1992).

Finally, in the market dominant model there is medium to low state provision of social services; moreover, there is a moderate level of responsibility placed on families for providing care. State intervention is characterized by extensive means tested programmes, whereby services are only provided for the most disadvantaged groups in the population. Actual provision is only partially delegated to the third sector and a strong state dominance remains. The selective character of state provision nevertheless leaves a large part of the demand for social care unsatisfied. It is addressed by non-profit organizations (which obtain a large part of their income from the sale of services) or more often by for-profit organizations. The size of the private market for services explains why, despite the low level of state spending and the modest supply of services from the third sector, little care is actually carried out in the family (although the level is somewhat higher than in Scandinavian countries). In this context, the role of the third sector is complementary to state provision, but it is not residual, as it is shown by the high level of funding that non-profit organizations obtain from private giving.

To conclude, the inclusion of the third sector in a comparative analysis of social care systems allows us to better understand how national social care systems are constructed. They are based on a complex combination of public policies and initiatives of civic and religious forces. The emerging picture is perhaps broader and more finely grained than an analysis centred exclusively on the family-versus-state dichotomy. The models of social care provision that emerge constitute different points of equilibrium. Therein, the third sector plays a crucial role, within the framework of public policies (as occurs in the state dominant and subsidiarity models), or outside it (as occurs in the third sector and market dominant models). The position of the third sector is therefore at times complementary to state intervention (and closely intertwined with public policies) and at times a substitute for it (and very weakly connected with public policies). Its presence cannot always be associated with an absence of state commitment, nor, on the other hand, with its presence: there are countries in which the strong commitment of the state to welfare policies is associated with strong third sector involvement, and there are others in which the strength of one is accompanied by the weakness of the other. Both in Scandinavian and continental countries (Germany above all) there is close integration between the state and the third sector; nevertheless, in the former the role of the third sector is complementary and residual, while in the latter direct state provision prevails. Nor can it be said that the third sector is strong only where it has strong state support: the cases of Italy and Spain show in fact that a strong third sector dominance of social care provision can exist alongside partial state funding and limited state commitment to welfare policies. The identification of different organizational models within national social care systems in which relations between the state and the third sector take on a specific shape, also confirms the idea that these relationships are associated with different models for covering social care needs of the population. The third sector takes on different roles and functions within these general models of coverage; they range from that of the 'public agent', which extends public policies through the provision of specific forms of organization (a role played above all in the state dominant and subsidiarity models), to that of a substitute for state provision, both in terms of direct supply and of finance (this role is evident above all in third sector and market dominant models).

The presence of the third sector, though in different roles, has allowed for a fuller provision of social care services than that provided directly by the state. The third sector has supplemented or substituted state supply, while reflecting the more general features of the larger welfare system in which it operates. The attention given to its presence allows to gain a better understanding of the nature of each social care model and has perhaps clarified the differences that exist between them.

2.4. THE ROLE OF THE THIRD SECTOR IN SOCIAL CARE: BEYOND PARTNERSHIP

Once the fundamental contribution made by the third sector in the provision of social care is recognized, what remains to be understood is the role it plays with respect to the other actors of welfare policies, and firstly with respect to state intervention. As seen in the previous section, the relationship between the state and the third sector differs greatly from country to country. Despite these differences, it seems possible to find some characteristics that are common to most of the countries considered in the study. This exploration is aimed at identifying the existence of a political space within which a typical model of relationship between the state and the third sector has grown.

The role of the third sector with regard to social care policies has long been considered as opposing or competing with the state (Weisbrod, 1988). The comparative literature on welfare policy has traditionally considered its presence alongside the relevance of the family and informal networks as characteristics of liberal welfare systems. Confirmation of this view came from the recurrent observation of the extraordinary richness of voluntary initiatives and associations in a country, like the United States, very poor in developing a state welfare system, while the scarcity of non-profit organizations in Scandinavian countries seemed to confirm the residual nature of the third sector as an alternative to the development of a strong welfare state. In these views, the existence of a third sector is considered, therefore, as an alternative to the development of a welfare state. The persistence of third sector organizations appeared as the survival of institutions and cultures associated with a vision of welfare that still sees social policies as charity; a continued existence which only finds opportunities for growth in welfare systems with little inclination toward universalism and the recognition of full social citizenship rights.

Sufficient empirical evidence has now been collected to refute this vision (Gidron et al., 1992; Kuhnle and Selle, 1992; Anheier and Seibel, 1990). This analysis confirms that the third sector has grown in many European countries thanks to the support of the state and *not* in opposition to it. If this state support was already evident in the social services field during the 'golden age' of maximum expansion of the welfare state (the twenty-year period following the end of World War II), there has been further growth in the last ten years, which coincides with the start of privatization policies. In many European countries, but also in the United States, state funding has become the main source of income for third sector organizations operating in the social services field. It accounts for 65 per cent of income in Germany, 49 per cent in Spain, 58 per cent in France, 57 per cent in Italy and 40 per cent in Great Britain. The corresponding figure in the United States is 51 per cent (Salamon et al., 1999), a level not so different from that of the countries considered in this study. On the other hand, finance from donations and voluntary contributions—considered typical of organizations founded on an independent basis and which run mostly on voluntary work—is a minority source of income, insufficient to provide financial security for the organizations that receive it. Nevertheless, the strong financial dependence on the state does not imply that third sector organizations are a mere instrument used by public authorities to implement welfare policies more efficiently and effectively. Although most non-profit organizations operate as 'public agents' on the base of state funding and a government mandate, they are far from constituting a mere appendage of state bureaucracies (Wolch, 1990). Many studies have showed that the large sums flowing from public administrations to non-profit organizations have not reduced the independence of the latter (Kramer, 1992). Despite the inevitability of a relative reciprocal loss of autonomy when there is an exchange of resources, Kramer (1994) has observed, for example, a substantial symmetry of interdependence. The past history of relations between the state and the third sector is characterized more by cooperation between the two sectors than by competition: the state furnishes the basic funding and the third sector the services that the state either is unable or unwilling to provide directly (Salamon, 1987b).

According to Kramer (1992), cooperation between the state and the third sector allowed an incremental expansion of welfare polices in a period— 1970s and 1980s—characterized historically by limited financial resources. In almost all Western European countries, non-profit organizations supplemented state action. The functions performed by these organizations were numerous: anticipating need, diversification of the service supply and specialization in the field, tutelage of groups of the population excluded from state programmes, experimentation of new forms of social care intervention, and support of a more effective use of state programmes. Many of these initiatives were progressively financed by the state and included in government planning, thus conferring important legitimation on the organizations that created them; others, on the other hand, were funded with no precise evaluation of their effectiveness and usefulness.

It is difficult, observing the growing merging of roles between the two sectors, to assess where the final responsibility for the supply of a considerable number of social services lies. According to some authors (Salamon, 1987b), cooperation between the state and the third sector has grown in parallel with an increasingly clearer distinction of responsibility between who provides the funding and who runs the services. However, so far, on the basis of the national cases presented in this book, what emerges is a considerable overlap of responsibility between the state and the main non-profit providers of social services. While at an official level, entrusting service provision to the third sector implies a shift of responsibility from public administrations to non-profit organizations for running services, in actual fact it has often favoured a 'symbiotic' relationship between the two sectors. It would therefore be incorrect to describe the relationship between the state and the third sector in terms of a partnership between an agency which funds and another that provides services on behalf of the former. While on the one hand responsibility for funding lies mainly with the state, responsibility for actual service provision is largely shared between government bureaucracies and non-profit organizations.

The most important political consequence of the massive involvement of the third sector in the implementation of social care policies is the development of a typical form of state regulation. A 'specialised network of decisions concerning specific subjects and problems' has developed (Franz, 1991, p. 490). The theoretically authoritative role of the state service has often been translated into a regime of 'shared government' (Franz, 1991), characterized by local and partial compromises between public and non-profit actors. The social services field has thus become a 'protected market', in which relations between the different actors (funders, services providers and clients) are mainly based on trust. It is a context that has favoured the diffusion in non-profit organizations of behaviour aimed more at conservation of the *status quo* rather than at investment and innovation. Moreover, third sector organizations have gained privileged access to decision making processes in mixed welfare regimes. Non-profit organizations have acquired positions of great influence over the last decade, succeeding in obtaining direct representation on government commissions and playing a decisive role in the development of new state programmes. The national cases presented in this book provide many examples and reflections on this subject.

In line with a pluralist perspective, it may be held that the increased political influence of the third sector allows priority to be given to goals in the public interest. In defending their own interests, non-profit organizations would in fact be defending the interests of the most socially vulnerable and excluded groups. On the other hand, the growth of financial links with the state has pushed the third sector increasingly further away from its role of safeguarding the interests of the most disadvantaged. The transformation of non-profit organizations from 'competitive groups' into 'corporative groups' (Cawson, 1982) is a side effect of granting them (sometimes explicitly and more often implicitly) public recognition, which has implied not just the right to be consulted by public authorities, but also joint responsibility for deciding and implementing social policies.

In conclusion, the development of contemporary social service systems in Europe has occurred in parallel with the growth of closer and more complex relations between the state and the third sector. The mixed statute of these systems lies not just in the existence of actors with different juridical and organizational standings who contribute to service provision, but it also means that the actual borders between the sectors has become increasingly uncertain, just as the levels of responsibility for and participation in policy making have overlapped. Systems of service provision have therefore developed which cannot be understood correctly by resorting to previous interpretations. The 'mix' indicates considerable variety in the supply system, to which a plurality of subjects contribute, each equipped with forms of organization and with cultural orientations that are very diversified and heterogeneous. On the one hand, this mix has generated confusion and difficulty in defining the aims and principles of the service system; on the other hand, it has paradoxically contributed to widening areas of experimentation and innovation.

The role played by the third sector in the field of social care is very peculiar. It certainly cannot be assimilated with the functions of the family and informal networks because of the high level of professionalism achieved and the close relations with public administrations. Furthermore, it cannot be defined as falling within the public sector, because of its very high degree of autonomy and the great influence it exerts on policy making. For a full understanding of the current position of the third sector, it must not be forgotten that the social origins of non-profit organizations are based on collective goals, on civic commitment to social goals, on desires for change (Wuthnow, 1991). The service provision aspect must be defined in relation to this original identity and is characterized by the religious or humanitarian values of the civic and social communities of which they are an expression (Seibel, 1989). Their relationship with public policies developed at a later stage and placed them in an intermediary position. Now they constitute 'a tension field where different influences compete, cross or have to be outbalanced' (Evers, 1995, p. 163). According to Evers, the specificity of third sector organizations lies in their occupying an intermediate position between the state, the market and the family (the latter inclusive of local communities), and in integrating and combining the original lines of action of each actor. It is therefore reductive to just 'stick' the identity of these organizations onto one of these components from which it acquires its norms and codes of behaviour, even if it is the dominating component. Furthermore, the particular type of combination depends on wider historical and social circumstances and is in any case constantly changing with the changing relationships between the different components.

Notes

1. Personal social service provision is actually considered by Gornick et al. (1997) as action designed to encourage the employment of mothers and more generally of women.
2. One complementary strategy employed by some countries is to encourage the purchase of care services on the private market by means of tax benefits and other measures; this strategy, however, runs up against the limits to the expansion of the private market for providing these services, and in any case, ends up favouring higher income families.
3. In these countries the third sector is actually concentrated in social services, accounting, on average, for 44 per cent of all non-profit sector employment (Salamon et al., 1999).
4. This attention is beginning to have some echoes in the comparative literature on welfare, where the existence of a fourth sector, consisting of non-profit organizations, is now acknowledged alongside the state, the market and the family (e.g. cf. Esping-Andersen, 1999). On the political side, there are now various European countries in which the third sector is recognized by the state to be consulted when social care policies are defined.
5. The considerable diffusion of these services allows to seek space and opportunities for the development of a third way to solve the dilemmas and difficulties with which social care policies are currently struggling, that goes well beyond the simple alternative between growth of state intervention and further overloading of the family.
6. A more general typology made on the same basis and assigning even more importance to the degree to which responsibility has been removed from the family, is proposed by Esping-Andersen (1999), which follows the well-known distinction between the three regimes of welfare capitalism described in Esping-Andersen (1990).
7. The typology contains four models: (a) *a state dominant model*, in which both functions are performed by the state; (b) *a dual model*, in which both the state and the third sector duplicate both functions with little communication between them; (c) *a cooperative*

model, in which the government funds and the third sector provides most of the services; and (d) *a third sector dominant model*, in which both functions are performed by the third sector. Most of the national cases, however, fall into the category of the dual or cooperative model, while the definition of only one cooperative model runs the risk of placing national cases that are very different, such as the United States and Germany, in the same category of model (Kuhnle and Selle, 1992).

8. This typology identifies: *an integrated dependence model*, characteristic of Scandinavian countries and of Germany and Holland, in which the services provided by the third sector are integrated into a more general and comprehensive welfare system; *a separate dependence model*, found in France and Italy, characterized by communicative and cultural distance between the third sector and the state; *an integrated autonomy model*, in which cultural affinity is accompanied by considerable operational and financial autonomy (in which none of the countries studied by the authors is included with the possible exception of the Netherlands); *a separate autonomy model*, characterized by cultural distance and financial independence, characteristic of Spain. The main problem with this tipology is the excessive concentration on relations between the state and the third sector and, again, the existence of cases that are more theoretical by than empirically verifiable.

9. The theoretical framework the authors use to support their approach is the historical analysis by Barrington Moore (1966) on the origins of Fascism and democracy and the comparative theory of Esping-Andersen (1990) on welfare regimes.

10. For example, the assignment of Italy to the social democratic model is difficult to justify, given the actual low level of state welfare spending.

11. Clearly, a classification of regimes on the basis of the amount of state welfare spending does not take account of the context in which the money is spent (in which sector and on what services), nor can it be considered a sufficiently representative indicator of the type of socio-economic embeddedness of the third sector.

12. The typology proposed, as shown in Table 2.2, is based on data that is mainly incomplete. Precise information on the level of state funding of non-profit organizations that provide specific services is lacking. The typology that follows should, therefore, be considered as only suggestive.

13. The fact that women work does not mean, of course, that they are free from responsibility at home to the same degree as men or their male partners. However, the rate of women in labour force clearly shows to what extent families can adopt a self-servicing strategy to meet the care needs of their members.

14. See also the chapters on Italy and Spain in this volume.

Chapter 3

A Contract Culture even in Scandinavia

MAGNE EIKÅS AND PER SELLE*

3.1. INTRODUCTION: FROM MUTUAL TRUST TO CONTRACTING

In this article we discuss the changing character of the Norwegian Welfare State. In particular, our concern is with the new organizing principles that regulate the relationship and cooperation between public authorities and voluntary organizations and businesses. We are concerned with the emerging tendency towards a breakdown of the 'monolithic' welfare state, in particular with the downgrading of the state's role as a welfare *producer*. This development provides an opportunity for old and new voluntary organizations and new commercial enterprises to move into the business of welfare through the delivery of contracted services with the public authorities. The emerging contract culture with its emphasis on competition, regulation through formal contracts and accountability, is changing the meaning of contracting between government and other sectors.

The history of cooperation between government and voluntary organizations in the field of social services[1] in Norway dates back to the mid-19th century. Even though voluntary organizations have played a significant role in Norwegian social policy for more than one hundred years, for a long time the

*MAGNE EIKÅS • Høgskulen i Sogn og Fjordane, Avdeling for Samfunnsfag, 6851 Sogndal, Norway.   PER SELLE • Norwegian Research Center in Organization and Management, Rosenbergsqt. 39, 5015 Bergen, Norway.

scope and nature of their contribution to welfare represented a lacuna in the welfare state research (Kuhnle and Selle, 1990).

This lack of research effort and the parallel lack of 'voluntary organization visibility' in the public debate on social policy are probably the main reasons why scholars abroad and at home, for a long time, came to believe that Norwegian social welfare was solely the story of services produced by two sectors: Government (at the national, regional and local levels) and the informal sector (family, friends and neighbours). Most social policy researchers have put Norway in the cluster of welfare states characterized by a predominant public sector with redistributive public institutions (Titmuss, 1974; Esping-Andersen, 1990).

Such welfare state typologies have recently been criticized for being overly simplistic. In Scandinavia Norwegian scholars such as Kuhnle and Selle (1992) and Swedish scholars such as Lundstrøm and Wijkstrøm (1997) have been concerned with the defectiveness of the dominant welfare state typologies in the international literature. They argue that as long as these typologies do not attempt to include the role of voluntary welfare organizations in a systematic manner, we will not obtain a reliable picture of differences and similarities between welfare states. These organizations have played an important, though often neglected, role within the Norwegian Welfare State.

Moreover, as long as these models do not take into consideration the role played by what we may term welfare market-actors, who have always delivered welfare services in Norway (though on a rather limited scale), we will not be able to present a realistic picture of our kind of welfare state. For instance, who is aware that the dental services for adults in Norway are services that are, and always have been, completely financed by the individuals and produced by dentists in a competitive commercial market (Erichsen, 1996)? Or that almost half of the annual labour (in man-years) in medical services at the local level is produced by private medical practitioners on contract with the local authorities (Fimreite and Stensvoll, 1998)? There exists a long tradition of contracting between government and individuals as representatives of professions at the local level in Norway. This tradition is now about to be expanded to encompass even larger commercial enterprises as part of the new contract culture.

In this article we will first provide a brief historical overview of some of the most characteristic features of voluntary social service organizations' contributions to social welfare services in Norway. We then outline the mechanisms of government: organization integration and cooperation. In order to understand the contemporary changes in the welfare state, which we think are comprehensive or even 'transformative', we believe it is vital to understand the difference between the 'old' system of cooperation, basically founded upon close integration and mutual trust, and the new contract culture with more focus on competition, time-limited contracts, legal control and accountability, but also greater ideological freedom regarding the content of the services provided by the organizations. Thus, in the main sections we focus on these recent developments. We also trace the origins of the emerging new contract culture, in which the key words are Mangement by Objectives (MBO) and New Public Management (NPM), with an emphasis on deregulation, decentralization, effectivity, privatization and contracting. These concepts, which to a large extent are imported from the vocabulary of business administration, are now penetrating the traditional institutions of the Norwegian Welfare State and the social-service-producing voluntary organizations alike. In particular, we will show how the contract culture is now about to penetrate one of the core areas of traditional public welfare, that is, care for the elderly, thus opening up a new market not only for voluntary organizations, but also for commercial enterprises.

3.2. THE HISTORICAL RELATIONSHIP BETWEEN GOVERNMENT AND VOLUNTARY SOCIAL SERVICE ORGANIZATIONS

The Voluntary Organizations' Contribution to Welfare

Organizations which originated in two important social movements in Norway, the teetotal movement and the Christian laymen movement, were among the pioneers in philanthropic social work in Norway. These movements date back to the 1840s (Seip, 1984). Their activities were directed at helping special groups such as poor and unemployed women, alcoholics, the handicapped, the homeless and other suffering people (Raaum, 1988; Blom, 1998).

The real momentum began with the founding of 'new' social organizations in the late 19th and early 20th centuries. The subsequent development has two main paths, the first of which involved the establishment of national, humanitarian organizations. These organizations first had rather narrow objectives, but later broadened their humanitarian purposes. Examples of such organizations are the National Organization for Female Volunteer Workers (1896) and the National Organization for People's Health (1910).[2] Both these organizations worked to combat the problem of tuberculosis. This work involved an expanded focus on prevention, for example, on the origins of illness and bad health, and thus made the organizations capable of continuing and expanding their work on a broader basis when the fight against tuberculosis was finally won. Being pioneers, both organizations were heavily involved in running hospitals, institutions for children, convalescent homes, work-training institutions and sanatoriums (Raaum, 1988; Blom, 1998). In some of these areas, such as institutions for sick children and the convalescent homes, the organizations were in charge of almost all the existing institutions at the time. Another important national humanitarian organization which broadened its humanitarian activities and services in this period was the Norwegian Red Cross.

The second line of development is the establishment of national, voluntary organizations for the functionally disabled. The first organizations were designed to help the 'classic' groups with strong and visible disabilities: the blind (1908), the deaf (1918) and the crippled (1931) (Ravneberg and Solvang, 1995). All these national organizations were based on former local and regional initiatives and organizations (Onarheim, 1990). After 1945 a large number of new organizations were formed, most often with very specialized purposes. The birth rate of such organizations was particularily high throughout the 1980s and 1990s, with an increase in all types of 'syndrome'-organizations. These organizations work closely with government and are now among the strongest supporters of the traditional welfare state. They have played successful roles as political advocates for the establishment of universal material welfare entitlements for the disabled, and they see the legitimacy of their rights as strongly connected to the legitimacy of the state in welfare matters.

The period after the second world war has been characterized by continuous expansion in the number of voluntary social service organizations. Thus, the growth in the public sector and the rise of the modern welfare state in this period have definitively not made the voluntary organizations superfluous. More than 50 per cent of today's organizations in this field were established during the 1960s and 1970s (Selle and Øymyr, 1995). The number of social service organizations at the national level rose from 44 in 1945 to 134 in 1985 (NOU, 1988: 17). In 1995 approximately 160 national organizations received economic support from the Ministry of Social Affairs (St meld nr 27, 1996–1997). This figure encompasses all kinds of voluntary organizations in the welfare area, ranging from huge humanitarian organizations with broad social welfare goals to smaller self-help and interest groups engaged in problems such as suicide, anxiety, drug addiction and psycho-social problems (ibid.). Some of these new self-help organizations are connected to public authorities in that they receive financial and professional help from the public sector. As a means of comparison, we might mention that the national organizations in the welfare area cover approximately 7 per cent of a total organizational population of 2,500 (Hallenstvedt and Trollvik, 1993).

At this point it is pertinent to ask the following question: In which welfare service areas have the organizations not only made very important contributions historically, but continue to be important *service producers*? We shall emphasize three in particular: care for mentally disabled, care for alcoholics and child welfare care. Measured in annual employee-years, institutions owned by voluntary organizations contributed 39.9 per cent, 63.4 per cent and 32.4 per cent, respectively, of the total number of employee-years in these areas in 1985 (NOU, 1988: 17, p. 120). However, the political decentralization of the responsibility for services for the mentally disabled, which were moved from the regional to the municipal level in 1991 (the HVPU reform), had one unintentional effect: the reform took place at a time when the dominant ideology was deinstitutionalization, normalization and more 'open care' (Sandvin and Søder, 1998). The essence of the ideology (open care) is that the mentally disabled, as far as possible, shall have their own homes in their own local communities, and that the services shall be structured and planned in accordance with this premise. This is the reason why voluntary organizations involved in the running of large institutions for the physically disabled faced a situation in which they were owners of empty buildings associated with an 'outdated' service and ideology. The ideology of deinstitutionalization described above has been strong throughout the 1980s and early 1990s, but is now under pressure. Thus, we are again observing a more favourable climate towards larger institutions (especially in psychiatric care and care for the elderly) which may allow room for new types of voluntary activity.

The Traditional Form of Cooperation

Looking back, voluntary organizations in Norway have always cooperated with public authorities, and thus influenced public policy (Kuhnle and Selle, 1990). Their genesis coincides with the early phase in the development of the Norwegian welfare state. Government accepted the importance of the organizations' work, while the organizations themselves not only accepted public responsibility for the social and health-care problems that they were involved in; they pushed in that direction. Often the boundaries between what was public and what was voluntary were very blurred. An early expression of this institutional intertwining is the fact that public officials were often instrumental in the establishment of voluntary organizations in the late 18th century, and they were often members of the organizations' executive boards (Try, 1985).

The broad humanitarian organizations were not 'forced' to cooperate with government. On the contrary, they have been key factors in the ideological change that gradually resulted in an overall public responsibility for social and health care problems. The organizations have been more interested in pragmatic problem-solving, for example, the improvement of social and health conditions, than in drawing up sharp boundaries against government in order to secure their own autonomy. This is true even for the organizations for disabled persons described above, where the question of organizational autonomy at times has been very important. However, since the implementation of the welfare state, the organizations have not been afraid of receiving public funds. Such funds have underscored their rights within the welfare state, rights closely linked to the comprehensive public responsibility within the field.

Government and voluntary organizations have, in the early phase of the welfare state, shared a set of basic goals and for that reason, the relationship has been rather pragmatic and peaceful, and not very contentious. The organizations have had a profound ideological influence on public policy in the welfare area, that is, the shift from private to public responsibility, and have often served as pioneers in the institutionalization of new forms of social services—services which later have often become a public responsibility (Seip, 1984; Blom, 1998). Very generally speaking, the historical development seems to be characterized by an integration based on mutual trust, and the organizations have gradually become more important in the implementation of public policy (Klausen and Selle, 1996).

The integration of government and many of the voluntary social service organizations has, in general, grown 'deeper' from the 1970s until today. The organizations have, in this period, become more dependent on government financial support for the implementation of their services and activities than they ever were before (Selle, 1998). This is not unique to Norway: it is a trend found in many other countries as well (Kramer et al., 1993; Salamon and Anheier, 1997). But what probably *has been* unique, compared to other countries, is the relatively high degree of institutional autonomy at the organizational level of the service-producing voluntary organizations. This may be due to their dual nature as service producers as well as membership-based, democratic organizations. The 'service units' of the organizations are in many cases organizationally separated from the 'mother organization', even if they both grew out from the old membership organization. However, even today there is an extensive overlap of board members. This structure applies to the majority of the national organizations in the field of social services (Lorentzen, 1994). This dual nature of the organizations makes it difficult for the public authorities to treat the organizations as a more or less standardized service-producing unit that can be relatively easily controlled, because the public authorities cannot legitimately interfere with the internal democratic structure and the democratic processes of the organizations (Selle and Øymyr, 1995).

Nevertheless, this increased economic dependence does have some important consequences for the voluntary organizations. Today, governmental economic support may, in some cases, be a question of 'to be or not to be' for the voluntary organizations, and for most of the social service institutions owned by voluntary organizations this is definitely the case. For instance, Selle and Øymyr (1995) have shown that the growth of voluntary organizations seems to be strongest in fields where they are most heavily financed, and thereby also legitimated, by public authorities. Accordingly, the growth of the voluntary sector today is largely dependent on public financing and close cooperation with governmental agencies. The gradual integration of voluntary social welfare organizations into an overall public system of finance and control has made it even less accurate than before to consider this sector to be a *completely independent alternative* to the public sector. On the contrary, this is a development that has resulted in hybrid organizational forms and welfare pluralism, in which 'boundaries' between the public sector and voluntary organizations often seem to be rather obscure. But there must be no mistaking the fact that the public authorities are most often the dominant part in this relationship, since they, to a large degree, control the organizations' finances through growing public transfers. Thus, within most sectors we do not observe a well-balanced partnership.

The result has been more formal institutional integration at the expense of the more informal integration. Even if 'new' voluntary organizations most often started out as independent actors, they soon became more or less integral parts of public policy, or at least they have become very dependent on public transfers. But this does not *necessarily* result in a severe loss of organizational autonomy. The degree of autonomy will, to a large extent, be defined by the organizations' own strategic choices, for example, in the way that they choose to interact and cooperate with public authorities (Skov Henriksen, 1996), as well as the interests and goals of the public authorities, which differ largely across sectors.

Voluntary organizations may be integrated with government in different ways: normatively, economically, professionally and administratively (Lorentzen, 1994). In our view, it is the financial integration that has been most crucial to the organizations, because historically, in most cases, the financial aspect is strongly related to the other types of integration (Kuhnle and Selle, 1990). Thus, in the following, we will present the major funding instruments public authorities in Norway have used (and are still using) to support the organizations. However, the connection between financial integration and the other forms of integration may, as we shall see in Sections 3.3. and 3.4, be weakened in the contracting system now emerging, while at the same time these financial instruments are undergoing deep change.

1. Basic Grants

Basic grants are the traditional public means that have been used to support *membership-based* voluntary organizations. These grants are usually described as 'free', which means that the public authorities (until now) have laid down few restrictions on *how* the organizations spend the money. Through this arrangement, government seeks to realise goals connected to participation, local organizational activities and democratic decision making (St meld nr 27, 1996–1997: 31). It is important that the means of support are framed in a way that secures the organizations a free and independent position in society (*ibid.*). The governmental expectations connected to the goals above, have (until now) not been formulated as distinct prerequisites for receiving grants. This means that there has been little obligation for the organizations to meet governmental expectations on requirements.

2. Grants for Running Institutions

Government is paying voluntary organizations currently for their service production in different fields, most of which is carried out at the local (municipal) level. If the organizations satisfy various governmental requirements and are part of, for example, public social and health care plans, they receive public grants that cover most of the operating costs connected to the running of the institutions. On some occasions, the organizations can also use public grants to finance loan investments, for example, in buildings and equipment. In fact, sometimes it is only the difference in formal ownership that makes such welfare service institutions different from public institutions. Many organizations have downplayed their ideology and value-base in the welfare state period in order to comply with the requirements of the authorities. Professional staffing in the institutions is often a prerequisite for receiving public grants. Service production is usually (though not always) regulated in specific contracts. These contracts between local government and the institutions have traditionally differed vastly in content, duration and degree of formalization, as well as the exercising of public control. This has caused the municipalities' employer and interest organization (Kommunenes Sentralforbund) to work out standardized contracts, which the municipalities are now about to introduce as a part of the new contract culture. But the organizational resistence to this change seems to have been rather strong at the local level. For instance, the local authorities in the city of Bergen, the second largest city in the country, have worked for a long time to implement a more coherent and formalized practice towards the voluntary organizations and foundations that are running welfare institutions.[3] This new type of legal and financial control seems to have been difficult to implement. There is, for instance, disagreement between local public authorities and the organizations as to the preferred duration of the contracts. In brief, it is in the interest of the organizations to establish long-term contracts which give them financial security, while it is in the interest of the local authorities to have short-term contracts which give them more freedom if they should want to switch between different suppliers.

3. Subsidies

We have now moved from *direct* public transfers to more *indirect* public payments. This category covers exemptions from various ordinary financial obligations such as taxes, reduced rent levels on leased buildings, free use of public buildings, sale of public buildings below market price, etc. (Lorentzen, 1994). There exists no empirical documentation on the total scope of such subsidies, but they are generally believed to be very significant. This also creates controversies between public authorities and organizations when, for example, buildings owned by the organizations are sold to public authorities or on the market. The problem that arises is the determination of a fair price, given the government subsidies that have been invested previously.

Before turning to how the new contract culture alters how public authorities support the voluntary organizations, we need to understand how this culture could develop in the first place. That is intimately connected to the introduction and implementation of MBO and NPM in the public sector. Let us, therefore, first describe what kind of influence MBO and NPM have had on the public sector in general, as well as on the voluntary organizations.

3.3. THE 'CONTRACT CULTURE'

Public Sector Change

It is difficult to single out one particular explanatory factor to explain why society seems to be moving in the direction of more strictly regulated 'contractual' relationships between different actors. But it seems obvious that the neo-liberal trends with emphasis on competition, market and cost-effectiveness are of great importance. We will describe and analyse one particular public reform that we believe *might* be one of the more influential parts of this neo-liberal ideology, that is, the introduction and implementation of MBO.[4]

The MBO reform was part of a more general trend towards 'modernization' of the public sector in Norway. This process has been labelled 'New Public Management' (Hood, 1991; Lægreid, 1997, 1999). The reform seems to have been one of the answers to the criticism of the public sector in general and the welfare state in particular. The main problems have been believed to be the ineffectivity and suboptimality of the public sector. It is the cost-side of the sector that is most in focus. The public sector is accused of being slow and ineffective. It is too rule-bound and the professions and their organizations are exercising too much power. The public sector is showing weak results and is lacking the kind of flexibility and 'user responsibility' that is necessary to bring it into line with the existing claims and demands in society. In other words, the traditional institutions of the welfare state are criticized for not being in line with the 'problem structure' of contemporary society. The solutions (the reforms) are to a large degree based on the import of models from the private sector, with a management-oriented philosophy, which is in line with international trends.

The most characteristic features of NPM were outlined in seven doctrines formulated by Christopher Hood (1991): (1) 'Hands-on professional management' in the public sector, which means active, visible and discretionary control from named persons at the top, who are free to 'manage'. (2) Explicit standards and measures of performance, which means definition of goals and indicators of success, preferably expressed in quantitative terms. (3) Greater emphasis on output control, which means resource allocations and rewards linked to measured performance. (4) A shift to disaggregetion of units in the public sector, which means a break-up of formerly monolithic units. (5) A shift to greater competition in the public sector, which means a move to term contracts and public tendering procedures. (6) An emphasis on private sector style management practices, which means moving away from 'military-style' public service ethics and, finally, (7) an emphasis on greater discipline and parsimony in resource use, which means cutting direct costs and raising labour discipline. A comparison across nations shows that Norway is among the nations demonstrating a rather clear shift towards NPM in the 1980s, together with nations like Sweden, Canada, New Zealand, Australia, UK, Denmark, France and the Netherlands (Hood, 1995). To sum up: a more flexible, result-oriented and cost-effective public sector is supposed to vitalize and rationalize the operation of the welfare state (Olsen, 1993). How did this mangement ideology and philosophy crystallize in Norwegian public policy?

In 1987 the Norwegian Government decided that all state institutions should introduce 'operational plans'[5] for their activities by the end of 1990 (Thorsvik, 1991). Through this decision, MBO became one of the main governmental tools in the aim to achieve the best possible use of public resources. The focus was clearly on reduced costs and improved cost-effectiveness. The decision was, to a large degree, based upon proposals that were put forward in a governmental report published three years earlier (NOU 1984: 23). This report basically stated that all the activities of the state should be governed through goal decisions and budget frames. Central government was to downplay its former way of governing through concern with details of the state institutions' performance. Instead, government was to give the institutions more freedom to choose the most suitable means to achieve their planned goals (deregulation and decentralization). Thus, the institutions were supposed to achieve more freedom but at the same time they were required to make plans and report on the results of their activities. The most influential prescriptions were formulated by a governmental agency (Statskonsult) in a report published in 1988. In this document, the central elements seem to be threefold (Thorsvik, 1991):

1. The institutions should develop a goal structure which groups, in a systematic manner, the different goals of the institutions. This is supposed to form the basis for precise quantifications of goal achievements.
2. Every institution should make an operational plan based on the formulated goal structure. This plan is to be worked out for one year at a time. It is supposed to show which results the institution wants to achieve, and how it is to achieve them.
3. The last part of this management strategy is the following up of results, defined as 'systematic registration, revision and analysis of results and cost information in an institution'. The latter is, according to Statskonsult, a prerequisite for a successful implementation of MBO as a governing tool (ibid.). If it is difficult, or impossible, to produce precise information on results and costs, MBO will not work as intended.

There is a certain ambiguity on the outcome of this governmental tool. Some have argued that very little has been achieved with regard to the underlying governmental goal: more efficient use of public resources (Olsen, 1996). And Per Lægreid (1999), for instance, claims that NPM has not affected civil service at the national level to any significant degree due to institutional resistance.

Others have argued that even though this instrument might not have had any direct impact on the performance of state institutions, it might have had some indirect impact, for example, making the people who work in state institutions more aware of the purpose and content of their activity (Thorsvik, 1991). Moreover, we have firm reason to believe that there is a significant difference between the civil servants at the central level (the Ministries) and the top leaders of the local administrations in the Norwegian municipalities (where most of the service production actually takes place), in their acknowledgement of MBO and NPM as useful tools in the implementation of cost-effective strategies. The introduction and implementation of a buyer–supplier model in a growing number of municipalities is one of the tools used to increase cost-effectiveness in the municipalities. So, while many municipalities are in the forefront here, others are still working in a fairly traditional way (see Section 3.4).

Regardless of the implementation and outcome so far, MBO and NPM are good examples of the *ideological* penetration of the market into the public sector. It is hard to imagine how the emerging contract culture could have come about without this influence. In fact, MBO and NPM are a defining part of the whole contract culture. The core of the market ideology, economic efficiency and competition, has expanded into areas where, traditionally, this kind of economic rationality has been excluded (Lægreid, 1997). There is no doubt that result measurement, evaluations, quantifications, control and accountability have become more common in public administration. New accounting systems emphasizing performance indicators of different kinds have been introduced. The development towards increased use of internal contracts in the public sector not only concerns individuals, but also regulates service delivery between different parts of an institution (e.g. between different departments).

Change within the Voluntary Sector

Parallel to this neo-liberal ideological shift in the public sector, there have been some important processes of change going on inside many of the social service voluntary organizations, as well as in other organizational fields. These changes are part of the same ideological packages as the MBO/ NPM and can be understood as prerequisites that make contracting possible on a larger scale. There are at least three changes that are important in our context: increased specialization, increased centralization and increased professionalization (Selle, 1998).

There has been a general trend towards increased specialization. New organizations, to a larger degree than before, choose a set of well-defined objectives and/or operational areas, directed at well-defined target groups. This development is particularly visible in organizations that have been recently formed, for instance in the explosive growth in the number of self-help and special interest organizations. Increased specialization is linked to two other features: growth in cooperating bodies and growth in the number of 'umbrella-organizations'. Specialized voluntary organizations increasingly feel the need for new types of coordinating institutions. For some organizations these coordinating institutions might be the first steps towards the merging of organizations. We see this development as a sign that public policy has become more important to these organizations, not only in terms of central policies at the national level, but at the regional and local levels as well. Both parties, the public authorities, as well as the voluntary organizations, are increasingly in need of effective and time-saving coordinating bodies (Selle, 1998).

The average number of members per organization is increasing. Contrary to the expectation that increased specialization would imply a decline in average membership ratio, the organizations are, in general, growing larger. There has been a general tendency towards organizational centralization at the local level. This is expressed in two influential and parallel processes:

1. The traditional model of local organizational units operating in the different communities is gradually changing. Former local units scattered

throughout the municipalities have increasingly been amalgamated into a single organizational unit at the municipal level (Selle and Øymyr, 1995).

2. The intermediate organizational level has become more important, not least as an adminstrative service-institution for the local organizational units. This is partly a consequence of the introduction of a 'new' regional, governmental level (fylkeskommunen) based on popular elections in 1975, but it is also an expression of a more general trend towards increased need for professional (full-time) employees in order to strengthen the organizations' effectiveness and competitiveness (Selle, 1998).

There has been a push towards more professionalization at all organizational levels in the voluntary sector. In this respect, the concept of professionalism may be said to cover two different circumstances: *activity* and *organization*. Time seems to have become more costly to the individual: thus there are rising expectations towards goal-attainment and effectivity. In brief, as time becomes a scarce resource, volunteers become more instrumental in their attitudes towards their organizational activity. And, correspondingly, the organizations demand more from their members in terms of voluntary work or they do not want volunteers at all, only economic contributions from members. The result is pressure on the traditional view of amateurishness and voluntarism.

Organizations are increasingly employing part-time and full-time workers. This is especially the case at the national and regional organizational levels, while at the local level this is not (so far) a dominant feature, with the exception of the institution-based services, of course. The results of this process are twofold: (1) a strengthening of the central level of the organizations, less 'power' to the members and more power to leaders and managers who are increasingly taking on a businesslike management style, and (2) possible conflicts between professionals and amateurs inside the organizations as these groups may come to represent different cultures (Selle and Øymyr, 1995). The 'language' of the market and the NPM ideology in the public sector are gradually becoming more common in voluntary organizations as well (Ulstein, 1998; Heitmann and Selle, 1999). As a result the traditional membership-based organizational model is put under pressure (Selle, 1998).

Since the early 1980s Norway has witnessed a growth in non-membership-based, professionalized, and highly centralized non-profit organizations in which mass mobilization was not as important as before. As this type of organization grew, and as many of the most important democratically structured, membership-based organizations suffered serious decline, it became apparent that the organizational model which had dominated traditionally was losing ground. As of the 1990s, we are witnessing the emergence of a qualitatively new organizational society, which, increasingly, lacks traditional characteristics, that is, being membership-based, democratically structured and based on local branch organizations. The membership-role is evolving. The tendency seems to be towards organizations which are less in need of large memberships, or whose 'members' are more loosely associated with the organizations. The result is, in other words, a new type of organization and a new type of member (Selle, 1998).

The observed symmetry between changes in the public sector and the changes within many (though not all) of the voluntary organizations could imply that many of these organizations are now 'prepared' to meet the new public demands for services, that is, the emphasis on cost-effectiveness, quality and accountability. We are not saying that the changes within the public sector are the main reason for the voluntary sector change: they are both part of a more overall societal change. However, close contact with and dependence on public money have, in general, speeded up the process of change within the voluntary sector. But this change will probably also make it more necessary for many of the organizations to further strengthen their administrative, economic and legal knowledge, either through the employment of new professionals or through the purchase of such expertise outside their own ranks.

To sum up: the developments that we have described in this section, that is, those that allow the formation of the contract culture, are all prerequisites for the *implementation* of contracts in the field of welfare, to which we will now turn.

3.4. THE IMPLEMENTATION OF CONTRACTS

The Changing Attitudes of Public Authorities towards Voluntary Organizations

During the last few years, four important white papers and public reports have been published concerning the changing relationship between voluntary organizations and government.[6] The proposals in these governmental documents clearly point in the direction of more use of public control and more focus on assessing the achievements of the voluntary organizations in terms of activity and *service* performance in general. The Norwegian government is now articulating its expectations towards the organizations more explicitly. Although the government does not want to change all basic grants to 'earmarked' financial support to specific organizational activities, the documents clearly express that not all current use of these grants is in accordance with governmental expectations and purposes (St meld nr 27, 1996–1997: 32).

The government emphasizes that the purpose of the financial support is not to help the organizations to acquire as many members as possible, but to promote a high level of activity and participation within the organizations. This may call for a change in the way grants are given in the future. The signals in the white paper point in the direction of giving basic grants more in accordance with the level of activity within the organization, and put less emphasis on the presented (and sometimes even false!) membership figures.

If we turn to the way government *controls* the organizations' use of basic grants we can also observe new signals in the white paper (St meld nr 27, 1996–1997). There have traditionally been rather weak governmental control instruments associated with basic grants. Control has basically been limited to ensuring that the organization has delivered accounts, audited by a registered accountant, and making sure, as far as possible, that the number of recorded members is correct. The new signals from the government suggest that this will not suffice in the future. In addition to the traditional control instruments, the government suggests that supervision should be supplemented by new control forms, for example, external and internal evaluation of the *level of activity* within the organization. In some cases, the government (Ministries) may also implement a closer dialogue with the organizations (St meld nr 27, 1996–1997: 33).

One of the most interesting signals in the white paper is a proclaimed change towards giving more of the financial support in the form of *project grants*. These grants are *time-restricted*. As the name indicates, they are usually made available for specific projects which the organizations may be engaged in for a limited period of time. But this does not necessarily mean that money is given only to well-defined and strictly organized projects. Under this category organizations may apply for funding for specific events, special services or experiments. The diversity under this category is vast, although the sum for the different projects may be relatively small. The criteria for support seem to leave considerable room for discretionary practice. In order to be judged 'worthy' of support, the applicant must have a project that is considered relevant to the public authorities. Moreover, public authorities may even *define* the area or activity to be considered relevant. The applicant must also be believed to be seriously committed to the project (St meld nr 27, 1996–1997: 25). A public report from Statskonsult (Rapport, 1995: 3) shows that project grants, as an instrument, have strengthened their position relative to the traditional basic grants (at the national level). But this displacement is not equally unambiguous in all Ministries, that is, in all organizational fields.

A transition to more frequent use of project grants, and thus more public control over organizational activities, which we believe is part of the NPM in the public sector, could imply a change of one of the most typical aspects of volunteering in Norway: a high degree of organizational autonomy coupled with nearness (relatively deep integration) with public authorities. Trust and informal relations between organizations and government have always been a prominent feature of organizational life in Norway. It is likely that a transition to project grants will weaken this traditional system of trust and promote formalization and control. However, the extent to which this will happen will largely depend on how the system of project grants is implemented, or more explicitly, how strongly the public control is implemented (Selle, 1998). We must also be aware of the possible difference in implementation between the national level (the Ministries) and the local level (the municipalities) in this respect.

The Knowledge Base: Limited, but with a Clear Direction

Our empirical knowledge as to what extent the contract culture has been implemented in the field of social services is at the moment rather scarce and marred by some uncertainties. This is especially the case at the local level, largely due to defective aggregated statistics and a lack of relevant and updated case studies. A few studies have been carried out, however, and we shall consider these in turn.

Five projects involving cooperation between local authorities and voluntary organizations in the field of social services have been carried out in the southern part of Norway (Repstad, 1998). The five projects (cases) in the study involved services for 'marginalised' youths, battered women, single mothers and people with disabilities. The researchers concluded that these projects were not characterized by written and 'formalized' agreements, but by more informal and oral agreements. The low degree of formalization was interpreted as an expression of the need for freedom of action (on both sides), as well as a sign of mutual trust. Consequently, this local study does not indicate that the contract culture (so far) has pentrated the relationship between organizations and public authorities in these particular communities. The 'old' means of cooperation based on personal contacts/overlapping positions, informal agreements and mutual trust still dominates the relationship. The studies demonstrate, in our view, the stucture of the old relationship between government and the voluntary sector, that is, the traditional one that the contract culture will change, and already has in many municipalities. Information exists that tells a different story.

A nationwide representative survey (Eikås, 2001) directed at the administrative leaders of the health and social services in the municipalities clearly indicates that formalized contracting with voluntary organizations and businesses is very common. In fact, formalized contracts are already slightly more common than informal and oral agreements (42.2 per cent against 38.2 per cent) and in many municipalities there has been formalized cooperation in the past too. The most common form is short-term contracts with a duration of 1–2 years (22 per cent of the municapalities), and many of the municipalities use both kinds of regulatory 'instruments' in their cooperation with other sectors. This study also shows that not only large, but even smaller municipalities report using formal contracts. As many as 18 per cent of the municipalities now use this instrument within the health and social sector. However, as we lack time-serial data, we are unable to grasp the dynamics of change statistically. Furthermore, since formal contracts are not unknown in the 'old' system, we cannot decide the extent to which these formal contracts are written in the spirit of the new contract culture.

We saw that contracts and agreements have been used when voluntary organizations have received public grants for running welfare institutions. This has, for instance, been the case for different voluntary organizations' involvement in care for the elderly at the local level in Norway. But these 'old' agreements between the organizations who have been running such welfare institutions and the public authorities are of quite another character compared to the 'new' system that is emerging now. The new system is far more detailed and formalized, and the claims on performance and results are more clearly expressed in written agreements. It is tempting to describe the difference between the 'old' and the 'new' way of contracting as a difference in the time span of cooperation, where the time horizon used to be 'from here to eternity', while it now is 'until tomorrow'. This is, of course, an exaggeration, but it pinpoints the fact that the element of potential competition is now about to transform the 'old' way of cooperation.

A general impression (in historical terms) is that voluntary organizations have had a relatively large degree of freedom in their use of public transfers. The former use of formal and informal contracts may be interpreted as an expression of generalized *trust*. Voluntary organizations may, in general, have been believed to be accountable and trustworthy: consequently, it has been deemed unnecessary to introduce different kinds of written agreements and more formalized contracts, and control has been rather weak. The move from the traditional form of cooperation building upon trust towards the new type of contract emphasizing control may still mean integration, but perhaps with clearer boundaries between sectors and institutions.

There have, undoubtedly, been recent development trends in Norway that clearly point in the direction of more use of 'contracting-out' of (former and new) public services in the field of social services, at the national as well as at the local level—and it is important to remember that most services are implemented at the local level. How the voluntary organizations are adapting to this new development and what the consequences might be for them is not yet possible to state unequivocally. The outcome might be different in different service fields. For instance, foreign aid organizations have increasingly

become successful partners with government. Groth (1999) shows that there
have been dramatic changes in the relationship between state and organizations from the mid-1960s up to the present. From a situation where the
organizations were marginal but autonomous, they have now become heavily
integrated with the government as contracted partners working as instruments in the fulfilment of governmental policy in foreign aid. Today NOK
1.6 billion are transferred from government to the organizations each year,
and public transfers are the main sources of income, for most of the organizations in this field. In this field, the relationship between government and
organizations has been characterized by harmony and consensus, rather than
conflict and antagonism, with respect to fundamental questions concerning
motives, goals and appropriate means of action. The special structural traits
related to the field of foreign-aid and the financial dependency on public
authorities have resulted in considerable closeness between organizations and
state, without making the organizations less flexible in their practical work
abroad. Nevertheless, the organizations have had to adjust to governmental
claims on formal control and evaluation of the organizational perfomance.
The result has been tendencies towards organizational isomorphism. Different
kinds of organizations are working pretty much in a similar way. They hire
professionals who are familiar with the codes and the 'language' in the field in
order to compete with other organizations on contracts and projects initiated
by government. Since the organizations seem to be aware of the possible dangers of isomorphism linked to the contract culture, they are now gradually
becoming more occupied with their image, using rhetoric in order to profile
their own values more clearly.

Groth (1999) concludes that even though the intertwining of state and
organizations is closer than before in terms of economic support and contracted agreements, this has not resulted in a severe loss of organizational
autonomy, as one might expect from theoretical assumptions on the consequences of such close cooperation. There are several reasons for this: Government has made itself almost completely dependent upon the organizations in
order to reach its goals in foreign aid. The organizations are working abroad,
far from Norway, which complicates close government supervision. Government itself has rather limited knowledge in a relatively new organizational
field. In this particular field, the organizations are more legitimate actors
than governmental agencies (such as NORAD) in the eyes of the Norwegian
people.

These are all factors that we will not find in the traditional field of social
services. Conflicts are, therefore, more likely to occur in this 'older' field,
where both public authorities and voluntary organizations may often have
well-developed knowledge and 'natural' ways of doing things. For instance, a
case study carried out by Lorentzen (1994) demonstrated how a contracted

collaboration between the government and the Norwegian Red Cross on the running of a centre for refugees (in the city of Oslo) collapsed after a short period of time, due to a number of conflicts. Such case studies are valuable and point out some very interesting issues and areas of potential conflict that may arise when voluntary organizations become contracting agents for the implementation of public policy.

A qualitatively oriented study of the interplay between local government and private actors has been carried out in three municipalities in the northern part of Norway (Nylehn and Støkken, 1996). This is a broad study including the interplay with private actors from all three sectors: private enterprises, the third sector and the informal sector. Since the empirical data they present builds largely on unstructured interviews with representatives from the different sectors, we are not given precise information on how the relationship between voluntary organizations and the local public authorities is regulated, for example, whether formal contracts/agreements are used to any significant degree. But several relevant findings may be singled out.

In the largest municipality, Bodø, there was, until recently, one private home for the elderly and infirm. It was organized as a private foundation and owned by a religious organization. This institution was almost 100 per cent dependent on funding from the municipality for the running of the institution. The municipality finally concluded that this was not really a satisfactory situation, since they were not able to include this institution in their plans on a completely equal footing with the other (public) institutions in this field. The municipality then decided to take over the operation and responsibility for the instititution, through an agreement in which ownership was still in the hands of the foundation, while the municipality rented the buildings (Nylehn and Støkken, 1996). This is a situation that is, probably, not unique. As the 'old' social service organizations face problems with recruiting new members it becomes increasingly difficult for them to be engaged in such demanding tasks as running nursing homes for elderly people. Even if they hire professionals to work in the institutions, they are still dependent on volunteers as a supplement in order to make it work. However, this does not mean that the public sector is taking over forever. The public sector may within the new ideological climate soon contract out institutions they have taken over.

On other occasions, the municipalities have considered the interplay with voluntary organizations and foundations to be 'a good bargain', even if their governing possibilities are rather limited. This is particularly the case in areas in which the municipality itself has very little to offer. Nylehn and Støkken (1996) state that it is hardly coincidental that so much of the private activity is played out in the area of child care and the care for alcoholics and drug addicts. These are areas in which the public authorities often experience their own powerlessness, and where more experimental and unorthodox methods undertaken by private actors do not clash with public domains and interests.

A third type of interplay is characterized by dilemma and ambivalence from the municipalities' point of view. Such a situation seems to arise for instance, when local, voluntary organizations or foundations start to build institutions for the care of the elderly, which they then expect the municipalities to take the full responsibility for once they have been finished. Although the municipalities in general are in favour of voluntary initiatives, they will not always approve of such projects, because they feel that they are caught up in activities that are not in line with their own plans and priorities. But at the same time, they cannot show a completely hostile attitude towards such initiatives, because that could imply a loss of support and political legitimacy among the citizens of the municipalities.

Furthermore, if we move from the organizational to the individual level, that is, the voluntary worker/member's relationship to their organization, it is possible to state that this relationship could also be taking on a more 'contractual character'. The new contract culture is general enough to be observed at all organizational levels. We have chosen one example to illustrate this development, but the tendency is seen in large parts of the voluntary sector and particularly within the social service field (Selle, 1998).

Since 1974 a 24-hour open 'crisis' telephone has been available for needy people in the city of Oslo. This service is run by a foundation: the Church's City Mission (Kirkens Bymisjon) and it is called 'Kirkens SOS'. The service employs several full-time, salaried employees and a large number of volunteers, including some clergymen. Every new person who wants to become a volunteer must take an introductory course. By the end of this course, everyone who decides to become a volunteer in this service has to sign a binding contract which is reciprocal. This contract regulates the relationship between the leadership and the volunteers and specifies how the volunteers are expected to relate to the service. It covers, for instance, issues such as loyalty to the purpose and objective of the organization, promises of confidentiality and the rotation of shifts. To be more specific, this implies that the volunteer, for instance, signs a contract in which s/he is required to work at least two shifts each month and to participate in (compulsory) group meetings twice a year. The volunteer is also required to take part in counselling groups once a month. The leader is required to give individual instruction. If a volunteer is not able to cover his/her shift, he must get another person to do so. After one year, the volunteer assesses his position and may leave after a period of three months if s/he desires (Haugland, 1992).

As we can see, the routines for entry into this particular organization are rather comprehensive, probably more so than in most other social service organizations. Applications, interviews, introductory courses and the subscription of contracts are essential parts of this organization's structure and they are very important in the process of socializing members. This case, nevertheless, clearly demonstrates the trend towards more professionalization inside the voluntary organizations, that is, a new form of contract between the individual and the organization. The tendencies in many other organizations, for example, the Red Cross, point in the same direction. We are now observing a more instrumental attitude from the members as well as the managers of the organizations, for instance in that members' work for the organizations is more strictly planned and regulated through schedules (Selle, 1998).

The developments that we have described in this section all boil down to the fact that voluntary organizations and their members and volunteers are, increasingly, for hire or prepared to be for hire (Lipsky and Smith, 1993). However, they are not the only ones.

3.5. THE NEW CHALLENGE FROM THE MARKET

The Cognitive Shift

We are now observing that voluntary organizations, which have been the dominating 'private' suppliers of welfare services, are being challenged by new commercial suppliers who are entering this area with a for-profit motivation. For instance, large international companies are now entering into care for the elderly (Bjerke and Eilertsen, 1998; Mietle, 1999). Thus, the result is now more competition, a larger number of potential suppliers, and more pluralism.

We believe that the ideological climate is now about to be changed in a fundamental way, especially in larger municipalities and cities in Norway, in favour of privatization and contracting-out. Since the mid-1980s local public authorities have had a positive attitude to the roles of voluntary organizations as alternative and complementary suppliers of welfare and as arenas for individual and collective 'democratic competence building' and personal growth. But their concern now (almost irrespective of political colour) seems basically to be how to supply the inhabitants in the municipalities with necessary *services*, no matter *who* the provider is. We do not question that they still acknowledge public responsibility in terms of *finance* and *control* in the field of social services, perhaps even more *legal* and *financial* control. However, most likely, the local authorities are now accepting less ideological control, for example, control with the content of the services. As a result of the ideological shift, politicians and managers in public sector agencies at the local level are now increasingly willing to buy core services from suppliers outside their own ranks, instead of *producing* the services themselves. This process of externalization has been given different labels: 'privatization', 'contracting-out', 'out-sourcing', 'purchaser–supplier model' and 'competition-exposure'. These are all concepts that, to a large degree, cover the same phenomenon, and they are an expression of the contract culture. Local public authorities, are of course, concerned with users' demands and the quality of services as well. It is assumed that the level of quality will not deteriorate and the hope is that it can be maintained at the same level as earlier or even improve.

This recent cognitive shift opens up solutions which seemed impossible to implement or were not seen at all ten years ago. The shift is now most prevalent at the local level, where it has 'matured' over the last ten years. The result is a step by step process in which voluntary organizations have been given new roles first, and then more space for commercial enterprises has been opened up, making it possible for them to move into new service areas in the Norwegian welfare state. These new market actors are now challenging both the voluntary organizations and the public agencies in the field of social services.

The Gradual Penetration of Business into Elderly Care

As mentioned in the introduction, private *commercial individual actors* have always been predominant suppliers in areas such as dental services. But in other areas, such as care for the elderly, *commercial enterprises*, which are something rather different from individual contractors, have been completely absent until recently. Voluntary organizations, on the other hand, have played an important role here, for example, in running nursing homes as well as day-care centres. Their contribution has been especially important, for example, in Oslo, the capital of Norway.

Three research reports (Kjerstad and Kristiansen, 1996; Bogen and Nyen, 1998; Bjerke and Eilertsen, 1998)[7], as well as the survey carried out by Eikås (2001) and a thesis published by Mietle (1999), substantiate that the changes described above really are at work at the local level in Norway, although they are in an initial phase. Bogen and Nyen's report shows that in 8 per cent of the municipalities there are private suppliers running nursing homes; support services, such as cleaning, laundry and catering, (where contracting is common) are not included in this figure. Only one municipality reports that residential care has been privatized. The figure includes both voluntary sector suppliers as well as commercial suppliers, but the majority is supplied by non-profit actors. So far, only 2 per cent of the municipalites report that there are commercial enterprises involved in the core services such as care for the elderly (nursing homes, etc). Eikås (2001) indicates that this has now increased to 5.0 per cent. For the 'support services' like laundry and kitchen the figure is 9.2 per cent.

The scope of the private services in the field of nursing homes seems, at the moment, to be rather modest. Only two municipalities with private suppliers in this area report that these suppliers cover more than 10 per cent of the total 'market' in this area. In most of the municipalities with non-public nursing homes, voluntary actors have always offered such services; thus, it is hardly correct to state that this is an expression of 'privatization': it is rather an expression of lack of 'communalization' in an earlier phase, although the municipalities have covered most of the running costs of these private nursing homes for a long time. On the other hand, in those few municipalities (7) where we can find commercial enterprises in this area, we find that these are services which where formerly produced by the local authorities themselves; thus we can state that this is privatization in a more genuine sense.

What characterizes those municipalities that have been breaking new ground in Norway, through the introduction of a buyer–supplier model on health and social services for the elderly? And what kind of experiences have they had with this model so far? The two cases presented in Bogen and Nyen (1998) suggest that these municipalities are relatively densely populated, with 50,000 inhabitants (municipality A) and 25,000 inhabitants (municipality B), respectively. In a Norwegian context, these are large municipalities. Both had a political majority of right-wing seats in the municipality councils at the time when the decision was made.

In 1996 the first municipality (A) awarded a contract to a large multinational commercial enterprise (ISS) for the running of a new nursing home for a period of five years. The building is owned by a foundation in which the municipality is one of the major shareholders. The contract was granted without any kind of competition between different suppliers. In 1997 the second municipality (B) awarded a contract to a large mulitinational commercial enterprise (Partena Care) for the running of a nursing home for a period of four years. The building is owned by the municipality. Two enterprises competed for the contract. This was the first step, but now the authorities of the municipality have taken a further step by putting out the *residential care* in one of the municipality districts on contract (*Bergens Tidende* 13th of December, 1998).

These two cases are examples of both ideologically and economically motivated changes that may have far-reaching consequences if they produce results that can satisfy the expectations of the administrators, politicians and inhabitants in the municipalities. The contracts in these two cases are estimated to give a cost-reduction of 10–20 per cent compared to the level estimated if the services were produced by the municipalities themselves. So far, there is no indication that the level of quality in these two contracted services is below that of the nursing home services produced by the municipalities themselves. The inhabitants seem to be very satisfied with the service they have been offered (*Bergens Tidende* 13th of December, 1998). This satisfaction corresponds to the general experiences reported by the chief executives (Bogen and Nyen, 1998) and the administrative leaders for health and social services (Eikås, 2001) in the Norwegian municipalities.

But it is too early to reach any definite conclusion on the matter of quality on the basis of these few cases. It is important to be aware of the fact that these cases are 'pilot-projects' with quite a lot of invested prestige, both on behalf of the private suppliers and the municipalities. Thus, the outcome of these projects will have a significant impact on the development of this new market in the future (Bjerke and Eilertsen, 1998). The municipalities are now working out systems for evaluating the quality of these services using a wide range of indicators. This is a complicated and difficult task, and since this is something new it is also impossible to compare with earlier situations. Thus, reliable comparisons can only be made when these quality performance indicators are operative for single case and comparative evaluations in the future. There is no doubt, however, that this process has made some of the municipalities more aware of the preferred content of their services and also of the possibilities for municipal units to win contracts in open competition in the future.

Why are we focussing on these few cases and these few municipalities that have opened up for commercial enterprises in this core field of the traditional welfare state? One important answer can be found in one of the surveys in Bogen and Nyen (1998). When the chief executives in the municipalities were asked how likely they thought it would be that their municipality in the next ten-year period would privatize services that at the moment were not privatized, as many as 75 per cent answered that this was likely to happen (Bogen and Nyen, 1998). And when asked how likely they thought this would be the case in the services for elderly people, as many as 20 per cent answered positively. Estimations made by Eikås (2001) indicate that the number of municipalities with 'privatized' health and social services will increase by 5 per cent in the near future and that this figure will be even higher in the long run. Thus, our conclusion is that it would be unreasonable to expect that the scope of 'privatized' services will be less comprehensive at the local level in the near future.

It is important to note, however, that resistance to this development is still relatively strong in some of the political parties in the municipalities, not to speak of some of the most powerful trade unions at the local level, for example, Norsk Kommuneforbund (*Verdens Gang* 25th of November, 1999). The survey carried out by Eikås (2001) demonstrates rather clearly that resistance in political parties and in trade unions are considered to be two of the most important factors in explaining the contemporary lack of contracting out of social services in the majority of the Norwegian municipalities. But it is even more important to underscore that the most important factor to explain lack of outcontracted services is rather pragmatic and not ideological, namely the lack of potential market actors in many (presumably small) municipalities (Eikås, 2001).

However, several recent articles in different newspapers indicate that the process of privatization is accelarating, especially in the larger municipalities. In Oslo, the capital city of Norway, with more than 500,000 inhabitants, the city council has decided to put out major parts of elderly care out on contract in three different political/administrative units of the city (*Klassekampen* 8th of December, 1998). In Trondheim, the third largest city in Norway situated in the middle of the country, two nursing homes are now being put out on contract (*Vårt Land* 3rd of February, 1999). In Bergen, which is the second largest city in Norway, with more than 250,000 inhabitants, the city council has proposed that the operation of one nursing home, owned and run by the municipality, shall be put out on contract in the near future. The chief executive in Bergen (Jan Refseth) confirmed in an interview with a local newspaper that private suppliers in 'soft' services, such as care for the elderly, will be more common in the future, and that Norway is in an initial phase of this development (*Bergensavisen* 5th of December, 1998).[8] He has later proposed that the running of all *new* nursing homes in the city should be contracted out in open competition (*Bergens Tidende* 13th of November, 1999).

We argue that the cognitive and political conditions for extensive change are already in place; mostly in the big municipalities. However, it is not unlikely that smaller municipalities will follow, for example, starting out with less controversial areas such as 'support services' (laundry, cleaning, kitchen, transport, etc.) We already know that 9.2 per cent of the municipalities in Norway have put such services out on contract to commercial enterprises and that some of these municipalities are relatively small units (Eikås, 1999).

3.6. CONCLUSIONS

In this article we have described and analysed trends that point in the direction of a 'contract culture', which is a prerequisite for the implementation of contracting out of (formerly) public services. The traditional Norwegian Welfare State is at the moment undergoing major changes. Elements of the NPM ideology are now breaking through at the local political level, where most of the responsibility for the welfare service production is placed.[9] The largest municipalities are in the lead position in this process. But concepts such as 'contracting (out)' and 'purchasing–supplier model' are about to become more than theoretical concepts to administrators and politicians in smaller municipalities too.

Are we now witnessing a fundamental change in mentality among local administrators (especially among the chief executives) and many politicians?

Who formulates the premise for the change—the bureaucrats or the politicians? The process of contracting-out seems to be accelerating at the local level. Will this imply that privatization actually may be implemented more rapidly and comprehensively than most people would have deemed possible only a few years ago—also in the labour-intensive area of social care? We know from the research on earlier periods of the welfare state that new solutions in the welfare policy are often implemented in some local municipalities first, and then become more broadly institutionalized (e.g. Nagel, 1991). Will this also be the result in this area?

It is not unlikely that the contract culture over the years will make many of the voluntary organizations in Norway more similar to the kind of service producing, non-profit organizations that are found in the Anglo-American countries (Lipsky and Smith, 1993; Taylor, 1992). In such organizations *membership* and *internal democratic influence* play a minor role. While this is already largely the case in the relatively 'new' organizational field of humanitarian foreign aid in Norway (Groth, 1999), we would expect a similar change in the field of social services and other organizational fields as well, although the institutional resistance in the field of social services is stronger, due to their legacy of internal democracy and 'non public-interference' with organizational matters (Selle, 1998).

Market actors, even big multinational companies, are now challenging both the traditional voluntary organizations, which for a long period of time have been engaged in the supply of social services and the traditional main 'producers', that is, the public agencies themselves. The question arises whether smaller, locally based commercial actors or local voluntary organizations will stand a chance in the competition with big, international companies in the 'welfare business'. Is it possible that they will form networks based on common interests and mutual dependency (Rhodes, 1997)? Will new types of organizational 'hybrids' including elements from all three sectors—government, market and voluntary sector—emerge at the local level to meet the new challenges?

What will happen in this area in the future is also dependent upon the position of the voluntary sector in the minds of local bureaucrats and politicians. If the predominant guiding principle is economic effectiveness, we believe that it is vital for the voluntary organization to demonstrate such effectiveness, but in combination with a more clear cut demonstration of its own values. We have seen that this is an organizational strategy that seems to have been rather successful in the field of foreign aid. If voluntary organizations do not show their distinctiveness towards administrators and politicians, that is, demonstrate that there are certain values and ideologies connected to their service production that makes them different from ordinary market actors and public agencies, the result may be local privatization based on commercial service producers. One reason may be that many users/clients would feel that many voluntary organizations would be too ideological, so that more 'neutral' market solutions are to be preferred.

It is too early to predict how the voluntary organizations will meet this new challenge. The general internal organizational changes that we have described will probably make the transition less difficult for some of the organizations. There are also some indications, however, that the organizations are aware of the new situation and that they are willing to act and adapt themselves accordingly. For instance, the 'Employer Organization of Private Organizations working for Government' (APO), which has over 600 member organizations and a total of 17,000 employees, published a report in 1997 (APO—report nr. 1 1997) dealing with this new challenge.[10] The report discusses the future use of more standardized contracts between the municipalities and the organizations that are running institutions in elderly care. It states that the contemporary arrangements regulating the relationship between many municipalities and the owners of private institutions can no longer continue, because of legal, economic and contractual obscurities. The report suggests that the voluntary organizations and foundations in this area are not willing to be 'put out of business' by new commercial actors without putting up a fight. If the situation in this area is typical for the changing relationship between voluntary organizations and government, in general, we would expect that the focus on more clearly defined legal and economic obligations and 'quality-performance' indicators will be evident in other social service areas as well.

Norway's welfare state is now moving, ideologically and in practice, away from a model which has been largely characterized by a dominating public responsiblity for welfare services in production, finance and control. Will a downplaying of the role of public authorities as welfare *producers* have severe impact on important social policy questions such as social rights, equity and equality? There is no doubt that competition, pluralism, market and effectiveness are playing a more substantial role than before. We seem to be moving away from the more traditional and standardized welfare system as witnessed in the 'golden age' of the welfare state. This was a system that was primarily based on the ideals of equality and equity and was commonly described as the social democratic model of welfare. Alternative welfare service producers are now more ideologically legitimate, and legal, economic and ideological mechanisms of (public) control are about to be changed from the 'old' system of informal agreements based on mutual trust and non-interference to a system based on elements from NPM and the new contract culture. This development means that it is hardly fruitful any longer to discuss only the relationship between voluntary organizations and government in the area of social services. Even in Norway, the whole triangle of public, voluntary and market sectors should be taken seriously in future welfare state discussions and research.

Notes

1. We use the term 'social service' organizations in this article. While the connotations and thus the implicit understanding of the area covered by this term may be relatively unproblematic in the continental and Anglo-American literature, this is not the case in Norway. The most common term in Norway is 'organizations in the field of social and health care.' In order to be in line with the international literature at large, we have chosen to omit the label 'health'. By doing so we will lose some precision, acknowledging that the boundary between social and health care is blurred and hard to define in a strict manner.
2. The Norwegian names are 'Norske kvinners sanitetsforening' and 'Nasjonalforeningen for folkehelsen'.
3. This information is based on an interview with two civil servants, a chief planner and a chief buyer, in the department for social and health care services in the city of Bergen.
4. MBO has been singled out as one of three organizational concepts that have become organizational 'superstandards' and that have penetrated all kinds of organizations worldwide during the 1980s and 1990s (Røvik, 1998).The two other superstandards are performance appraisals and total quality mangement (*ibid.*).
5. In the Norwegian language this was called 'virksomhetsplaner' (VP).
6. These white papers and reports are: NOU 1995: 19: *Statlige tilskuddsordninger til barne-og ungdomsorganisasjoner*. St.meld nr 27 (1996–1997): *Om statens forhold til frivillige organisasjoner*. Statskonsult (Rapport 1995: 3): *Statlige overføringer til frivillige organisasjoner*. Statskonsult (Rapport 1996: 4): *Statlig støttepolitikk og endringer i det frivillige organisajonslivet*.
7. The first report, which was mainly based on a postal questionnaire to a selection of Norwegian municipalities, was initiated and financed by the employer and interest organization of the Norwegian municipalities (Kommunenes Sentralforbund). It was carried out by SNF (Stiftelesen for næringslivsforskning). The latter report (mainly based on telephone interviews) was initiated and financed by the interest organization of the employees in Norwegian municipalities (Norsk Kommuneforbund). It was carried out by FAFO (Fagbevegelsens forskningssenter). The third report analysed the use of competition and commercial actors in care for the elderly in Norway. It was initiated by the main trade union of Norwegian nurses (Norsk sykepleierforbund).
8. In a comparative Scandinavian perspective, Sweden is the country that has gone furthest in the direction of privatization in this area. More than half of the municipalities in Sweden have put social services out on contract. Almost 10 per cent of the nursing homes are now run by private actors. The process started in 1992, when the conservative party (Moderatarna) won the majority of the seats in a number of municipalities and county councils. The social democratic party was ideologically opposed to these new social 'solutions' during the first two or three years, but today the ideological controversies have more or less died down (*Vårt Land* 3rd of February, 1999).
9. No doubt, this process has been slower and less comprehensive than in Sweden, probably due to factors like a 'sounder' national economy and a lower amount of the GNP spent on public services in the early 1990s, and less due to severe ideological differences between the two countries.

10. This organization has now been merged with another organization (HSH) which is the main organization for corporations engaged in commercial trade and service production. The director of APO, Gustav Berntsen, stated after the merger that his member organizations must now become more directed at *business administration* (*Aftenposten* 9th of February, 1998).

Chapter 4

Government, the Third Sector and the Contract Culture: The UK Experience so far[1]

MARILYN TAYLOR*

4.1. INTRODUCTION

The language of 'contracts' and of the 'contract culture' is one which has a resonance for third sector organizations[2] in many parts of the world, as markets or quasi-markets come to dominate the provision of welfare. But it is important to recognize that it can mean different things. Building on Lyons (1997), there are three main trends associated with the use of the term:

- increased government support for third sector organizations (with implications for increased state control);
- the transfer of services formerly provided by the state to third sector organizations;
- a change in the terms and conditions under which government funding is provided to third sector organizations.

All these trends have been visible in the UK over the past twenty years. A number of circumstances combined to make the introduction of welfare markets inevitable. Increased demand, particularly the increasing proportion of older people in the population, but also the longer life expectancies of

*MARILYN TAYLOR • Health and Social Policy Research Centre, University of Brighton, Falmer, BNI 9PH, United Kingdom.

disabled people and people with chronic illnesses were one factor. Increased expectations were another: as basic standards of welfare were assured by universal provision, welfare consumers grew dissatisfied with its uniformity and what they saw as the dominance of producer over consumer needs. At the same time, a sharp ideological shift to the right in government attacked the 'dependency' that state welfare was seen to foster and its supposed sapping of personal responsibility.

But the extent of the shift in welfare in the UK can be exaggerated (Batsleer and Paton, 1997). While there has been a significant increase in government funding to third sector organizations in the UK over recent years, government has been a significant source of support to the sector for a considerable time and this feature of the contract culture is nothing new. This is particularly true of social care, where there has been a mixed economy of welfare for many years. In this field, although the balance of provision is shifting from the state to the independent sectors (the for-profit sector is also a major provider of state-funded care), the change is one of degree rather than of substance. On the other hand, there is concern about the extent to which the financial burden of services will be transferred along with its delivery and the extent to which the third sector will be expected to substitute for the state rather than complement its services.

What is significant about the 'contract culture' in the UK is therefore not the introduction of government funding to the third sector, but a potential change in the nature of that funding as the third sector is increasingly seen as a mainstream service provider. Lewis argues (1995, p. 6): 'while a commitment to a mixed economy of welfare in which the part played by the state sector is played down is not new, a situation in which the state determines the conditions of provision without taking responsibility is new.'

Prior to the 1990s, the perception is that, with some exceptions, government funding to the majority of local third sector organizations largely took the form of grant-aid for services which complemented mainstream state services. As such, it came with relatively few strings attached. From the late 1980s, the nature of funding has changed: from a gift or investment, based on services specified largely by the third sector organization, to a purchase, with the service and the terms and conditions under which it is provided, specified by the government purchaser. While this offers new opportunities to third sector organizations, it has also given rise to concern within the sector that, from being partners, with a complementary and independent role in welfare, third sector organizations will become agents, providing services defined and circumscribed by the state.

The advent of the New Labour government in 1997 has added a new chapter to the tale with the its search for a 'third way' which will move policy from a 'contract culture' (Giddens, 1998) to a 'partnership' culture. The significance of the third sector as a provider and partner has been underlined in a range of policies and also in the launch of a national 'compact' between government and the third sector which provides a framework of basic principles to govern future relationships (Home office 1998). There is little sign of a move away from markets in welfare—if anything the pace of change has accelerated. But a new dimension has been added with the introduction of a 'best value' regime in local government which recognizes the need to consider quality as well as price in service delivery.

This chapter draws on a range of recent research in the UK to assess the extent and implications of these changes and the impact that they have had on third sector organizations in the UK. The first part of the chapter charts the changing relationship between government and third sector social care organizations over time and describes the key changes that introduced the 'contract culture', examining their significance for both government and the third sector. It then describes in more detail the arrangements which govern the relationship between government and the state in social care under current policies. The second part assesses the impact that these changes have had on third sector social care organizations in the UK and their users. In doing so, it looks first at the place of the third sector as a provider within the new welfare mix, then at its role in partnership and policy making. The paper ends by assessing how far the new government's agenda will mark a further change of direction for third sector organizations in social care.

4.2. THE CHANGING RELATIONSHIP

In 1991, Batley described the UK local government system as lying midway between the US and its European neighbours. Indeed, Esping-Andersen's characterization of the UK alongside the US as a 'liberal' welfare regime (Esping-Andersen, 1990) has been challenged by a number of commentators in this country, who argue that the liberal philosophy which the Pilgrim Fathers took with them to the US in the 17th century has been diluted in the UK by a number of other currents over the centuries (Bagguley, 1994). Hirschman (1982) argues that, across the globe, there are cycles of 'publicness' and 'privateness' in social development and the history of welfare in the UK provides ample evidence of this. Political commentators point to a continuing ambivalence between a social liberalism which sees welfare as a safety net for the failures of a dominant market system on the one hand, and a modern social democracy which has more redistributive ambitions—an ambivalence encapsulated in the current search for a 'third way'. Classification is equally difficult when it comes to the place of the third sector in welfare. Kendall and Almond (1998) point out that the dominance of government as a funder places the UK sector firmly in line with its European counterparts. But they argue that the 'corporatist' model that still holds sway in many European countries cannot be applied to government-third sector relationships in the UK, while the extent of for-profit welfare provision in the UK is not matched anywhere in mainland Europe.

From Government to Market

The author has mapped out the historical development of the relationship between government and the third sector in earlier papers (Taylor, 1997; Taylor and Bassi, 1996). To summarize, the relationship between the state and the third sector in the UK was for a long time what Gidron et al. (1992) would call a 'dual' system, in which the two sectors were seen as having parallel but independent roles. Charity and mutual aid provided for the deserving and provident poor; the state acted as a last resort (and deterrent) for the 'undeserving poor'. But even in the golden age of philanthropy, as the 19th century appeared to be, the state was assuming a more central role as a regulator and financier, particularly in public health and education, and more gradually as a provider. While the third sector continued to have an important role alongside the state in the early part of this century, the transfer of responsibilities to government gathered pace throughout the first half of the 20th century until, in the 1940s, a raft of legislation ushered in the British welfare state, with the state taking primary responsibility for both the financing and delivery of welfare, particularly in the fields of health, education and income maintenance.

Underlying the move to a government dominant system was a gradual recognition of the failure of charity and mutual aid to provide for the health and welfare of the population. However, it became clear in the 1960s that a government-dominant system was failing to meet the welfare needs of the post-war generation—in a sense the welfare state was the victim of its own success as the aspirations of its citizens rose. In 1979, a right-wing government was elected into power, committed to the introduction of market principles into welfare. Over the first three terms of this government (but mostly in the third), it privatized government assets and services, introduced compulsory competitive tendering into many local authority services and created internal markets in those policy fields—like health—where privatization was not a feasible or political option. While the extent of the transfer of responsibility has to be seen in proportion—the overwhelming majority of the UK population still depend on the state for health, education and income maintenance—there is no doubting the significance of the ideological shift or the concern generated by this 'sudden and abrupt change of gear' (6 and Kendall, 1997).

There were four main aspects to the introduction of contracts and the wider 'contract culture' in the UK:

- a split between purchaser and provider roles, encouraging the transfer of mainstream delivery to independent providers where possible;

- promoting competition between providers;
- formalization of funding agreements to specify and monitor the quality and/or quantity of the provider's service;
- a greater emphasis on consumer rights and consumer choice.

6 (1997) suggests that the main goals of the introduction of contracts, according to its advocates, were greater efficiency and accountability of public services. He also mentions greater targeting of finite resources. But he goes on to say that there is little evidence as yet that any of these have been achieved by contracting (or indeed any previous system) and argues both that the major rationale for the introduction of the 'contract culture' was political—an inevitable response to the gap between expectations and what the state and open-ended funding was able to deliver.

The reforms were accompanied by a culture shift away from a 'public service orientation' in local government to a 'new managerialism', drawing heavily on perceived commercial practice. The language of cost centres, performance targets, outsourcing, and marketing swept through public authorities with considerable speed: 'Public sector managers were to be taught a lesson in management and their textbook was to be the example of private sector practice' (Walsh et al., 1997). There are some who would argue that, in the UK, the language of the market was taken on by the public sector with scant regard for experience at the cutting edge of business. The concern of the market enthusiasts at central and local level with strict rules of competition appeared to ignore leading edge commercial practice which encourages relational contracts and the building of trust with suppliers (Clegg, 1990; Ring and van de Ven, 1992).

'Customer care' was an integral part of this language, characterized by an emphasis on consumer charters and consumer rights. While this encouraged a shift from producer-dominated services to more service user control, however, it also signified a shift from the 'citizen' to the 'consumer', from collective to individual rights and responsibilities, with the democratic system the servant of the market rather than vice versa. Local government powers were further eroded by a series of policies which encouraged the devolution of service management to consumers (parents and governors in the case of schools; tenants in the case of public housing) or bypassed the local democratic system altogether (e.g. setting up appointed bodies at local level to oversee regeneration initiatives). A wholesale local government reorganization was also carried out in the mid-1990s, changing the predominantly two-tier system outside the main conurbations to a unitary system in Scotland and Wales and a mixed system in England.

However, there were limits to the transfer of welfare responsibilities from state to market. Firstly, the emphasis of legislation in the 1980s was on the withdrawal of the state from service delivery. To privatise the financing of welfare was not yet politically expedient. There was some enabling legislation to provide incentives for people to opt out of or top-up state provisions, but take-up was low in a country where the balance of public opinion was firmly in favour of state responsibility for health and education. Nonetheless, a strong ideological attack on the 'dependency culture' which the state was said to have fostered began to shift the terms of the debate from citizenship rights to responsibilities, placing a growing emphasis on the responsibility of individuals to provide for their future and on the responsibilities of 'active citizens' and families as the first line of defence in the face of adversity.

Secondly, the language of the market was accompanied and in some ways bounded by a parallel language of partnership. Encouraged initially by the Thatcher government as a way of opening local government to the influence of business interests in economic development and education policies, partnership has, over the years, brought a variety of stakeholders into policy making and implementation across the welfare field. By the 1990s, new government funding for urban regeneration initiatives and housing development was made conditional upon evidence of partnership between agencies operating at local level and of community involvement.

A New Beginning?

The 'contract culture' was steered through by a radical right-wing government pursuing a liberal market philosophy. The election in May 1997 of a 'new Labour' government marked growing dissatisfaction with this philosophy, with its lack of investment in public services and with the growing polarization between rich and poor in society. But the new government did not turn the clock back. Indeed, it could be argued that the size of its Parliamentary majority allowed the new government to scrutinize aspects of the welfare system which were politically out of bounds for a right wing government. Thus, the need to bring the welfare budget under control was central to this government's plans. A major initiative to move people from welfare to work began to formulate the right to a basic income, while a major review of the benefits systems included a search for ways of encouraging those who could make their own provision for health and care needs and a signalled likely end to the principle of universalism that marked state welfare. Pressures on care and health services budgets forced more targeting in provision and attention began to shift from the privatization of service delivery to the privatization of finance for those who can afford it. Although the report of a Commission set up to consider the future of long-term care argued for shared responsibility between the state and the individual, this has only been accepted for nursing care in England and Wales.

Nonetheless, there were changes of emphasis with the new government. The aggressively individualist rhetoric of the 1980s, marked by Margaret Thatcher's often-quoted comment that 'there is no such thing as society', has given way to a growing interest in communities. Arguments over the existence and definition of poverty under a Thatcher government determined to reduce the amount of dependency on state welfare have been displaced. Instead the Blair government has addressed the increasing polarization in society between rich and poor by setting up of a high-profile unit to tackle social exclusion. The managerialist language of the 1980s and early 1990s has been tempered with a commitment to move from 'a contract culture to a partnership culture', which has spread across all policy fields and sought to bring about 'a wholesale breakdown of institutional barriers'. For the third sector, this has been reinforced through the development of a 'compact' between government and the third sector (Home Office, 1998).

Meanwhile concern about the inflexibility of compulsory competitive tendering and its neglect of service quality in favour of price led to the development of a new concept of 'best value' as the crucial factor in determining the pattern of welfare delivery. There is now a duty on local authorities to obtain best value across all their services and to demonstrate to local people that services are 'economic, efficient and effective'. The new regime is not intrinsically opposed to competition, but requires authorities to review all services according to four Cs:

- to **challenge** the purpose of each service,
- to **compare** their authority's performance with other authorities,
- to **consult** with the community, and
- to provide for **competition** where appropriate.

There is the prospect of more financial independence for local authorities, if they can demonstrate better performance in delivering services people want, at a price they are willing to pay (DETR, 1998; NCVO, 1998). The initiative was piloted in 53 local authorities—a small minority explicitly addressed grants and other payments to third sector organizations as part of the overall package.

The third sector will be affected as a provider, expected to demonstrate value according to the criteria that are developed. It is also being consulted alongside business, service users and other stakeholders as part of the 'community'.

'Best value' is part of a package of local government modernization to encourage a more outward looking role. The modernization agenda is encouraging widespread consultation with citizens and other stakeholders, has given new powers to local government and also political reform, encouraging a more 'cabinet-style' form of government at local level, with a parallel emphasis on the scrutiny role of the majority of elected local councillors (Gaster et al., 1999). The oppositional stance of the previous administration has gone, but a strong commitment to sending in 'hit squads' when minimum service standards are not met (from the commercial and non-profit sector) underlines suggests that local government is not out of the woods yet.[3]

4.3. THE CONTRACT CULTURE IN SOCIAL CARE

The Context of Change

While the policies described above apply to social care as much as to other welfare fields, the pendulum between state and private responsibility has never swung quite so far in this field. A mixed economy was evident in this field throughout the post-war period. Social care was not a priority for the reforming post-war state, compared with the universal services of health, education and social security, and the State continued to rely on the assets of the third sector to shelter the 'deserving poor'. The third sector was the repository of specialist expertise, its provision was acknowledged to be of superior quality for most care groups and it was not politically expedient to allow third sector provision to disappear without providing an alternative (Kendall and Knapp, 1996). Nonetheless, the capacity of local government social services grew into the 1970s, when adult and children's services were combined into large new departments in local authorities which had themselves been consolidated into fewer and larger units. The third sector began to find alternative roles for itself in the fields of prevention, after-care and advocacy (Younghusband, 1978)—policing the boundaries of state welfare.

The development of social care during this period was strongly influenced not only by political ideology but also by demographic change and the deinstitutionalization of care. 'Care in the community' was the result both of the escalating costs of care and changing views about the acceptability of incarcerating vulnerable people in institutions divorced from the rest of the community. Its growth forged a new social work profession, largely institutionalized within the new social services departments. But the resettlement of institutions in the fields of mental health and learning difficulties also provided fertile new ground for the third sector. De-institutionalization also changed the nature of child care—residential places in third sector childcare organizations fell from 25,000 in 1953 to 300 in 1985 (Kendall and Knapp, 1996).

Introducing Care Markets

The Changing Financial Regime

During the 1970s and 1980s, the pattern of residential care provision for older people changed dramatically. During the early years of the welfare state, funding for residential and nursing care came from local government (through its own services or support to third sector organizations) or from the health service through hospital care. However, as both local authorities and hospitals looked for savings in the context of public expenditure cuts and rising demand, those in need of care looked increasingly to the social security system to fund their long-term care on a reimbursement basis. With no ceiling on social security payments, the costs of residential care to the government shot up during 1970s and 1980s.

Faced with the burgeoning costs of care to the state, the NHS and Community Care Act 1990 introduced a new system whereby finance for social care was transferred from the central government social security system to local government. The legislation encouraged a quasi-market system with local authorities acting as purchasers. The legislation also involved major reforms to the National Health Service,[4] with the introduction of an internal market and the separation of purchasing from provider roles. Guidance following the Act required local authorities to increase the amount of independent provision in order to expand choice, and to regulate providers through the use of contracts (Department of Health/Price Waterhouse, 1991). The transfer of residential care delivery from the state to the private (and third) sectors was ensured through a requirement under the Act that 85 per cent of the monies transferred from central government with the new legislation were to be spent in the independent sector—existing independent sector provision was further safeguarded by a Special Transitional Grant to maintain levels of provision, although as Wistow et al. (1996) point out, this was not new money and represented a minute proportion of the total community care budget.[5] There was no compulsory competitive tendering, but with the tax and subsidy incentives firmly favouring non-statutory delivery, a number of authorities transferred all or part of their own provision to housing associations or not-for-profit trusts.

Wolfgang Seibel's theory of mellow weakness (1989) suggests that governments use contracts with the third sector as a way of appearing to tackle problems that are unresolvable. An explosion of caring costs in the 1980s, combined with demographic change and increased expectations left central government exposed. But the 'fall guy' in the community care reforms was local government rather than the third sector. By shifting the responsibility for the financing of social care onto local government (against the prevailing policy trend to strip local government of powers), central government was handing on a poisoned chalice, especially given its continued control over local government finance. The reforms took place under conditions of considerable distrust, as central government introduced waves of legislation to reduce local government powers (Wolch, 1990; Walsh et al., 1997; Taylor and Bassi, 1996) in other policy areas and forced it into competition with private sector providers. While the picture has changed considerably—Wistow et al. (1999) argue that 'we are all market enthusiasts now'—attitudes die hard and questions remain as to how far changed views in middle and senior management have filtered throughout social services departments as front-line workers see their role change from service provision to care management (Statham, 1996).

Choice was a key feature of the reforms and this was to be achieved not only through the transfer of delivery, but also by the introduction of a needs-based assessment for all adults in need of care, separate from the subsequent decision about whether or how to meet these needs from public funds. These rights to assessment were recently extended to carers. The severe financial constraints that have accompanied these changes have, however, limited both eligibility for care and the extent of choice (Statham, 1996). The risk of a legal challenge if authorities identify needs they cannot meet has increasingly tied assessment to the availability of resources, despite the intention of the Act. The introduction of Direct Payments legislation for adults under 65 provided some disabled people with the opportunity to purchase their services directly rather than through a local authority purchaser and it is now proposed to extend this to people over 65. But increasingly, the benefits of the Act in terms of choice and quality are confined to those in most need. There is also some evidence to suggest that, despite the intention of the Act to give people the opportunity to stay in their own homes, the lack of a domiciliary care market in many areas meant that cost, availability and simplicity conspire to dictate a residential placement. As Statham (1996, p. 13–14) points out: it appears that choice has increased in terms of which residential care home a person enters, but not for community services.

The resource shortage has been intensified by boundary disputes between local and health authorities, with 'cost-shunting' by health authorities as they redefine community services as 'social care' and seek to free up hospital beds. Many local authorities have introduced charging policies to ease pressure on tight budgets and sometimes to allow for improvements in standards (Baldwin and Lunt, 1996) and Statham comments on the inequities caused by the considerable variation between authorities across the country. The debate about national welfare reforms, meanwhile, has considered alternative ways of funding community care, particularly for older people, with the potential introduction of compulsory insurance schemes which will begin to shift the responsibility for finance to individuals above a certain income threshold. Recommendations by the Royal Commission on Long-Term Care that the state should accept responsibility for the long term personal care of older people were rejected by government, which was only prepared to accept responsibility for nursing care. Meanwhile, the introduction in 1999 of increased funds for 'modernization' may have eased the financial pressure, but much of this money is tied to specific conditions and targets and preliminary feedback from local authorities suggested that it is unlikely to relieve pressure overall.

Unlike many other local authority services, social services were not subject to compulsory competitive tendering (CCT), although legislation proposed by the outgoing Conservative government in 1997 would have extended CCT to this field. They will, however, be subject to the 'best value' regime (although the NHS is not yet included). Statham commented in 1996 on the plethora of standards governing social services departments. A number of high-profile media stories on child abuse, mental health and older people have kept the need to protect vulnerable people high on the agenda and there is a strong emphasis in government on standards, with the introduction of a General Social Care Council and independent regional Commissions for Care Standards.

Community Care Planning

In social care, the drive towards markets and competition has taken place within a framework of long-established joint planning processes, with their potential to control the unfettered progress of market forces. Government introduced a system of joint planning between public health and social care authorities as far back as 1974. In the 1980s, joint planning was extended to include third sector organizations. The 1990 NHS and Community Care Act built on this in its requirement that local authorities should draw up annual Community Care Plans in consultation with third sector and private sector providers, users and carers. A number of authorities invested in the third sector infrastructure for joint planning through funding support workers and/or supported the development of user forums and user involvement.

More recent developments in health policy will change the shape of community care planning. The introduction of 'primary care groups' as the major purchasers of primary health care and community health services has brought a major new player onto the community care scene. There is still a strong emphasis on partnership. Primary care groups have third sector representation as do a limited number of health action zones, introduced on a pilot basis to develop a coordinated approach to health. However, general practitioners (GPs),who will dominate the primary care groups (PCGs), do not have a particularly strong record of partnership working with either social services (Statham, 1996) or the third sector: The consistent view is that, at present, the close involvement of GP fund holders in community care has been very much a matter of committed individuals rather than structures.

'Best value' is also changing the nature of consultation, with some commentators suggesting that it can encourage a focus on what is provided, rather than the finer detail of structures and procedures: Users will move from being the people who are listened to in order to ensure they will purchase a service to being people who need to be engaged in finding solutions to problems (Chapman et al., 1999).

However, the same authors note that the extension of consultation to a wider group of stakeholders—including the for-profit sector and the general public could swamp the voice of third sector organizations, and the more excluded groups. The proliferation of partnerships, meanwhile, is placing heavy demands on the third sector infrastructure and particularly on smaller, community- and user-based organizations. The issue for many third sector groups, therefore, may no longer be **whether** they are consulted, but the quality of consultation processes and the extent to which they are able to make themselves heard.

4.4. ANALYSIS OF CURRENT IMPACT

In the UK, there is a growing body of research that addresses issues of contracting and the third sector. But there are a number of factors which make it difficult to draw firm conclusions from these studies. Firstly, the past eight years represent a period of transition between different models of welfare. Both purchasers and providers have been learning how to handle new requirements and it may be, as 6 argues, that the key policy goals will only be achieved later on (6, 1997). Sabatier (1993) argues that policy change needs to be studied over a decade or more to establish its impact, a view confirmed by Statham (1996, p. 1): 'bedding down the current changes will probably take another decade.'

A second, complicating factor is the impact of other changes. The major reorganization of local government, set in train in the 1990s by the Conservative government, means that the authority responsible for social services has changed in many localities, with unitary authorities taking over responsibility from shire counties. The national health service has also experienced continuous reorganization. The introduction of 'best value' and of PCGs, now Primary Care Trusts are adding further dimensions to the emerging picture. The introduction of care trusts is now likely to revolutionize the delivery of social care services.

A third complicating factor is the considerable variation between authorities, policy fields and organizations, which makes it hard to generalize, particularly since many studies offer in-depth case studies of particular localities. Some studies (e.g. Unwin and Westland, 1996; Kumar, 1997) are considerably more positive about the impact of contracts than are others (e.g. Russell and Scott, 1997; Walsh et al., 1997) or indeed than anecdotal evidence suggests in many localities. Walsh et al., note that, despite the centralized guidelines which accompanied the NHS and Community Care Act reforms, there is more scope for local influence in social care contracts than in contracts in other fields, which are subject to compulsory competitive tendering. Commentators identified a spectrum from those who are 'market enthusiasts', (some of whom also see the market as a vehicle for keeping costs down) to objectors committed to preserving state welfare (Wistow et al., 1994; see also Bemrose and MacKeith, 1996; Taylor and Lansley, 1992).

Wistow et al. now see all local authorities as market enthusiasts (Wistow et al., 1999), but they still note considerable variation in practice. A reading of the various studies would suggest that there is still a spectrum of approaches— from those local authorities who see third sector organizations merely as agents of their own policies to those who see them as partners. At the former end of the spectrum, the language of the market is likely to be interpreted rigidly, serv- ices to be judged by economy rather than quality, and the financial sustainabil- ity of the sector to become a secondary consideration. Moving toward the latter end, authorities are likely to be committed to a more participatory approach, consulting with third sector organizations over the planning and commission- ing of care and with individual organizations over the specification and moni- toring of contracts. There are also variations within authorities. Statham, for example (1996), asks how far the commitment to change has filtered down the authority, from senior management champions to the front-line.

So what can be said of the experience so far? Fears were expressed at the outset of contracting that the third sector would lose its presumed virtues—of flexibility, closeness to the consumer, innovation—and be a cheap substitute for the state (Taylor, 1990; Gutch, 1992; Statham, 1996). The picture is much more complicated than that. Davis Smith and Hedley (1994), for example, report that 40 per cent of the organizations they studied experienced the new arrangements as an improvement; only 10 per cent felt they were worse off as a result. However, a number of researchers feel the impact of the changes has been ambiguous (see, particularly, Scott and Russell, 2001; Mocroft, 1998), while the impact on service users—who are supposed to have benefited from the introduction of a social care market appears to have been negligible (Kumar, 1997; Deakin, 1996a). In the following section, the impact is analysed firstly in terms of the sector's contribution to service delivery and secondly in terms of its contribution to the development of policy and its ability to give a voice to service users and excluded communities.

4.5. THE THIRD SECTOR IN WELFARE DELIVERY

Market Share

The advent of the contract culture has been marked by a sustained rise in income from local government to the third sector, both in real terms and as a proportion of local authority spending. This rise predated the NHS and Community Care Act (government funding to the sector doubled in real terms between 1979 and 1987 but faltered in the late 1980s), but has gathered momentum since the implementation of the Act. As a proportion of total local authority expenditure, spending on the sector grew from 1.7 per cent in 1989–1990 to 2.84 per cent in 1996–1997 (Mocroft, 1998). A comparison of local government funding for the year ending 1992/1993 and 1995/1996 shows an overall increase of 47 per cent in the field of social care, with fees increasing most rapidly, but grants also rising in real terms (Mocroft, 1998). 6 and Kendall (1997) note that the proportion of local government budgets being used to fund third sector delivery is higher than ever before and recent NCVO figures suggest an overall increase in funding from the social services budget of 6 per cent in real terms between 1993/1994 and 1994/1995, and 18 per cent over 1995/1996. However, there are signs that the rush of funds into the sector following the 1990 NHS and Community Act is reaching a plateau. Mocroft's 1998 figures (Mocroft, 1998) note a drop of 7 per cent in local authority social services department spending on the sector between 1995–1996 and 1996–1997 and reductions in other local authority budgets are greater. It is important to remember that, while an increasing proportion of local authority funding to the third sector comes from social services (56 per cent in 1996–1997), social care is also provided by more generalist organizations who may be funded from other sources—this is especially true of black and ethnic minority and other community-based organizations.

It is clear that there is an accelerating trend for local authority funded services in adult care to be delivered by non-statutory organizations. The increase in the use of third sector and for-profit organizations for services to vulnerable adults has been greater in residential care than in domiciliary services. By 1995, local authority was funding more places in externally-delivered residential care than in-house. But, as the overall level of resources directed into local authority domiciliary care has increased, these resources too have been used to fund independent sector services. The independent sector's market share is expected to increase across the board as post 1993 placements rise (1993 was the year in which the 1990 NHS and Community Care Act was fully implemented).

This would seem to be good news for the third sector. However, while in the UK, personal social services have been the most rapidly growing component of the third sector and enjoyed increased funding from the local authority, points out that the main beneficiary of increased local authority spending on the independent sector is the for-profit sector—the same is also true of health authority spending on the sector. This was true before the implementation of the 1990 Act—the increase in independent care provision for older people in the 1980s left the third sector as the smallest provider in this field in 1990, especially in residential care where it represented only 10–12 per cent of the total market (a decline of a third over the 1980s). With the transfer of services encouraged by the 1990 NHS Community Care Act, the third sector had an initial short-term advantage (Johnson et al., 1998), especially in services to non-elderly adults. There was a historical bias to funding the third sector to provide local authority funded services and evidence suggested that public sector purchasers favoured the third sector because of its commitment to public sector values of welfare, altruism and public duty (Wistow et al., 1996). However, this is by no means assured in the long run. Research in 1994 already found a growing interest in for-profit providers from newly appointed commissioning managers (Hoyes et al., 1994) and the evidence suggests that for-profit providers are now entering the care of non-elderly adults on a larger scale.

Mocroft (1998) injects another cautionary note. In many cases, he argues, the expansion of funding to the third sector reflects the transfer into the voluntary sector of former council establishments or services: As a result, the 'traditional' or pre-existing voluntary sector found that in practice, grant-aid budgets were squeezed ever more tightly because of the general restrictions on council spending. Figures comparing the different fields are difficult to come by. In 1990/1991, Kendall and Knapp found that government spending on children's services in the sector was only two-thirds the level of its spending on elderly care in the sector. NCVO research finds that between 1994 and 1996, local government funding to the sector in the field of community care rose slightly faster than spending on children's services (Hems and Passey, 1998), while Russell et al. (1995) found that, in their sample of 17 third sector agencies, government funding had grown faster in the field of elderly care than it had in children's services. While the sector remains a significant player in the child care field, there is little evidence of the transfer of services from the public sector seen in the care of adults. A stream of scandals in public sector children's homes has provided an opening for a greater mix of provision, but public and media concern about child abuse demands that the state retain a strong regulatory role and there is still an ethical resistance to contracting out, particularly to the private sector.

The third sector has always been a significant provider in services for disabled adults. Kendall and Knapp (1996) report that, in 1990, the sector was the largest provider of staffed residential care for adults with disabilities and a 'substantial' provider of mental health services. The state has never been a major provider of services to marginalized adults (drugs and alcohol services, single homelessness, etc.), and this means that transfer of service delivery in this field has never been a key issue. However, the 'contracts culture' has had a significant influence as grants are turned into service level agreements and the tightening of conditions on the payment of welfare benefits has reduced budget flexibility for organizations providing hostel accommodation on a reimbursement basis. The complexity of services and the crisis nature of intervention in these fields makes them difficult to fit into the provisions of the Community Care Act. It is difficult to separate assessment and provision and it is difficult to make a clear distinction between purchaser and provider, especially for young people who simply are not picked up by statutory services (Kendall and Knapp, 1996). There is some similarity between the pattern in this field and mental health, which is also characterized by crisis intervention and complexity of role, although the picture here is closer to that of adult services. In all these fields, the sector has also retained a strong campaigning role.

Overall, findings from research so far suggest that the social care market has not been highly competitive as yet, at least in the fields where third sector organizations operate. Johnson et al. (1998) report that in some rural areas and specialist fields, the third sector is the only credible supplier of many services. Hems and Passey's NCVO survey (1998) suggests that only one in four third sector providers are losing competitive tenders, while four out of five report that their existing contracts are being renewed. By and large, their survey suggests that private and third sectors are often operating in different sectors of the market and most of the competition that was reported by respondents to their survey appeared to come from the public sector.

Financial Sustainability

However, while the third sector's competitiveness within its own areas of interest may not yet be at issue, its financial sustainability is. In a financial climate where most authorities are feeling the pinch, it is not surprising that most studies report that third sector organizations feel they are doing more for less. Resources are being targeted at those most in need and intensive packages are most likely to be delivered through the third sector and private sector (Statham, 1996). However, the fact that clients are more dependent and administration costs are high has often not been reflected in costings. Although third sector organizations are now thought to be getting more sophisticated in these costings, the NCVO survey suggests that contract renewals, far from reflecting this increased sophistication, are not keeping up with inflation. The result is that third sector organizations say they are topping up contract payments. Furthermore, where contracts are being lost, the NCVO survey suggests that they are being lost to the public sector on cost grounds (Hems and Passey, 1998).

Scott and Russell (2001) report that, although the general funding trend in their studies is upwards, this masks considerable volatility in funding in the intervening years and a decline in real terms for 40 per cent of their sample organizations. Funding patterns are characterized by uncertainty, with contracts and service agreements often short-term in nature and funding decisions taken late in the day. This uncertainty may, as one chief executive of a major national charity argued, stimulate creativity and innovation, but it is hardly the basis for a dependable service. Funding is tied ever more closely to the delivery of particular services. A number of studies find that in the move from grants to contracts, financial support for the general aims of funded organizations and their core administrative and development costs is giving way to an emphasis on specification and 'core business'. Gaster et al. (1999) find that this emphasis on specialist and short-term funding is even greater in health authorities. They also suggest that generic organizations are undervalued—a particular problem for black and minority ethnic organizations, where generalist organizations provide for a range of community needs and others who do not fit into recognized client categories. While there are alternative sources of funding for these organizations outside social services departments and health authorities, Mocroft's finding that other local authority sources of funding are declining more steeply than those available from social services gives cause for concern (Mocroft, 1998).

Social care funding does not only come from specialist social services funders. The advent of the National Lottery, new policies for regeneration funding from central government,[6] funds attached to New Labour initiatives like the New Deal for Jobs, and initiatives targeted at specific localities—the various health and education action zones or the New Deal for Regeneration—offer alternative sources of income, at least in the medium-term. While regeneration programmes in the 1980s were increasingly geared towards economic objectives, the current emphasis on tackling social exclusion recognizes the need for a multi-faceted approach.

There is a commitment in the national compact between government and the voluntary sector (Home Office, 1998), to 'the value of long-term, multi-year funding, where appropriate, to assist longer-term planning and stability.' But a lot will depend on how the national compact is rolled out at local level. There is particular concern about the implications for revenue funding when time-limited grants like the Lottery grants run out. Ongoing work tends to be less attractive to Lottery boards and flagship policy initiatives and, while new 'modernization' funds recently announced for local authority social services will benefit some areas, the prospect for local authorities taking up the slack left by short-term funders more generally is extremely limited. Targeting, meanwhile, and the need for measurable outcomes, mean that preventative work, although its worth is generally recognized, is regarded as something of a luxury. Prevention, of course, has been a major element of the third sector contribution to welfare (Younghusband, 1978). Walsh et al. (1997) find that most contracts in the care of older people have been spot contracts, and it is care for older people which has tended to dominate the development of contracts as a whole. In the field of disability, by contrast, there is likely to be greater involvement with providers and formal or informal groups of trusted providers are developing, especially in the wake of the resettlement of mental hospitals and institutions for people with learning disabilities. However, Gaster et al. (1999) report that, while the use of spot contracts overall still accounts for less of the social services budget than block contracts, it seems to be on the increase. The advance of direct payments for care will also increase the use of 'spot' payments.

Spot contracts can be a mixed blessing. They can be a lifeline for small specialist organizations. Block contracts tend to favour larger organizations and may make it more difficult for smaller organizations to maintain niche markets (e.g. for black and ethnic minority elders or disabled people). But spot contracts are difficult for smaller organizations to manage. Gaster et al. (1999) report that the use of spot contracts 'created uncertainty and inhibited long-term planning' and there is anecdotal evidence of organizations having to lay-off staff halfway through the year because of their inability to manage demand. Spot contracts may offer the individual the most choice in the short term, but will restrict choice in the longer run if those organizations who cannot carry the costs of flexibility close. Quality may also suffer if spot contracts means employing staff on a more casual basis.

Some studies suggest that organizations with contracts are becoming increasingly dependent on this one source (see e.g. Hems and Passey, 1998; Scott and Russell, 1998). If this is the case, they may lose their place in an increasingly competitive marketplace for private donations. They may also lose their fund-raising skills (Taylor et al., 1995). The NCVO study (Hems and Passey, 1998) finds that organizations without contracts are more optimistic about prospects of future funding than are those with contracts.

A new factor in the sustainability equation has come onto the scene in the shape of a national minimum wage. This is another example of the paradoxical nature of policy change. While many third sector organizations will welcome the intention of the legislation, they may find it difficult to comply. It will be interesting to see who is expected to carry the costs of the minimum wage—whether these are passed down to the provider or covered by purchasers. In an atmosphere of continuing financial constraint, the prospects for providers (especially if cheapness is part of their attraction) are not too encouraging.

Diversity

The contract culture may have encouraged growth in the UK third sector, but has that growth been spread across the sector? The weight of opinion so far suggests that larger organizations stand to gain most from the spread of contracts, especially in a competitive market—they have the resources to underpin development and administrative costs and even to cut costs to capture a niche in the market. They are likely to have the in-house skills needed to gear up to contracting and the resources to accommodate demands for additional safety measures, quality controls and qualified staff. They can also exercise more power in contract negotiations and are more likely to have the resources to engage in consultancy and joint planning exercises. The pressure for economies of scale as the market matures is demonstrated in the housing field in the UK, where many housing associations are now entering into mergers. Nicholas Deakin—who headed the Commission on the Future of the Voluntary Sector (1996)—is quoted in the professional press as saying that 'a gap has opened up between organizations who have successfully adapted to the culture of contracts and those who have not: 'Smaller organizations and those catering for black and ethnic minority groups, or unpopular causes, are at risk of being among the losers' he argues (*Community Care*, 1999a).

Research findings on size and funding success do not, however, present a clear picture. The smallest organizations, who constitute the vast majority of UK third sector organizations, survive on very low incomes and there are many community-based, user-based and advocacy organizations who may not want to 'take the government shilling' and want to promote different values to those of professional services—for example, the independent living movement for disabled people and many black and minority ethnic groups. For those that do, those which have found a niche—however small—may be well-placed to benefit from continued government support. Hems and Passey's data suggest that the organizations that are likely to be the most challenged by the contract culture are medium-sized organizations. While there are signs of modest growth in organizations with annual incomes under £100,000 (who are also the least likely to have contracts), it is 'the middle ground that is being squeezed'. In their survey it is these organizations who are the most dependent on contracts and, as we have seen, this also means they are likely to be the least confident about future funding.

There is a logic to Hems and Passey's conclusion about the problems of middle-sized organizations. It is middle-sized organizations who are having to make the hard choices about whether to move into contracts or not and whether to grow in response to new opportunities or not. It is those organizations that are not large enough to have significant economies of scale or significant assets, but who have liabilities in the shape of employees and premises who are most vulnerable to fluctuations in the market and to competition from the larger non-profits. However, we need more evidence on this.

Scott and Russell (whose local organizations range between incomes of £7000 and £309,000) find no association between size and funding success. They emphasize the importance of understanding local context and the 'connectedness' (socially and politically) of individuals, groups and agencies in analysing funding patterns. But they also emphasize the disadvantages experienced by smaller organizations in managing contracts: Many do not have specialist full-time finance workers. But they face heavy demands in managing and monitoring budgets.

As increasingly professional standards are required and work is increasingly subjected to quality controls, some commentators fear that volunteers will be lost. Will management committees be increasingly stocked with professionals, accountants and lawyers? Will front-line volunteers be replaced by paid staff who can be regulated? The evidence on this so far is again contradictory. Russell and Scott (1997) find evidence that contracting offers the prospect of increasing satisfaction to the longer-term volunteers that they studied, but they also find increasing polarization between trustees and paid managers, paid workers and volunteers, skilled and unskilled volunteers. They cite managers who freely admit to replacing 'amateur' trustees with professionals and question how far the regulation required of contracting can be matched with the motivations of volunteers. A survey of volunteering in the late 1990s (Davis Smith, 1998) suggests a decline in volunteering within the health and social welfare field. It also suggests that fewer volunteers are putting in more hours, and thus run a higher risk of burn-out. Davis Smith's finding that volunteers are more instrumental in their approach to volunteering seems to match the more instrumental approach by funders and providers that is implicit in Russell and Scott's work.

4.6. PARTNER OR AGENT?

The research evidence is that there has been much less distortion than third sector organizations feared either in relation to the content of their work or the way they do it.

Goals

Most studies agree that there is little evidence to support fears of widespread distortion of the goals of third sector organizations (see e.g. Richardson, 1995). Half the contracts studied by Russell and Scott (1997) reported were conversions of existing grants—a finding reinforced in a recent NCVO study (Hems and Passey, 1998). Providers in a number of studies report that their campaigning and advocacy roles are not affected. Guidelines produced jointly by the Association of Directors of Social Services and a range of third sector intermediary bodies in 1995 underline the importance of the sector's campaigning role as does the national compact, but one or two studies suggest that, while there may be no overt censorship, the sheer weight of contract administration may squeeze out campaigning activities (Lewis,

1993) and that there might be self-censorship. It is also possible that, if third sector providers become more like businesses, there may be a shift from advocacy for the marginalized user to advocacy for market share, although there is no evidence as yet for this.

Goals can, however, be distorted if organizations change direction in order to chase the money and Richardson (1995) finds some evidence of this. Several studies report the pressure on small organizations to expand and change the nature of the services they offer: a small lunch or social club run once or twice a week may find itself moving into day care on a daily basis (Prins, 1995) which changes the nature of the commitment, of the task and of the organization. In other cases organizations who ran a range of activities may now find it easier to get services funded than preventive work (Statham, 1996).

Research does suggest, however, that third sector organizations are now dealing with more dependent clients. While this may be seen as a positive development in terms of reaching the most needy people, it may have implications for their original service users. There is evidence, too, that contracts force third sector organizations to limit their services to the locality covered by the purchaser (Richardson, 1995).

It is easier to resist the pressure towards distortion if alternative funding is available. An NCVO study of purchasers (Hems and Passey, 1998) reports that purchasers are maintaining grants for start-up costs, new initiatives, advocacy and campaigning—a finding, which is in turn reinforced by Unwin and Westland. Available statistics suggest that, in the late 1990s, non-contract funding was still available from government—local authority grants were still rising, albeit at a slower rate than fees (see below). There are, as we have seen, alternative sources of funds—although usually time-limited. The fact that only half the respondents to the 1998 NCVO survey of third sector organizations were involved in contracts suggests that there is no headlong dash into the contracts market.

Operation

Walsh et al. (1997, p. 140) report that the contract culture has brought 'pressure to formalize relationships and to demonstrate value for money'. Several studies report benefits for providers in terms of clarity, but Deakin (1996b). warns that the obverse of clarity might be inflexibility. Most studies find that contract specifications tend to be drawn up in negotiation with third sector organizations (see e.g. Kumar, 1997). Scott and Russell (1998) report that 'Where the reputation, market niche, size and managerial competence were high, there was evidence of successful negotiation'.

In areas where the market is underdeveloped, some third sector organizations can dictate their own terms—Walsh et al. (1997) report that, in some areas, the larger providers can be 'little short of dismissive of the registration process', while Johnson et al. (1998) argue that sanctions are unlikely to be used where suppliers are limited.

On the other hand, there is common agreement that the preparation, negotiation and administration of contracts has placed a considerable administrative burden on organizations, especially smaller organizations. Administrative problems can also be caused by inconsistent policies between different local authority departments who may be funding the same organization. The need to develop multiple funding strategies noted both by Scott and Russell (1999) and Gaster et al. (1999) is likely to exacerbate these problems.

Kumar (1997) reports that third sector organizations are not finding the accountability demands of purchasers overbearing (Kumar, 1997). It may be the case that purchasers and providers are learning together how to make contracts work. It may be that larger national charities—of the kind that Kumar studied—can absorb the additional requirements of contract accountability more readily. There is also a tendency in the literature to exaggerate the boundaries between the two sectors. This paper has already noted the multiple links between the public and third sectors and Kumar reports that contract managers from both sectors tend to meet informally and move in the same circles. Wistow et al. (1996) comment that, even before the introduction of the reforms, third sector organizations often had local authority elected councillors on their management committees, although as roles and interests become more carefully delineated under a contract regime, this is under much greater scrutiny. They also note that the involvement of third sector organizations in joint planning for community care from the 1980s onwards allowed for considerable mutual learning and paved the way for a smoother transition to the 'contract' culture than might otherwise have been the case. 'In recent years,' they go on to say, 'third sector organizations and local authorities have tended to operate alongside each other within social networks, in which mutual dependence has been recognized by both parties'. At the same time, the reforms have brought with them changes in the employment market. Several studies report what appears to be increasing movement of senior personnel across sectoral lines (Kumar, 1997; Taylor et al., 1995; Leat, 1995; Scott and Russell, 2001). This may apply particularly to the larger national third sector organizations, which were the subject of Kumar's study. Knight (1993), for example, argues that large not-for-profit firms have more in common with their public sector paymasters and the commercial sector than with their third sector roots.

Does this mean that the fears of over-regulation that were expressed at the outset of contracting are unjustified? The evidence for coercive isomorphism—with the purchasers forcing providers to behave in particular ways—is not convincing. But the rise of the new managerialism that has accompanied the contract culture brings with it a potential for normative and mimetic isomorphism among both purchasers and providers[7]—what one third sector chief executive called 'cultural take-over by stealth'. Thus, Walsh et al. (1997) note the importance of norms in times of instability and the way language has been used to 'structure the way in which people have perceived the issues'. Scott and Russell (1998) note the hegemony of the financial language of contracting and associated systems of accounting. They express concern over the extent to which handling money has had to become a more specialized activity in organizations, with its own systems and culture. Many studies report the advance of commercial and marketing values and the drive to be more businesslike (see e.g. Taylor et al., 1995). Business management degrees have become *de rigeur* for senior managers in the third sector and in the fight to keep ahead in the market, trustees and senior managers have been recruited from the for-profit sector (Leat, 1995).

In human services that are notoriously difficult to define, the tendency to fall back on financial and input data is well documented (Scott and Meyer, 1993; Deakin and Walsh, 1996; Chapman et al., 1999). There is a tendency to believe that what cannot be costed or measured does not count. Yet there is much in social care that is difficult to measure. Harding and Beresford (1996) comment that 'people who use services are consistently saying that what gives a service its quality is the nature and style of the worker and the relationship'. The possibility of service failure, the attention of the media when mistakes are made and the fact that large amounts of public money are being spent tends to make purchasers risk-averse. Systems are introduced without reference to the primary task—the emphasis is on getting the structure right—and accountability is passed down the system, with a plethora of standards governing the caring task (Statham, 1996).

Blackmore et al. (1995) demonstrate how this culture spreads, despite concerns that it is inappropriate. They contrast a general statement about not being too prescriptive from local government associations in the UK with suggested guidelines on day care specifications from the same associations which run to 20 sections and 21 pages! Against this background, fears that detailed regulation and performance indicators may discourage innovation, development and advocacy (Johnson et al., 1998) may yet be justified.

The growing preoccupation with quality in public services over the 1990s (Gaster, 1995; Johnson et al., 1998) may offer an approach that is more sensitive to the different dimensions of human services. This emphasis on quality is reinforced in defining 'best value' as something which goes beyond price. Where quality definition is part of a negotiated process between purchaser and provider, there is potential for enhancement of the services provided. However, Johnson et al. (1998) express reservations. They argue that quality tends to be defined by the purchaser and is politically and managerially driven, with cost-effectiveness as a key dimension. They also find that a commitment to involve users in definitions of quality, which could address the concerns expressed by Harding and Beresford above, is not matched by effective strategies for achieving this objective.

User Responsiveness

One of the most striking features of the development of the third sector over the past ten years or so has been the growth in organizations of service users and of the disability movement, challenging traditional professional practice and developing new approaches to independent living (Oliver, 1996). Cost apart, one of the main arguments behind the community care reforms was said to be the need to improve choice for and accountability to users, but Johnson et al.'s finding just quoted suggests that this has not necessarily been the outcome—for a number of reasons. Lewis and Glennerster (1996) point out that, while the contract culture places more emphasis on accountability requirements, it is not clear about who should be accountable to whom. Johnson et al. (1998) remind us that choice is exercized by customer proxies (i.e. local and health authority purchasers) rather than customers. Most research focuses on the impact of the reforms on providers and purchasers; little is concerned with the impact on the users whom the reforms were supposed to benefit. The research that does provide this focus finds that contracts have so far brought little benefit for users (Walsh et al., 1997; Kumar, 1997). Indeed, Robson et al. (1997) demonstrate how far third sector organizations themselves have to go to involve users fully in their operations. They found that while an increasing number of third sector organizations were introducing consumerist measures like satisfaction surveys and complaints procedures, relatively few organizations were involving users in governance structures. On the other hand, recent NCVO research suggests that user involvement in management committees is on the increase (Hems and Passey, 1998). Direct payments legislation should also give users more say.

There is, of course, little evidence that giving users a greater say privileges the third sector. Several studies argue that **what** is provided and **how** it is provided is much more important than **who** does the providing. It is also important to note that user empowerment is strongest in the field of physical disabilities and mental health where the user movement itself is strongest. Less progress has been made in services for older people and children.

4.7. THE THIRD SECTOR IN GOVERNANCE

This report has already commented that moves towards the market were tempered and to some extent in tension with parallel moves towards partnership. More practically, the experience of contracting must be set in the context of joint planning, intended to involve both provider organizations and consumers in the assessment of local need, the mapping of local provision and planning for the future. It is the reconciliation of the tensions between the market and democracy which lies at the heart of the search for a 'third way' in government.

How has the contract culture affected the involvement of third sector organizations in the governance of welfare? The emphasis on partnership has provided scope for increased collaboration with government at all levels, and there is evidence that in some localities, this has generated gains for the sector (Unwin and Westland, 1996; Essex, 1998) especially where there is already a tradition of joint planning to build on. There are opportunities now for third sector organizations to define the terms on which they engage and the shape of welfare provision. As the future of social services departments in their present guise becomes increasingly uncertain, local authorities—and social services departments within them—need to embrace partnership as a survival strategy.

But research on partnership in general suggests that the rhetoric of partnership still outstrips the reality (Taylor, 1997). Outside the joint planning arena, social services departments have not been a major player in partnerships (Zipfel, 1994; Statham, 1996). Whether in joint planning or in relation to wider issues, like regeneration, partnership has not proved easy. Third sector organizations find that the rules of the game are set by statutory partners and they are always struggling to get to grips with unfamiliar systems. Many organizations face difficult choices between the more privileged access to decision making that partnership may offer and the loss of independence that can result. It is a process that can take valuable time away from their front-line work, especially as the number of areas in which consultation is required grows and partnerships proliferate. The paradox for many is that, the more they are admitted into the arenas where decisions are made, the less they are able to sustain contact with the constituency which gives them legitimacy in those forums.

There is a sense in which third sector organizations are the victims of their own success as they are pulled into more and more decision-making forums and have to find ways of engaging without being incorporated. Often they find they are in the wrong game altogether—the real decisions are hammered out in the corridors of power and the committees on which they find themselves are simply a rubber stamp. Even where there is goodwill on the local authority side, partnerships tend to be dominated by funding and service delivery considerations (Gaster et al., 1999; Craig et al., 1999) and the contribution that third sector organizations can make is tempered by the fact that they are often in receipt of government funding and may not wish to rock the boat.

One asset for the UK third sector in the drive toward partnership has been the existence of a long-established infrastructure within the sector. Local development and coordinating organizations exist in most parts of the country and although they may not reflect the views of all local organizations (black and minority ethnic organizations often feel excluded from what tend to be white, middle class organizations), they do provide a recognized means through which third sector views can be sought and represented and a model for other forms of cooperation within the sector. It is through this and similar networks that third sector input into joint planning has been coordinated and local coordinators employed to support local organizations in making their views heard.

However, there is a tension between the market mechanisms that dominate the contract culture and moves towards partnership. The language of joint planning has been superseded in a number of localities by an emphasis on joint commissioning, influenced by the superior purchasing power of health authorities and their market driven perspective. Joint commissioning is more of a market model and, in this context, third sector organizations can be seen as having potential vested interests as providers (see e.g. Lewis and Glennerster, 1996; Gaster et al., 1999). From this perspective, the contribution they can make as development agencies, advocates, support agencies or in offering a voice to the wider community is easily overlooked.

In this sense, partnership may be getting sucked back into the market. And there are other senses in which the move to partnership remains firmly within a market framework. Recent years have seen a growth in new forms of democracy, using focus groups, panels, market surveys and similar mechanisms to revive a representative democracy that has become somewhat tired and discredited at local level. Health authorities, who have been leaders in the move to joint commissioning, have been particularly enthusiastic about the new participative forms. Both this government and its predecessor have placed great emphasis on 'citizen' or consumer charters which lay out the rights of users and the standards they can expect. Modernising Social Services—the government current proposals for community care—also lay emphasis on satisfaction surveys.

These new exercises in democracy have considerable potential to involve consumers and the public more in influencing the way services are planned and provided, but this form of consumer participation does not of itself constitute democracy. Health authorities are not politically accountable at local level—their members are elected rather than appointed and their culture is managerial in nature. These exercises need to flow alongside and feed into the representative democracy that has been discredited at local level.

However, other partnerships are mushrooming in local government, and these are less likely to follow the market model. Indeed, some commentators have seen the spread of partnership across policy fields, and particularly in regeneration, as the foundation for new forms of governance in the 21st century, which bring together the range of stakeholders in the locality, with the local authority in an enabling rather than controlling role. A range of proposals to involve communities, service users and voluntary organizations in partnerships for health improvement, Sure Start (a Programme for under 5s), the New Deal for Communities, and new forms of neighbourhood management which seek to join up services at local level (SEU, 2001) may now be creating an important contrary climate to the commissioning model described earlier and provide a new context for the social care planning of the future.

4.8. SUMMARY

The picture that comes out of research on the impact of the 'contract culture' so far is ambiguous—whichever aspect we explore. It suggests that there are advantages and disadvantages for those involved. Thus, while the amount of government money flowing into the sector is still increasing, third sector organizations are generally doing more for less and funding can be volatile, which raises questions about the sustainability of the contribution that the third sector is making to care. While there is evidence that there is considerable scope for negotiation in drawing up contracts, there is contrary evidence of a 'ratcheting up' of regulation as new systems bed down and of a 'cultural take-over by stealth'—as the more successful operators in the third sector absorb the language of the new managerialism and learn the rules of the game.

The evidence also tells us that there are winners and losers. While the evidence is still difficult to read, there is concern that, except in niche markets, the larger organizations, whose cultures are most compatible with those of purchasers, will be the main beneficiaries of the transfer, along with for-profits, who must be taken into account in any analysis of the UK welfare mix. In reality, it is likely that for the entrepreneurial third sector manager, who is prepared to speak the language of the 'new managerialism', there will be much to win. It is equally certain that many organizations will be left struggling in uncertainty.

Involvement in partnership allows third sector organizations to make a contribution not only in delivering services but also in the formulation of policy and quality standards—determining the rules of the game. However, many still feel excluded from the real arenas of decision making and there are tensions between the language of the market and the language of democracy. The current emphasis on partnership is opening new doors and there is evidence of genuine progress in leading edge authorities, especially where local government has invested in the sector over a period of time

(Unwin and Westland, 1996). Elsewhere there is a continued sense that the reality falls far short of the rhetoric of joint planning and that third sector organizations, whether provider or user organizations, continue to be marginalized or coopted onto purchaser agendas. Where the market is the dominant model, the dominance of the new managerialist ethos, especially in health authorities, may emphasize joint commissioning rather than joint planning, with third sector organizations excluded because of their vested interest as providers.

There is clearly more work to be done on tracking the changing picture as the changes that arose from the 1990 Act settle down and as subsequent policy changes add their own gloss to the situation. Many factors have influenced the progress of the contract culture in the UK: the relationship with other key players, notably health authorities; the structure of the local social care market; local government reorganization, which has changed the authority responsible for social care in many areas; and the strength of the local third sector infrastructure. These factors are likely to be interlinked—a culture which encourages multi-agency working will often encourage partnership with third sector organizations. A well-developed local market will often be linked with a history of statutory investment in the sector as will a well-developed third sector infrastructure (Taylor, 1998). One recent study (Essex, 1997) suggests that effective third sector participation in planning and provision is also related to the presence or absence of a range of opportunities for individual statutory/third sector relationships outside the funding relationship, among which a strong inter-agency planning structure may be key. Where investment has traditionally been low, or where the third sector has traditionally been seen as the 'volunteer' sector, there is little social capital on which to build either an effective market or an effective third sector voice.

The contradictory nature of the evidence may be explained by the third sector's tendency to exaggerate the negative consequences of change (see e.g. Kramer, 1994). Alternatively, it may reflect the considerable variation both within the sector and between authorities across the country. But there is a deeper explanation. The search for a 'third way' between the market and the state brings with it a number of real tensions. The position of the third sector between public and private means that it will find itself holding the tensions and ambiguities inherent in this search (Taylor, 1997) and reflecting different resolutions of these tensions:

- between universality and targeting those in most need (**who is served**);
- between the need to be publicly accountable and the need for flexibility (**how they are served**);
- between the need for minimum standards and the option for a diversity of types of provision (**what is provided**); between professionalism and the voluntary principle;

- between choice (which includes access to a range of providers) and the economies of scale that the market demands (**who provides**);
- between the interests of the consumer and the interests of the citizen.

These are the tensions which any welfare system must address and no amount of rhetoric about partnership can disguise the fact that the public sector and the third sector often have different interests in addressing them. While ideologues still look for resolutions which favour one force over another, the focus now seems increasingly to be on an attempt to find the best of all worlds. But this 'third way' remains elusive.

4.9. THE FUTURE

The adoption of the language of markets throughout government in the UK has been as striking as the more substantive changes. As such, the 'contract culture' is set to continue, whatever the new government's commitment to a move from a 'contract culture' to a 'partnership culture'. It is also important to remember that the third sector has no automatic right to statutory funding. But the capacity of the third sector to release a diversity of resources for welfare and to give voice to different groups in the population can make an important contribution to this effectiveness and it is in these terms that the impact of the contract culture must ultimately be judged.

Experience to date suggest that, in both respects, the third sector faces a number of challenges in the immediate future.

Financing Welfare

Continually constrained budgets, with third sector organizations topping up public funds, have implications for sustainability even of basic services. Unless there is a recognition of the need for social investment in order to create a vibrant social market, much will depend either on the ability of third sector organizations themselves to find alternative funds or the capacity of individuals to fund their own welfare.

What is Funded

As public funding is increasingly targeted at those in most need, a second challenge emerges. A major contribution of the third sector in the past has been in its complementary and preventative roles. Although preventative work has the capacity to save money in the longer term, the continued emphasis on targeting is likely to place considerable limits on public support for these functions and these, too will depend on the ability of third sector organizations to find alternative, and often precarious, sources of funds.

Government's current emphasis on combating social exclusion has led to a number of initiatives to find new and imaginative approaches to public spending in targeted areas, and to target public spending more effectively on those who suffer most from exclusion. These emphasize the need for 'joined up thinking' across service boundaries and the need to 'bend' mainstream spending as well as injecting new funds (SEU, 2001). Indeed, they could provide the prototypes for the wholesale breakdown in agency boundaries that this government seems to be looking for. It may be that these will provide the capacity to provide the supportive background against which priority needs can be met, but these are themselves targeted programmes—targeted to localities in most need. It remains to be seen how effective this will be in changing the way government approaches the provision of welfare and how far it will be possible to spread good practice from targeted areas to the population at large.

Market Structure

Third sector housing associations, including those who specialize in social care, face increasing pressure toward merger, with competition favouring the larger service providers. In the context of increasing competition from private care firms, will the same apply to all providers in the social care field? In some parts of the country, coalitions have been formed to give smaller organizations access to economies of scale. However, this is not widespread in the UK.

Market Regulation

Insofar as regulatory regimes tend to push accountability and risk down the system, third sector organizations may face increasingly intrusive monitoring, which favours the easily measurable—this does not guarantee quality for users. Financial constraints meanwhile could shift the responsibility for quality and the delivery of 'best value' (or the blame for the lack of it) from the purchaser to the provider. The introduction of 'best value' which, with its bid to replace competition on price with competition on value, lays emphasis on widespread consultation in arriving at definitions of value is encouraging, but much will depend on how local authorities handle a complex consultation process if it is not to turn into a further layer of bureaucracy dictated by what is easiest to measure. The government's new 'non-ideological' slogan is 'what counts is what works', but how will 'best value' define 'what works' and whose values will count? While business is clearly seen as a crucial stakeholder, the position of the third sector is less clearly defined and some commentators have suggested that the widening of the definition of stakeholder may mean that the voices of marginalized users and those who work with them will still not be heard.

Governance

There are dilemmas both for the internal management of third sector organizations and for their participation in wider decision-making forums. Internally, there are dangers that the professionalization and technical expertise required for effective management of contracts may exclude those without business or legal expertise, who may find themselves marginalized. Externally, there is the danger that access to the arenas where key decisions are made will divorce organizations from their constituencies.

The User Voice

The state remains the purchaser for the most vulnerable service users and neither the increased use of market research mechanisms nor delivery by third sector organizations of themselves guarantee user empowerment. Chapman et al. (1999) express concern that the emphasis on consulting with a wide range of stakeholders may in fact disadvantage the most excluded. The commitment to user involvement is not yet matched by effective channels for involvement in most areas. The growth of individual consumerism is not sufficient to give service users more power over their services, although Direct Payments for Care may be a significant step forward, if available to enough people, with the information and consumer rights that this demands. Support will continue to be needed for user-based organizations which can give users the confidence, knowledge and skills they need to make informed choices and to ensure those choices are honoured. It will also be needed to ensure that providers are able to make the space to ensure that their users have the voice and influence they choose to have.

There are other changes ahead. The UK welfare mix has been one where the state role in finance has been significant, which has made the local authority as much the 'client' of the third sector provider as the user him or herself. With the introduction of direct payments and the possible reform of the income maintenance system, however, this may not be the case into the future. Indeed, even state responsibility for finance is no longer a foregone conclusion. Charges for social care became commonplace under the last government and, although a powerful disability lobby has moved the reform of disability benefits beyond the bounds of the politically acceptable for now, this is likely to be a temporary reprieve. Also, while recent reports suggest that the prospect of a demographic time-bomb is exaggerated in the UK (Royal Commission on Long-term Care, 1999), the unwillingness of the markets to countenance rising public expenditure is likely to drive the search for welfare reform further. If personal responsibility through private insurance is seen as the way forward, we can expect this to provide a further boost to for-profit care, with residual third sector and statutory care targeted at those groups who fall through the net and subjected to ever stricter financial control.[8]

This paper demonstrates that, even in the most favourable circumstances, the language of partnership masks very real tensions: between the need for a stable market and the need for responsiveness to individual need (as illustrated in the discussion of block and spot contracts); between the need for public accountability in the delivery of care and the desire of partner organizations for flexibility; between professionalism and the voluntary principle; between the need for standards and the need for diversity; between accountability and trust. The third sector is, by definition, marked by these tensions, situated as it is on at the boundaries between public and private (Evers, 1995; Taylor, 1997). While ideological solutions have in the past tended to look for resolutions which favour public or private, government, market or civil society, the changing balance between the different sectors over recent years offers the opportunity to find the best of all worlds, a commitment shared by the current UK government. But this third way remains elusive.

Notes

1. I would like to acknowledge the help of Philip Haynes in preparing this paper, especially in discussing issues of current trends in community care planning.
2. In the UK, the term generally used for the third sector is the 'voluntary' sector and these terms will be used interchangeably throughout this paper.
3. Local government in the UK does not have constitutional independence and is very much the 'creature' of central government in the UK compared to many other European countries (Batley and Stoker, 1991; Taylor and Bassi, 1996).
4. Health authorities in the UK are separate from local authorities. Their governing body is appointed, not elected and they are part of the National Health Service. The line between social care and health is by no means easy to draw and, although joint care planning and commissioning require the two bodies to work together, there have been considerable tensions between the two bodies.
5. This was to have been phased out after the first three years, but has been extended every year for the following three years.
6. Until 1994, there were more than 20 different sources of central government funding for regeneration. In 1994, these were pulled together into a Single Regeneration Budget Challenge Fund, with an annual bidding round. While there was no new money attached, this has made funding for regeneration more accessible in principle, although the required outcomes still emphasize jobs and training opportunities rather than social regeneration. In 2002, responsibility for this funding has been transferred to Regional Development Agencies, but some new funding for neighbourhood renewal is available in the Neighbourhood Renewal and Community Empowerment Funds administered by the new Neighbourhood Renewal Unit in the Department for Transport, Local Government and the Regions.
7. DiMaggio and Powell (1983) coined the term institutional isomorphism to describe the tendency for organizations in the same field to develop similar characteristics. They distinguished three kinds of isomorphism: coercive (enforced), mimetic (imitating successful organizations), and normative (where particular norms become hegemonic and organizations adhere to them because 'that is the way things are done'.
8. The Royal Commission on Long Term Care, which reported in March 1999, suggests that responsibility for provision should be shared between the state and individuals, with individuals responsible for living costs and housing and the state responsible for 'personal care'. However, in England and Wales, the state has only accepted responsibility for nursing care. Only in Scotland, does it also accept responsibility for personal care.

Chapter 5

Dilemmas of Public/Private Partnership in France

EDITH ARCHAMBAULT AND JUDITH BOUMENDIL*

5.1. INTRODUCTION

The field of social services is characterized in France by a mixed structure, which has favoured the enormous growth in this field of the third sector. The Johns Hopkins Project has shown that 'social services', that is facilities for specific groups of people such as families, handicapped, elderly, young people and adults in social difficulty, income support and maintenance, emergency and relief, and charities, is by far the major area of non-profit involvement, in spite of the sustained expansion of governmental provision in this field.[1] This field accounted for 29 per cent of the third sector's operating expenditures in 1990 and 38.5 per cent of total third sector employment, employing about 300,000 wage earners. Apart from being the largest field of non-profit labour, non-profit employment in this field dominates employment in the area of social services (58 per cent of total employment) and has almost doubled since 1980, contrasting with a significant decrease in general employment.

The development of a mixed delivery system in the field of social services can partly be explained by a voluntarist policy toward decentralization, which contradicts a thousand-year-old tradition of *etatism*.[2]

---

*EDITH ARCHAMBAULT and JUDITH BOUMENDIL • Université de Paris 1 – Sorbonne, Matisse, Maison des Sciences Economiques, 106 Bd de l'Hopital, 75647 Paris Cedex 13, France.

The decentralization Acts (1982–1983) redistributed the responsibilities between the state and local communities.[3] New activities and new resources were transferred to the local governments. Among these activities, culture and arts, sports, education and training services are important areas, but the social welfare services outside the social security, that is *aide sociale*[4] transferred to the *département*[5] and of course local development, became the 'game preserve' of local government.

State intervention is now more targeted and the state's participation in the financing of personal social services is slowly decreasing. As Tchernonog stated (1992), the division of responsibilities in social policy in France is defined as follows: 'central social policy targets the major functions of risk coverage through compulsory insurance, income redistribution among population groups and regulation, the welfare system acting as a counterweight to the economic system. At the local level, action is targeted at social management of the community: the actors at municipal level adjust their tactics on the basis of the shortcomings observed in central government action and provide aid or services which are complementary to national aid'.

In a context of budgetary crisis and facing these new responsibilities, local governments contracted out the provision of many services. Since they have been contracting with for-profit providers for equipment, open spaces management, public construction and economic services, they have favoured the partnership with non-profit organizations[6] for cultural and educational concerns and above all for social and employment policies.

This delegation of services allows the local authorities for cutting down the costs by evading the severe regulations ruling public sector employment (impossibility of dismissing workers once hired, higher wages for unskilled workers than in the private sector); another reason is to escape the heavy rules of public accounting which inhibit innovation. Public financing at the local level also implies a tighter patronage and even a political dependence.

The weight of state budget and the growing role of public local authorities in the provision and financing of social services which are more and more provided by non-profit organizations, demonstrates that the area of social services is characterized by a system of strong interdependence between non-profit organizations and public agencies. As a consequence, the way their financial and political relationship are structured is of major importance.

After a rapid overview of the historical background, the main object of this chapter is to analyse the type of relationship that have been developed between the government, at its different levels, and the non-profit organizations, in the recent years, and the consequences of these new relationships on the traditional functions of non-profit organizations.

5.2. HISTORICAL BACKGROUND

The French Welfare System

The French welfare system is more recent than the German or the British ones. The interwar period was the beginning of statutory social insurance in France. After World War I, the recovery of Alsace and Lorraine, lost in 1870 war and since ruled by German law, created a new problem: those regions benefited from the German social insurance set up by Bismarck (sickness and industrial injuries insurance; retirement and disability pensions). In 1918, France had no social insurance, except for industrial injuries, and had to choose between specific rules for the two newly recovered regions or the generalization of social insurance. Of course, this last solution was chosen by a centralized government.

This is why, the first social insurance followed the German pattern: compulsory sickness insurance, disability and old age insurance for the low-income salaried employees. A specificity of the French system is family allowances, at the philanthropic employers' suggestion. These were also prompted by a birth-raising policy since the birth-rate in France had been steadily dropping: during the interwar period, it got below the death rate.

After World War II, this 'bismarckian' social insurance system was replaced by a more comprehensive social security, influenced by the system that Lord Beveridge set up in UK. Initially intended for the salaried population, the social security scheme previewed an extension to the whole population, which occurred about 1970. From the very beginning, the benefits from social security were a large part of household income: 15 per cent in 1949 and this relative part increased to 35 per cent in 1996 on a total of 2360 billion FF. (363 billion Euros). Retirement and old-age benefits are the most important part (42 per cent), followed by health reimbursement and third party payments (33 per cent), family benefits (15 per cent), unemployment insurance and solidarity allowances (8 per cent) and minimum income (2 per cent). Related to GDP, social protection expenses are 30 per cent and France ranks third on twelve European countries *ex-aequo* with Germany, after Denmark and Netherlands. So the welfare state is an important reality in France. Regular polls show that French people are attached to the principle of social security.

The creation of the social security scheme in 1945 called into question the role of the mutual societies, which had been very active in social insurance management since 1930. Mutual societies are still very active in social protection. First, social security sickness insurance reimburses health expenses of households, but the patient's contribution amounts to 20 or 30 per cent. This contribution is covered by mutual societies for their members.

Similarly, the mutual societies expand to full income guarantee in case of sickness, accident or death. Second, the extension of social security to the whole population was slower than planned, which explains why some special social security systems are completely run by mutual societies: it is the case for civil servants, students, self-employed people and farmers. Mutual societies are not only a complement to social security, they were and still are also very active in the field of medical and social prevention: drug and alcoholism prevention, modern birth control, regular medical check-ups, poliomyelitis or tuberculosis prevention, or now AIDS prevention, are fields where mutual societies and associations were first; social security followed. In the post-war period, mutual societies and associations also began to run social establishments, mainly for the handicapped and the elderly.

The Provision of Personal Social Services in France: A System Based on Pluralism

Government responsibility in public welfare is a deeply rooted idea in France. French history is characterized by a thousand year old conflict between the state and any form of intermediate body, especially those linked to the Church, inherited from the *Ancien Régime* and above all from the French Revolution. This conflict lasted until very recently. This context explains that the main characteristic of the French welfare system is its centralization, and why the French system remains a Jacobin one.

But this pattern did not dominate in the field of social services. Indeed, contrasting with an everlasting school war,[7] peaceful relationships rapidly dominated between the state and the Church in the social welfare area on a contractual basis with social security or other social funds. The Church progressively ceased to run welfare establishments or services directly and the state or associations replaced it. This secularization trend began during the French Revolution and ended mid-20th century. In catholic welfare establishments or services, paid staff replaced volunteer nuns. From the 1950s and 1960s on, with the constant economic growth and with demographic and socio-cultural changes, civil society appeared to be more eager to initiate the provision of special services. The 1960s were also a time of institutional and political debate, and of the emergence of *laissez-faire* ideologies, questioning the opportunity of a state-centralized policy in every public field. Critics of the welfare state denounced the inefficiency of public policies, their waste, the weight of bureaucracy, and most of all the inadequacy of public procedures to cope with new or evolving needs. According to Ullman (1993) 'delegation to non-profit organizations has been the result of a deliberate effort on the part of political elites to improve the functioning and extend the scope of both social service provision and of French democracy (...). It results in part from the responses of policy makers to the set of challenges faced by all modern welfare states. It began, however, with the efforts of French political elites to right the imbalance between an overly centralized and insular state and a weak and fragmented civil society'. The public powers were also surpassed by the growing demand for social services linked with the comprehension of the need for more choice and flexible supply. Then, non-profit organizations became to intervene in the provision of special types of services.

The field of the services for handicapped people, in this sense, presents interesting specificities. After the 1901 Act granting the freedom of association in France, the first self-help and interest groups for handicapped people emerged, composed of the handicapped themselves, their parents and families, advocating an autonomous and global policy toward the handicapped. These groups were also centred around the issue of the right to work and to earn a living. As there was no core legislation for handicapped people apart from laws concerning the disabled veterans (1919) and those involved in on-the-job accidents (1898), non-profit organizations pursued advocacy for the economic independence of handicapped adults. In the 1950s and 1960s, with the implementation of social security schemes, the pioneer organizations of handicapped people began to mix the provision of services with advocacy, creating facilities and services (especially home services and work facilities). These associations rapidly received a formal public acknowledgement through the status of *reconnaissance d'utilité publique* (the official label of associations recognized as being of public utility, see hereafter). Then they obtained a continuous flow of public funds through state financing or third-party payments. They were also actors in the writing of the very comprehensive Law of 1975 intended for handicapped people (see hereafter).

This situation is obviously linked to a huge increase in the expenditures of the public programmes. The development of family day-nurseries is more recent. Born in the mainstream of 1968 events, this movement[8] corresponds primarily to a refusal of the public traditional day-care centres, which were generally based on a strong medicalization. In the 1980s, these family day-nurseries tried to stabilize their structure and functioning and progressively obtained a public financing, since public powers became interested in their objects in terms of socialization, and their relatively low costing. They are now subject to agreement (see hereafter), and financed partly by the families, partly by the state.

Recently, the Government has introduced new and significant legislation which encouraged the formation of non-profit organizations in the field of social services. Let us quote two examples:

- 1989: Law encouraging 'intermediary' associations supplying jobs to people experiencing social difficulties: unskilled young people, potential or former delinquents or drug addicts;

- 1992: Legislation encouraging (by social contributions cuts) the creation of 'neighbourhood jobs' by households, such as housekeeping,
  nursing care for children, the disabled, the elderly.

As many households could only afford a part-time job, many non-profits were
created to convert part-time to full-time by multiplying employers. They also
provide training and fulfill administrative tasks instead of the elderly or disabled employer.

5.3. THE FUNCTIONING MECHANISMS OF THE
   WELFARE MIX

The General Structure of the Field of Social Services

The general pattern in France now in the field of social services is one in
which the state provides the standard and basic services directed toward the
entire population or which present one or various of these characteristics:

- a rather strong consensus on their importance and usefulness;
- a direct link with the 'regalian' functions of the state: for example, services linked with justice such as services for juvenile delinquents are
  generally taken care of by the state, since other services are partially
  delegated to non-profit organizations. The state is indeed reluctant to
  lose the direct control on these activities.
- the medicalized services and those which present a relatively high
  level of technicity.

The state at its different levels delegates the delivery of personal and specialized services directed toward minority groups and socially endangered populations, or responsibilities in responding to new, less defined and highly
specialized social needs, especially those involving moral support for socially
disadvantaged populations and family relations. But the state almost always
provides the bulk of resources, through direct financial support or reimbursement by social security.

The debate questioning the level of statutory direct involvement in the
delivery of services is not relevant in France since the Welfare state is not
questioned so much as in other European countries. There is a rather large
consensus on the necessity to maintain the statutory role in most types of
services. The only threats against this situation comes from some private
insurance company leaders or ultra-liberal trade unions claiming somehow
for privatization of social security and more competition in the delivery of
social services. But these attempts remain quite restrained.

Institutional care is still the cornerstone in providing social services in France. Residential facilities are those which have really shaped the area. The majority of the establishments were set up mainly during the 1950s and 1960s, which is also the most prominent era of rapid government expenditure expansion. Today, the set-up of new establishments is less frequent, because of the financial constraints of public funding, but also since the needs are nearly satisfied (Archambault, 1997). The third reason is that the general discourse of policy makers is based on a voluntarist policy toward deinstitutionalization and a larger openness of the structures to the 'normal life'.

The Mixed Provision of Personal Social Services

According to the estimates produced by the Johns Hopkins Project, in 1990 non-profit organizations providing social services employed about 300,000 FTE wage earners, that is 58 per cent of the employment in this field. It is much more difficult to estimate the number of non-profit organizations in this field; they may number as much as 60,000.

As shown in Table 5.1, non-profit organizations provide the bulk of services for handicapped people, that is almost 90 per cent of the establishments and 85 per cent of employment. Establishments for handicapped people are highly specialized in France: almost each type of disability involves a special type of facility.[9] Services to disadvantaged adults with psycho-social problems are also a quasi monopoly for non-profit organizations: about 87 per cent of

Table 5.1. The Share of Public Agencies, Non-profit Organizations, and other Private Organizations in the Delivery of Personal Social Services in France (1996)

Status of the Organizations	Types of Service	Public Agencies(%)	Associations (%)	Private (%)
Handicapped people	Number of establishments	8.1	89.1	2.8
	Employment	11.0	85.2	3.8
Protection of children	Number of establishments	14.3	82.6	3.1
	Employment	26.3	70.3	3.4
Adults in social difficulty	Number of establishments	11.3	86.5	2.1
	Employment	17.1	81.0	1.9
Elderly homes	Number of beds	58.0	29.1	12.8
	Employment	59.5	27.8	12.7
Child day care	Number of establishments	60	40	
Housekeeping services	Number of establishments	30	60	10
Home care services	Number of beds	n.d.	70	n.d.
Family home help	Number of services	n.d.	96	n.d.

Source: SESI, Uniopss.
n.d.—not determined.

the establishments and 70 per cent of employment. Residential services for adults in social difficulty (*Centre d'Hébergement et de Réadaptation Sociale*) shelter adults and families with psychological or social problems with the aim of helping them recover their autonomy. Originally, they were intended for ex-prostitutes, but they progressively opened their doors to homeless families including battered women and their children, and now to any person living on the fringes of society.

Establishments for *children experiencing social difficulty* provide home care for pregnant teen-agers or isolated mothers in social difficulty, foster care, some receive deprived or neglected children. Clubs and centres dealing with the prevention of delinquency (*clubs et équipes de prévention*) present the originality of being directly settled in highly deprived areas. Associations account for about 83 per cent of all establishments conceived for this purpose, and 70 per cent of all wage earners. Public establishments are quite frequent in the field of care for children in difficulty (they manage 14.3 per cent of the total number of establishments), especially for the establishments providing foster care (*pouponnières à caractère social, foyer de l'enfance*), partly because these activities are connected to educational matters, a domain of the public sector and partly because they are in the field of justice decisions following-up, another domain of the public sector.

The part that non-profit organizations play in facilities for the elderly is smaller (29 per cent of beds) and public agencies prevail in this field. An explanation of this direct public provision of residential facilities directed toward these persons is given by Tchernonog (1994) who explains that elderly people represent a politically skilful social group and have a much higher 'voting power' than that of people in social difficulty, and the unemployed. Another explanation is that during the last decade, many hospital beds were in excess and have been converted in hospital nursing homes (*long séjour*). Private firms are also beginning to be attracted by the management of homes for the elderly, since the income of the elderly has dramatically grown in the last decades.[10] Powerful hotel trades (such as Sodexho, specialized in collective services for firms, Accor, Lyonnaise des Eaux, Vivendi) are screaming at the high income clients. This situation has consequences on the financial equilibrium of non-profit organizations leading establishments for the elderly, as we will see. But rapidly, these private companies have been facing solvability problems, as even high income elderly people are not ready to pay for these services.

The recent development of home care services is at the origin of strong and interesting debates, and involves particular roles for non-profit organizations. A new system of home care services, which particularly aims at maintaining elderly and dependent people, has developed significantly since 1984. It is organized into the peak organization UNASSAD (*Services de Soins A Domicile*). From the part of the State, the development of these services corresponded to a double observation: on one hand, a huge unemployment of non-qualified people, and on the other hand unsatisfied needs. Home care services are delivered at 70 per cent by the third sector, and about 118,000 people are employed by non-profit organizations for these services. Housekeeping services may be at 60 per cent non-profit ones.

Non-profit organizations have different ways of intervention in this field:

- provide the services directly, by employing people;
- not directly employ people, but put in contact a potential employee with a client and help this client in his employer's tasks (administration, management and so on).

These non-profit organizations are called associations mandataires. This last type of activity is currently developing much more than the first one.

As far as day-care facilities are concerned, the situation of France is very specific because of the early school attendance of children from 2 to 6 years old. This specificity is due to the existence of a very efficient pre-elementary school (école maternelle): 2,450,000 children between 2 and 6 were at school in 1995, 88 per cent in public pre-schools, 12 per cent in private non-profit pre-schools. The indicator in Table 5.1 concerns only those children below the age of 2 and the non at-school children above this age, attending crèches, day-nurseries, family day-nurseries or nursery centres. The third sector receives about 40 per cent, and the public sector 60 per cent of the 200,000 children in such facilities. Child-care is then more public-oriented than residential services. There were about 720 parents-nurseries receiving about 10,000 children in 1994 (SESI, 1995). But non-profit organizations have been at the initiative of the creation of two-third of the places in facilities in the last ten years. For these establishments, there is some kind of competition between public and non-profit establishments and non-profit nurseries often claim for a financial equal treatment between them and public establishments.

Finally, 'integration problems group' care, that is, for example, the rehabilitation of the suburbs, the integration of immigrants through literacy and training programmes, the help to the drug-addicts or alcoholics, and so on, are also emerging areas of social services. Residential facilities are frequently run by associations since these services involve high level skills based on the personal relationship, a domain for non-profit organizations' competencies. As for the 'light services' and counselling, even if the data are lacking in these fields which have a multipurpose dimension, one can say that, as they are generally under the responsibility of the local governments, these activities are also frequently contracted out to non-profit organizations.

For-profit organizations play a marginal role in the provision of personal social services, because of the frequent insolvency of the client, and the priority of non-profit involvement. But one can remark a new determination from the French body of private employers, represented by the Union CNPF

(*Centre national du Patronat francais*), to push private for-profit firms to provide home services, as this union has declared in a report on this subject.

The Role of the Third Sector

In exchange for this crucial service delivery function performed by the third sector, the state covers a large part of the expenditures of NPOs.

Table 5.2 reports the estimates of the Johns Hopkins Project (Archambault, 1997).

As shown in Table 5.2, the bulk of the resources comes from the government or the social security schemes. The establishments are funded either through per diem reimbursement by social security, or through grants, as in-kind support and global, and sometimes rather symbolic grants tend to dominate for small-sized local non-profit organizations. The larger the organization, the larger the public support will be. On the contrary, users fees are quite low in France, but they vary among the services. For example, clients' fees are rather significant in homes for the elderly (clients finance about two-third of the service). In the case of home services for elderly and handicapped people, the clients' contribution increases with the income, but health home care services are totally funded by public money.

To understand the role that non-profit organizations play in the field of social services, it must be taken on board that this field is characterized by a strong heterogeneity in the types of services, which also involves strong differences in the relationship that non-profit organizations and public entities share.

Table 5.2. Financing of the Non-profit Organizations Providing
Personal Social Services in France in 1990

Types of Resources	Million F	%	%
State	3,662	5.8	10
Local governments	7,025	11.2	19
Social security	27,066	43.2	71
Total public resources	37,753	60.2	100
Private donative	2,989	4.8	12
Fees and sales	14,482	23.1	58
Membership dues	6,677	10.7	27
Investment income	774	1.2	3
Total private resources	24,922	39.8	100
Total	62,675	100	

Source: Archambault, 1997.

First of all, the distinction between the non-profit establishments and residential facilities and the associations providing services without institutionalization, and especially 'light services', is fundamental. We should always keep in mind this distinction, as it conditions the attitudes and dilemmas of partnership.

Schematically, the first ones—the establishments run by non-profit organizations—are more or less para-public associations. The level of government financing is very high, generally through the social security scheme or financing by the *Département*.[11] The organizations are heavily regulated by state procedures (agreements and so on, see hereafter).

On the other hand, the small-sized health or social services have more diversified resources and are therefore more independent of the state. But they frequently share quite strong relationship with local communities. The regulation procedures are less frequent.

This distinction between structures and light services can also help in understanding the degree of institutionalization of a field: the emergent fields are generally based on small organizations run by volunteers. Then, when the need is acknowledged by the state, and more generally by the Nation, the government begins to finance the activities, and then establishments are created, as in France institutional care is the cornerstone. The establishments are run mainly by professionals. So the distinction between light and weight services also partly involves a distinction between 'new-emerging-innovating' services and 'traditional-institutionalized' ones.

Finally, as we will see below, the types of financial relationship between non-profit organizations and the government are also linked to this differentiation: the first ones are financed through grants, contracts and third party payments by the state or social security, as the other ones are subsidized through general grants, sometimes rather symbolic, or even by in-kind support such as free housing or equipment.

The Public Regulation

The large scale delegation in the field of social services to non-profit organizations is accompanied by various regulations related to the creation, costs and activities (standards of quality, qualification and recruitment of employees...) of non-profit establishments. This field is indeed one of the most regulated areas of activity in France as non-profit organizations are filling a public 'social mission' (*mission de service public*).

Different kinds of procedures allow the state for defining a general regulation of the field:

1. As part of the general social security scheme, social establishments are submitted to a process of authorization, called habilitation, involving

an *a priori* control of their project and its feasibility, and then leading
to the state financing (*accréditation*).

2. The status of *reconnaissance d'utilité publique*, is the official label of
associations recognized as being of public utility; many associations
providing social services are entitled to this status, which is quite difficult to obtain and not frequent in other fields (Théry, 1986).

3. The majority of the associations active in this field have also to
receive an agreement (*agrément*). The agreement is, first, a kind of
official recognition of the quality of activities performed in special
fields; but overall and very often, these activities are possible only if
the organizations carrying them out are agreed (*agréées*). It ought to
be stressed here that these controls are imposed upon the aforesaid
activities, and not especially upon the associations, and that the
requested standards have a pecuniary counterpart.

In these cases, the administration has a discretionary power of decision: it
thus grants a kind of monopoly to perform some activities, that is to authorize (or not authorize) a given organization to fix its aim in the fields concerned and carry out the corresponding activities, and consequently to forbid
all others to do so.

On one hand, the result is that the state administration keeps a very
close control on the agreed organization, and becomes a kind of partner for it:
the association is then a legal entity, half private entity, half part of the public
administration; strong conditions of morality and financial solvency are
demanded; and similarly for their insurance. Special statutes and by-laws have
to be accepted by the membership and, in some cases, the President and some
members of the board are appointed by a Minister; the books, the activity and
the general operation of the grouping are controlled by the controllers of the
state administration (*Inspection générale des affaires sociales, cour des comptes*).

On the other hand, the agreement opens the door to the public funding;
the agreed associations may receive donations and legacies, even if they are not
reconnues d'utilité publique. Finally, the agreement allows some associations to
bring actions before court for advocating causes in relation to their aim—a very
special exception to the French legal principle that no one is allowed to advocate before Court somebody else's cause (*nul ne plaide par procureur*): for
example, this is the case with the associations for handicapped people.

In the field of social services, this agreement gives non-profit organizations an automatic (and automatically renewed) access to public funding,
covering almost all expenditure involved in running the establishments,
either through per diem reimbursement or through global grants. Global
grants are distributed to establishments which are under the responsibility of
the state, and per diem reimbursements are provided by social security

system. To conclude, one can say on the one hand, that for these managing associations, the fundings are quite routinized, but on the other hand, that associations are agents of the government.

The Financial Relationship and Characteristics of Money Transfers

As we have already stated, the type of partnership primarily depends on the type of services provided, and the kind of public authority in cause.

The social establishments have strong revenues coming mainly from the state grants or per diem reimbursement from social security through. The per diem reimbursement are based on complex systems of contracts: the reimbursement depends on the type of structure and the number of residents. Each year, the amount of this reimbursement is revised by public administration (révision des taux directeurs).

The government subsidies for almost 100 per cent of the staff and operating costs but more and more non-profit organizations have to find financing for their investment expenses.[12] This is why these establishments are strongly regulated and controlled by government or the local authority in charge of them. First of all, as we have already seen, the set-up of establishments is submitted to the a priori authorization (habilitation) of the government. There are also serious norms on the recruitment of wage earners, and in the majority of the cases, non-profit organizations cannot choose their beneficiaries, since the demands are directly taken care of by public institutions which dispatch them then. There are a posteriori controls on the way the money is used, on the number of users and so on.

But with regards to the state's regulation, in the absence of direct incentives to maintain low costs, the effectiveness of public regulation is quite minimal, since the state is only involved in a global and quite segmented regulation of the field by developing 'a set of micro-measures' (Stiker, 1998). This lack of control and public regulation can partly be explained either by the difficulty, in this field, of finding criteria for specification and monitoring of quality and cost-effectiveness (see hereafter) or by the lack of economic incentives to control performance other than a strict financial measure of activity. The consequence is also a mutual dependence between the non-profit organizations—the main providers—and the state—the almost unique funder.

The mode of regulation in the social services since the 1960s, has been based on the continuous creation of establishments, and on the heavy equipment needed to supply them. This risk averse strategy has been quite efficient in a period of growth, but becomes unbearable in a situation of recession, as it brings with it a deep growth in operating costs and a structural increase in the size of the organizations.

Since the Decentralization Acts, non-profit organizations are also seen by the Government as important partners for local authorities and as the best private entities to restore social cohesion and prevent the social exclusion of frail or deprived populations in a period of growing unemployment. Non-profits are considered closer to people's needs than an impersonal bureaucracy; they are able to detect the coming issues and to propose innovative solutions. As they can react quicker than heavy public agencies, they can face emergency issues. In these types of delegation, the responsibilities are generally shared. But non-profit organizations are sometimes worried about the proximity of the new financers who are much more demanding in terms of reporting.

We have very few information on the level of contractualization in France and the normalization of the relationship between non-profit organizations and government agencies at local level. There are still very few studies on that subject. We have no information on the frequency of contracts, compared to global grants.

In the partnership between non-profit organizations and local communities, there seems to be a shift from global grants, rather discretionary, to special financing based on contracts; general activity contracts with reciprocal commitments are more and more taking the place of the classic system of general year-to-year funding. There are very few tenders, and more mutual agreements, except in the field of services for elderly people, in which they are developing. This is a request from the trade union of French employers (see earlier) to develop competition in the field of social services, and especially the field of home care services, but this movement is very slow for the moment.

For small non-profit organizations, especially for the activities linked with the support of groups, advocacy or 'watchdog' roles of non-profit organizations, global grants, rather discretionary, are distributed. In very small organizations, this financing is generally symbolic or based on in-kind help. These are year to year funds, and for the moment the major part of the funding is year-to-year contracts. This involves fragility of the financial structure of the associations.

The decentralization has somehow changed the relationship between the public powers and the associations, especially in the field of social services. Indeed, non-profit organizations are now much more proximate from their funder and controls is becoming more easy for local authorities. They are sometimes submitted to the political patronage of local leaders who take advantage of their purchasing power. So advantages and drawbacks are balanced.

Tchernonog (1992) explained the situation of monitoring in the field of social services in France: 'Supervision is very flexible and varied from case to case: in most instances, the extent and forms of supervision depend on the amount of the grant. Supervision can range from a simple a posteriori check on the use made of subsidies to actual participation in running the organization. Until very recently, most annual grants were renewed automatically, with an adjustment that depended on price trends, the granting and renewal of the annual grant being usually subject to submission of the organization's accounts and an annual report. This is a traditional form of supervision which has long existed, but the growing use of non-profit organizations has resulted in their ties with the municipal authorities becoming increasingly formal, contracts or agreements now frequently making for a formal relationship. Of the 580,000 organizations which are partners of municipal authorities, about 170,000 have signed contracts or agreements. Councillors or local officials, who are automatically members of the organization, take a very active part in the management of those organizations which receive substantial support. This is not a posteriori supervision, but the organization is managed with the assistance of the municipal authorities; the presence of the latter's representatives in the governing body denotes their active involvement.'

But once again, the development of agreements, contracts and so on is also rather deceiving: there are rarely real negotiations between the partners, but more often standard contracts based on administrative norms. Reporting is then quite limited.

New Managerialism and Evaluation Procedures

So far there has been no competition between the actors in the field of social service. The general attention on competition in France is rather linked to a process pushing toward efficiency, monitoring and so on, which has been called 'New managerialism' or 'entrepreneurial model'. It seems now necessary to show that the public money is well used.

There is now a quite strong emphasis put on efficiency in all the non-profit fields. The market mechanisms have guided the search of a more effective model of management. For example, the development of evaluation procedures, of marketing rules, new tools, and so on is coming from the private for-profit sector; these procedures involve a change in the way non-profit organizations are recognized; they are more and more considered as real 'enterprises' even in the field of social services, which was at first reluctant to these procedures. There is now a tendency to consider them as real enterprises, managing services, using the same arms as for-profit organizations. Chauviere (1997) concludes that 'this is why social services are no more out of the market. Market is now to be considered as the new "big organizer" of social relationship for the allocation of disposable resources and for the measurement of the efficiency of the action in the field of social services, as much as in other fields' (p. 7). The attempt to modify the central law regarding social establishments tracing back to 1975[13] is clearly linked to this movement: the government wants to find out how to control more closely the 'quality' of the services, by fixing norms and regular evaluation of the results.

We can observe also a bottom-up approach: many non-profit organizations' leaders, with the impulse of public powers, are developing special contracts for guaranteeing the quality of their services: this is especially the case in the fields of home care and establishments for handicapped people: these projects are called *démarche qualité* (quality process). The criterion includes equity principles.

Demand Policy and Emergence of For-profit Providers: The Risk of Anti-selection

As we have already stated, for-profit providers still play a low role in the provision of personal social services. However, as needs and demand for social services will obviously keep increasing in the next decades, because of an ageing population, and especially of an ageing handicapped population, profit-making companies will probably be interested in some of the fields. Up to this time, two fields have been developed: homes for the elderly and home services, and especially housework and family services, since subsidies or social contribution cuts have existed since 1992 to encourage the development of these 'proximity services'.

Public regulation is of crucial importance in the way the division of responsibilities has been evolving. Indeed, for the area of home services, the Right Government (1993–1997) encouraged—through tax incentives—the involvement of private firms in this area, which is supposed to give a dynamic impulse to this field. Two risks can be forecast: on the one hand, non-profit organizations may one day be confined to unprofitable activities, and the companies would 'cream' the market for the rich or the less disabled, and let the non-profit organizations handle the assistance to poor people; on the other hand, to compete with firms, non-profit organizations could be tempted to select the solvent clients, or the powerful groups of clients, to the detriment of equity. These risks of anti-selection exist in other fields and are all the more worrisome in a period of deep social exclusion and increase of poverty. It is why since 1997, the socialist government has reduced this tax incentives.

Moreover, during the 1993–1997 period, public authorities tend to try to impulse a competitive regulation—creating new markets—instead of a public one by programmes directed toward the demand solvency instead of an organization of the supply. This means giving direct grants to the persons involved rather than aid to organizations and structures. The financial constraints also lead to a rediscovery of the role that families can play in the provision of services. Since 1996, in the field of home services, the beneficiaries have been authorized to hire their employees directly through a system of 'service vouchers' (*chéques service*) combining the fee paid by the household with public financial support. The new *Prestation spécifique dépendance* (Law of January, 1997)—PSD (specific allowance for dependence) an allowance directly given to elderly people in need of home care services, also corresponds to this new policy. This allowance implies a financial contribution of the user who is also employer, and a complementary financing from the *Aide sociale*. Non-profit organizations active in the field of home services consider that the implementation of the PSD involves a destructuration of the supply, as it is not at all based on the supply already provided by non-profit organizations, and a deprofessionalization of a field which was just in construction. This goes also against non-profit organizations' stability in the field.

These new procedures tend to produce a slow transition from a societal conception of social welfare to a 'consumerist and individualistic' one. But the reverse trend can also be observed since the Left came back, as considerations of equity prevail.

5.4. THE INVOLVEMENT OF NON-PROFIT ORGANIZATIONS IN THE DEFINITION OF POLICIES

Non-profit organizations have recently played a leading role in the definition of social policy in France. Many examples can be found. In the majority of the fields, the attitude of the state has been that of letting the existing organizations organize the field to restrict the costs, and then of taking on the funding responsibility. For that reason, one can assume that this field corresponds to the 'partnership type' of relationship between the state and the non-profit organizations, defined by Gidron et al.[14] (1992). But the state always gives the final coherence of the policy.

An example is the law guaranteeing a minimum income in France, tracing back to 1988. This official acknowledgement has followed a long-term de facto cooperation between non-profit organizations and public authorities, especially in employment policy and health and social activities. Associations helped employment policy by running, with large public financing, job-training programmes, especially for unskilled workers.

Ullman (1992) stated that 'the policy to combat poverty [...] involved non-profit organizations more fully than ever before in the process of policy formulation and implementation'. First the *Secours catholique* showed evidence on increasing poverty in Paris; during the cold winter of 1983 the government announced a poverty plan, providing special funding to charities supplying emergency services (*Secours catholique, Restaurants du coeur, Aide à toute détresse Quart Monde*, Salvation Army), distributing food aid, especially

EEC agricultural surplus via non-profit organizations and extending financial assistance to the homeless and other people with housing difficulties.

From 1984 to 1987, the non-profit organizations involved in the poverty plans met local government officials and social housing managers under the auspices of UNIOPSS to develop a more durable poverty policy under the form of a guaranteed minimum income. In deprived industrial areas, such as the northern departments or Lorraine, the third sector cooperated with local government to provide help and income support to the unemployed new poor.

The report of J. Wresinski, adopted in 1987 by the economic and social council, is the fruit of this brainstorming and the first draft of the 1988 minimum income for integration (RMI) policy. Father Joseph Wresinski was the very charismatic founder of *ATD-Quart-Monde*,[15] a charity fighting extreme poverty, in which the volunteers commit themselves to live several years where and how the poor live. The Wresinski report (1987) recommended the extension of local experiments of minimum income with the participation of non-profits to enable the poor to join the mainstream. The Wresinski report asked for 'a tight collaboration between various partners engaged in the fight against poverty'.

In the 1988 Act, the non-profits are empowered to accept applications for RMI and to draw-up 'integration contracts', just as local governments or social welfare agencies. They were in fact very active in the implementation of this social policy. However, they complained of being considered as ranking under public or semi-public partners.

More recently, we can also observe that the new 'emplois-jeunes'[16] had had experience in non-profit organizations before their legal implementation, and now, non-profit organizations are explicitly identified as potential employers for these new contracts.

Another example is the recent *politique de la ville*, a policy promoting improved urban conditions in deprived suburbs which are becoming more and more immigrant and ethnic minorities ghettos. Large housing blocks were built by the quasi-public agency HLM (*habitations à loyer modéré*), during the 1950s and the 1960s to meet the post-war housing shortage. In the late 1960s and the 1970s, immigrants, previously in shanty towns, replaced the working-class families moving to better quality housing. With the growing unemployment which affects primarily immigrant workers, the suburbs became drug-addiction, drug-dealing and high delinquency areas. The housing became damaged and simultaneously the Communist Party and Catholic volunteer networks weakened. In a sense, the non-profit network replaced them in the mid-1980s. This non-profit network at the local level is a mix of old associations such as the multipurpose social centres and new associations such as anti-racialist, ethnic and more precisely Muslim associations or neighbourhood and local development associations. These associations were involved in the National Council of the Prevention of Delinquency and combined in 1990 to form an Interministerial Delegation concerning City Issues and Social Urban Development. Subsidized by the national *Fonds d'Action Sociale* and by local governments the associations in deprived suburbs of big cities are viewed as the way to restore social cohesion and to prevent social exclusion, especially for the young people.

In the recent years they have developed literacy and adults training programmes, school help to the children of immigrants, sports clubs and recreation clubs, Muslim activities, education and mutual help for women, legal assistance and aid for administrative problems. The local government encouraged by in-kind and financial support the creation of such non-profit organizations when they were non-existent.

The presence of the non-profit networks in these areas explains partially that social explosions were more limited than in other countries facing the same urban issues.

In this second case, non-profit organizations are used as substitutes of the public responsibility. The state uses contracting as 'survivors kit'. Bourdieu et al. (1993) indeed showed the omnipresence of associations in the day-to-day life of the underprivileged contrasting with the failure withdrawal of public agencies in the deprived areas. Another example can be the programmes aimed to unemployed people in very bad economic conditions, and far from the labour market. For these people, non-profit organizations receive funding without special commitment.

5.5. THE CHANGING STRUCTURE OF THE THIRD SECTOR

The Traditional Structure

Generally speaking, the structuration of the French third sector is rather recent and quite limited. It has been strongly favoured by the socialist government in the 1980s, which wanted to encourage the awareness of non-profit organizations, and the unity of the broader regrouping of *Economie sociale* (grouping associations, mutual insurance societies, cooperatives and foundations). In the 1960s and 1970s, the overall policy toward social economy consisted on encouragement to the creation of umbrella organizations enhancing the visibility of social economy, or federating funds.

Examples are:

- The *Comité national de liaison des activités mutualistes coopératives et associatives* (CNLAMCA), created in 1970 (National committee to link cooperatives, mutuals and non-profit organizations and to represent them in front of the public authorities).

- The *Délégation à l'Economie Sociale* (1981), an interministerial agency.
- A general fund to promote associative life and training programmes for volunteers (*Fonds national pour le développement de la vie associative*), created in 1982 and financed by a tax on horse races bets (*pari mutuel urbain*).
- The *Conseil national de la vie associative* (CNVA) which is the representative body of the non-profit sector before the government. The members of this body are appointed by the government and not elected by the organizations, which is rather symbolic of the traditional administrative procedures in France.

In 1995, the government also stressed its acknowledgement of the non-profit sector since the former Prime Minister created four workshops composed of members of the government and representatives of the third sector in order to provide recommendations on various topics such as the promotion of volunteerism, the funding of associations, the development of employment in the third sector and the European integration.

Generally speaking, the third sector remains *quite segmented* in France. There are also few networks. The average French non-profit organization is smaller than the British or German ones. But contrary to this general picture, the field of social services is one of the most structured among the non-profit fields, and there are some very powerful federative structures. The numerous associations active in the field of social services have indeed rapidly become part of networks or federated structures. Almost all these associations have gathered together in a unique and powerful federation, the *Union nationale interfédérale des oeuvres privées sanitaires et sociales*, UNIOPSS (the National Federation of Non-profit Organizations in the Health and Social Sectors) set up in 1947.[17] This umbrella organization gathers 7,000 associations which employ 300,000 people FTE and provide services to 450,000 users. UNIOPSS is almost the unique example of that kind of network and is now recognized by the government as an essential partner in the field of health and social services. Other umbrella organizations exist in most of the subfields: for example, the *Union nationale des associations de parents d'enfants inadaptés* (Federation of the associations of parents of mentally disabled children) set up in 1960 is considered as the most powerful lobbying force among associations. Social educators and social workers have also their peak organizations, example: the *Association nationale des éducateurs de jeunes inadaptés* (National association of educators of maladjusted children). The *Association des paralysés de France* (French Association for the Physically Handicapped), set up in 1933, is not an umbrella organization, but an association with a major economic force. The area of home services has also its umbrella organizations: UNASSAD, UNADMR, FRADAR.

The Impact of Contractualization on the Traditional Functions of Non-profit Organizations

The development of contractualization has consequences on the traditional functions of non-profit organizations. The institutionalization and professionalization of non-profit organizations sometimes lead to a degradation of the traditional associational forms.

These changes affect the special contributions of non-profit organizations and their internal organization. Non-profit organizations are sometimes instrumentalized by public powers. The instrumentalization is linked to the situation of crisis: as many studies have proved that non-profit organizations still create jobs in a period of general unemployment, government sometimes considers them only as agents of their employment policy. The financing of non-profit organizations is frequently guided by a target of job creation, without any other concern for the global coherence of the association's project. The aims of public administration for the financing of non-profit organizations, especially in the field of social services is generally twofold: restricting the cost, and developing employment.

Non-profit organizations also depend on the definition of public programmes; in the field of social services, they generally have to adapt their project to public policy. This means that they are confined in logics of social emergency. Public policy then influences their missions and objectives. Afchain (1997) defines three eras in the development of non-profit organizations in the field of social services, which can help us understand the evolution of the aims, methods and acknowledgement of non-profit organizations.

The first era is that of the pioneers: period of 'luxury and virtuous causes, made by 'saints and heroes'. This era was characterized by an identification between professionals and militants; then came the era of suspicion and denunciation, connected to the appearance of the concept of evaluation. The last phase is that of the drift to 'economism'. In the non-profit bureaucratic structures, the directors of non-profit establishments, who were educators or psychosociologists are now real 'firm leaders' and are recruited for their managing abilities.

Advocacy or Bureaucratization?

Confronted with strong public regulations in terms of accountability and technicity, non-profit organizations asking for public money are subjected to bureaucratic isomorphism: some of them[18] have become professional organizations and rely less on volunteers. The financial dependency is also a source of inertia, as some of the organizations have turned out to be as institutionalized and as rigid as the public bureaucracies are. Their capacity to react to new situations is sometimes low, and their advocacy role is declining. But this institutional isomorphism is linked with the characteristics of the money transfers, and especially concerns the 'managing associations'. But one has to say that there is no automatic link between the importance of public financing and the degree of autonomy of the non-profit organization.

Once again, the evolution of the associations of handicapped people can serve as example of the role and project of the associations. Since they were based on advocacy and voluntary participation in the 1950s, the majority of non-profit organizations in this field are now quasi-public organizations, and their main concerns are linked with management. There is nowadays no tendency for the self-help groups to increase their membership, as the rights of handicapped people and their interests are well protected. Moreover, the search for group identity, initially at the root of these movements, now seems to have almost disappeared. Therefore, the democratic base of the establishments is sometimes quite small. Because of the decline of voluntary participation, and of the decrease in attendance at general meetings of the members, these establishments have also become disconnected from their member base and sometimes feel at a distance from family preferences and users' rights to the detriment of equity. In these bureaucratized organizations, disabled members of the board are fewer than in more recent and less bureaucratized organizations.

Roughly speaking, the provision of services is sometimes considered as inconsistent with the advocacy role by non-profit leaders themselves; that is why we generally observe a kind of specialization among non-profit organizations: the organizations managing establishments create some branches whose aim is only the advocacy. This type of organization has also its own ways of financing, through grants without special commitment.

Moreover, there has been a recent tendency to develop networks and meetings pointing out 'the specificities of non-profit organizations' and defining their functions and autonomy in front of public agencies or privates firms. This movement tries to reaffirm the values of non-profit organizations in so far as producers of services and social movements at the same time. These networks reinforce the identity of the third sector.

Stability or Possibility of Innovation?

The innovation function of non-profit organizations is linked to their capacity to *react rapidly* to a changing environment and to afford non-bureaucratic answers to new social issues. Non-profit organizations reveal the insolvent needs which cannot be expressed in the market and find ways to cope with them, as they are deeply rooted in local communities.

One has also to emphasize non-profit organizations' capacity to seize a social problem in a multipurpose dimension, contrary to the administrations which compartmentalize the policies: employment, income, health, social and family position, housing, education and skills. Examples can be found in many fields: for example, 'intermediary associations' produce goods or services in the sectors overlooked by businesses and at the same time, they supply temporary jobs and training to people in social difficulty: unskilled young people, potential or former delinquents, drug addicts etc. These associations participate in the fight against social marginalization, and in employment policy.

Once again, it is very important in the analysis of the role of non-profit organizations in terms of innovation to distinguish institutions and managing associations and the other social services. The building-up of institutions which has long been the cornerstone of the field of social services, has been both a source of innovation and paralysis.

There is now a tendency against the institutionalization of handicapped people which is considered as a way of imprisonment of disabled people. These kinds or organizations are now frequently considered as involving limitation in the innovation process.

The division of responsibilities between large and small organizations is also true in terms of innovation, even if the link is not systematic since some large organizations can also be innovative: the small ones are frequently devoted to innovation and experimentation, with global grants and few controls. The largest are devoted to the management of institutions; they are less adaptive, and less sensitive to environment. Bloch-Lainé (1994) insisted on the ability of the association to be short-lived (*éphémère*) and therefore less institutionalized and more able to give impetus for social change than public agencies. This is all the more important as France is a very bureaucratic country. Generally speaking, at the level of financing, experimentation and management are also split into two distinctive categories. Experimentation receives special financing and is submitted to a special evaluation.

Professionalization or Volunteering?

The early secularization in France of social services has been accompanied by a movement toward professionalization, which is still occurring now. Nurses and nuns have been salaried. Social services is a field characterized by the fact that all the professional carriers have begun by voluntary activities. The first 'social workers', before and during World War I, were catholic single volunteer women. After the war, the qualification of these women has been acknowledged, they received a social visibility, and a new profession has been created identified by professional organizations, vocational education and specific diplomas. One of the most innovating role of non-profit organizations is indeed to initiate and experiment with new types of jobs and to create new skills, especially relational skills which are becoming more and more important on the labour market. For instance, being a former alcoholic, drug addict or prostitute qualifies the volunteer to fight against these social diseases and assist the victims; of course, this kind of qualification is not written in curriculum vitae for the labour market. Indeed this role of prospecting new jobs is essentially played by volunteers, and then by the wage earners of non-profit organizations. But the public financing is also partly responsible for this movement toward professionalization, since it involves the understanding of the financing circuits, the drawing of regular reports, the negotiation for the funds and so on. Finally, the initiative of the creation of non-profit organizations has also come from professionals who wanted to create their own job.

Generally speaking, volunteers are now rarely involved in the management of establishments since agreements and contracts impose professional skills. In these organizations, volunteer involvement is limited to the participation in the board of directors or to visiting the handicapped, and they have no function in the establishment itself. This is partly due to the predomination of professionals and to the heavy regulation. But volunteers are still very active in the advocacy organizations or small structures.

But we cannot speak of a process of devoluntarization; indeed, surveys show that volunteering and employment of professionals develop concomitantly in the field of social services: facilities for specific groups of people such as families, handicapped, elderly, young people and adults, in social difficulty, income support and maintenance, emergency and relief, and charities represented in 1996 about 14 per cent of total volunteering in France, that is about 161,000 people FTE (Archambault and Boumendil, 1997). The ratio of volunteers/professionals is even increasing. But volunteers are specially involved in management, coordination, and representation activities in organizations hiring a staff while they are more multipurpose in organizations without salaried.

5.6. CONCLUSION

To conclude, we dare say that the introduction of a 'contract culture' is not a main issue for the French non-profit sector, as it is for the British or the Italian ones (Kramer, 1992). In spite of the decentralization process and of the timid entry of non-profit companies in some subfields as residential care or home services intended for the elderly, the non-profit organizations remain more challenged by the public than by the market economy. Inside the partnership with the central or the local government, incentives and targets mix quantity, quality and equity. Competition is not very hard and invitation to tender is not as common as in some countries and it is not considered by the state as the best way to contract. In this context, what are the main trends facing social services non-profit organizations?

First, European integration is more and more a reality for the largest non-profit organizations and, at this level, they will face a more active competition and will be involved in bidding and invitations to tender. By the European bias, a more market-oriented behaviour may happen, associated with a greater part of earned income resources.

Second, the long-term issue of unemployment policy will result in orienting non-profit organizations toward this aim. We can already observe eviction effects between the employment target and more traditional concerns or more diversified populations. The reluctance today of many non-profit organizations to be involved in the 'emplois jeunes' programme can be understood as the fear to lose their main object.

Third, the progressive lowering of working time will afford more leisure time and more time for volunteer work. These two trends are in favour of the creation and development of non-profit organizations. The image of non-profit organizations is of course decisive to transform this potential into real development. So transparency, reporting and reliability of associations are at the agenda.

Last, the ageing of the population is challenging France as every industrialized country, giving opportunity to new services: elderly recreation, residential care, health services, home assistance and protection against dependence. The ageing of some specific populations is a specific challenge such as the ageing of physically or mentally handicapped persons who died early before. The financing of these new services is also a main issue, as the weight of compulsory levies is now considered as too heavy to be raised anymore. So the fees may be raised as well as other market resources.

Notes

1. But this area is also that of the major expansion of the Welfare State: according to Eurostat, in 1992, France was the second European country after Denmark (31.4 per cent) in terms of level of public social spending: about 29 per cent of French GDP.
2. Indeed, centuries of conflict between the state and any form of intermediate bodies explain the strong centralization in France; the central government fought successively against:

   • regional governments and religious minorities (Protestants and Jews) during the Old Regime,
   • the corporations, and the Church and its congregations, which ran non-profit schools and hospitals until the 1789 Revolution,
   • during the 19th century, the State fought against the labour movement and the political associations. It is only at the turning point of the 20th century, that the third sector ceased to be illegal, with the still-living 1901 Act.

   This historical sketch explains why most of the non-profit sector is relatively recent.
3. Three levels of local government exist in France: the *communes*—the town councils (about 36,000), the *départements*—the counties (96), and the *régions* (22).

4. *Aide sociale* is the term used for the social welfare money or in-kind transfers outside the Social Security scheme. It is based on the principle of assistance and proximity, as opposed to insurance on which social security schemes rely. It is financed by taxes and not by social contribution.

5. Which has received a transfer of funds.

6. That is most of all associations run by the 1901 Act, since there are very few foundations in France (less than 500). Mutuals also play a significant role in running social establishments.

7. The 'school war' is one of the most ancient and sensible quarrels which agitates France from time to time throughout the 19th and the 20th centuries. From a monopoly of the church in the field of education till the 19th century to a republican school fighting against the catholic influence during the end of 19th century and the first part of the 20th century, the education sector in France takes roots in a tumultuous history. Indeed, after the 1905 Disestablishment of the Church, the conflict between Catholicism and republican ideology focused on school and became more and more political. Even nowadays, the position towards private schools is still a sensitive issue between the Right and the Left.

8. The first facilities created by the parents were named wild nurseries.

9. The establishments provide internship, day care, night care, care in social emergency cases, home care, housekeeping services, and work facilities for the adults. Work facilities include workshops offering an activity with adapted work conditions to seriously handicapped adults (*Centres d'aide par le travail et ateliers protégés*) and centres providing training and vocational rehabilitation to less-gravely handicapped adults with the aim of improving their labour skills in order to integrate them into the labour market (*centres de éducation, réadaptation et formation professionnelle, équipe de préparation et de suite du reclassement*).

10. The average per capita income of elderly people is now higher than the average per capita income of the working population.

11. The *Département* is the level of local government which is more active in financing social services, through *Aide sociale*.

12. This is why they are now developing their fund-raising activity, when it was not necessary in the 1960s or 1970s.

13. The 1975 Act on the management of social institutions initiated a real public policy towards social establishments in France. It fixed the evolution of the per-diem reimbursement among the establishments, and various rules related to these institutions.

14. Gidron, Kramer and Salamon identify four types of third sector/government relationship in the delivery and financing of the services: the Government Dominant model, in which the government is the main provider and financer of the services, opposed to the third sector dominant model. In between these two opposite models lie mixed cases: the dual model in which non-profit organizations and government act in different spheres, with few interactions between them, and the collaborative model, where roughly speaking the non-profit organizations provide the services, and the government finance them.

15. *Quart-Monde*, fourth World, is a neologism suggesting that the Third World is inside France also.

16. The *emplois jeunes* is a public programme which has recently been implemented by the government to fight against unemployment among young people. New contracts of five years in government administration, local communities and associations are proposed to 18–25 year olds. The government wants to create or incite about 700,000 jobs (350,000 in public agencies and 350,000 in private entities).

17. Contrary to Germany, for example, this umbrella organization has no political or religious affiliation.

18. The largest ones, the national ones, those which mix advocacy with service provision, and obviously, the establishments themselves.

Chapter 6

The New Partnership: The Changing Relationship between State and the Third Sector in the Scenario of New Social Policies in Italy

UGO ASCOLI, EMMANUELE PAVOLINI AND COSTANZO RANCI*

6.1. INTRODUCTION

The second half of the 1980s and the 1990s will be remembered in Italy as the period in which privatization assumed increasingly significant proportions as the dominant political strategy in the field of welfare policies (Pasquinelli, 1993). The move towards privatization has been drastic and generalized. It has radically reversed the tendency to extend government intervention that had characterized the growth of the Italian welfare system since the end of the World War II. Until the 1970s, politicians had not only acquiesced to the expansion of welfare spending but had encouraged it. Nevertheless, during the last decade the worsening of fiscal problems and growing political instability (the result of scandals caused by investigations into political corruption) weakened

*UGO ASCOLI ● Universita di Ancona, Facolta di economia, Piazzale Martelli, n. 8, 60121 Ancona, Italy.   EMMANUELE PAVOLINI ● Istituto di Studi Storici, Sociologici e Linguistici, Facolta di Economia, Universita degli Studi di Ancona, Piazzale Martelli, n. 8, 60121 Ancona, Italy. COSTANZO RANCI ● Politecnico di Milano, DIAP, via Bonardi 3, 20133 Milano, Italy.

the social consensus surrounding the welfare state and gave room to proposals for radical change (Borzaga et al., 1996).

While the dismantling of the old welfare model turned out to be a very difficult and costly operation in political and electoral terms, the appeal for a general strategy to privatize the administrative institutions responsible for implementing welfare policies was more concrete and effective. Privatization was, in fact, presented as the best solution to the crisis of the welfare state, which appeared to have increasingly fewer resources and was less capable of responding to the multiple needs of contemporary society. The dominant opinion was that the limitations of the welfare state were caused, above all, by the excessive bureaucracy of public administrations and the extent to which government managed services directly (Ascoli and Pasquinelli, 1993). A further cause was seen in the dominance of a universalistic approach which had the effect of privileging middle class beneficiaries rather than the poorest. Privatization, thus, seemed to be the best strategy for slimming down the welfare state, which would, according to this opinion, be accompanied by an improvement in its efficiency, putting an end also to the overwhelming direct interference of political parties.

In reality, there are different versions of privatization. These range from very liberal versions, based on the belief that the introduction of competitive mechanisms constitutes the best way to improve the efficiency and effectiveness of services, to more moderate versions in which the introduction of market mechanisms is accompanied by the definition of mutually agreed criteria for the quality of services provided.

On a concrete level, privatization has so far translated above all into greater attention being paid to the efficiency of service provision. This led policy makers to award contracts for the provision of public services to private agencies, and mainly to non-profit organizations. Innovative administrative procedures have also been adopted, aimed at introducing more controls over the cost of existing services, above all when these are provided under contract by private organizations. These controls have been sought by introducing greater competition in contractor selection procedures and by subjecting contractors to more rigid financial accountability.

The meaning of the current privatization can only be fully understood if the recent transformations are seen in the context of Italian social services policies, in general. This is taken as a starting point for outlining, first of all, the historical background in which the current transformations are taking place (Section 6.2). A discussion is then given of transformations that have occurred in recent years, looking at changes in the general structure of relations between the state and the third sector (Section 6.3), the development of financial and contractual relations (Section 6.4) and then the new form taken on by the third sector (Section 6.5). Finally, we look at the dilemmas left open by the new regime of partnership between public and private and at the most probable future developments (Section 6.6).

6.2. HISTORICAL BACKGROUND

The Partnership

As opposed to other European countries, the responsibility of the state in the Italian social services system has been historically very limited. Though the Italian Constitution gives the state the responsibility for providing citizens with assistance and welfare, there was, in fact until October 2000, no national law which stated objectives and means for public intervention in the field; consequently there has been, and there is still now, considerable fragmentation of responsibilities among local authorities and great disparities in the level and effectiveness of welfare policies across the country (Ranci, 1999).

A second characteristic of the Italian social service system is its concentration on direct money transfers to families and the consequent poor development of direct service provision. In 1994, 88 per cent of total assistance expenditure (73.588 billions of Lire) consisted of money transfers to families. Only 12 per cent of total expenditure was used to provide direct services, the provision of which is mainly the responsibility of local government administrations (Commissione di indagine sulla povertà e sull'emarginazione, 1997).

As a consequence of the limited commitment of the state to social service provision, non-profit organizations have acquired a significant role in this sector. Proof of this is given by the statistics. In 1991, the expenditure on social service provision was L. 4.661 billion (IRS, 1992); in the same year, the total revenue of non-profit organizations providing social services was estimated at L. 6.199 billion (Barbetta, 1996), 57 per cent of which was provided by state funding. Therefore, while the state retains a crucial role in financing the system (providing 63 per cent of total expenditure on social services), direct state provision plays only a marginal role (accounting for only 15 per cent of total service provision) (Table 6.1).

These figures seem to confirm the idea that the Italian social services system constitutes a good example of a 'partnership' between the state and the

Table 6.1. Percentage of State and Third Sector Finance and Provision of Social Sevices (1991)

Functions	State	Third Sector
Finance	63.6	36.4
Direct provision	15.4	84.6

third sector, in which the former is responsible for funding but leaves actual management and provision of services largely to non-profit organizations (Gidron et al., 1992).

Two aspects which distinguish the Italian 'regime' of partnership historically from those of other countries should nevertheless be taken into account (Ranci, 1994). First, there has been, until recently, a lack of a uniform national policy. While, on the one hand, this has contributed to a scarcity of investment to support social policies, on the other it has encouraged financial support of a third sector which has no clear public policy goals. Second, the state recognition offered to non-profit organizations involved in the implementation of public policies has been more pragmatic than political, based more on the granting of appropriate funding in exchange for service provision than any involvement of the organizations in policy and finance decisions concerning the programmes in which they participate. These two aspects are examined in more detail below.

Financial Relations between State and Third Sector

Public finance still represents the main source of income for almost all non-profit social service structures: according to the Johns Hopkins research (Barbetta, 1996), it accounts for 58 per cent of their total income (25 per cent comes from fees, 5.6 per cent from donations). Public funding accounts for 50 per cent of the income of residential care institutions, 57 per cent for voluntary associations and more than 70 per cent of income for organizations providing more specialized services (such as residential care for drug addicts or community services for the elderly).

State finance to non-profit organizations (NPOs) has historically occurred through four different channels:

(i) *state transfers*: the transfer of public funds to organizations that, despite their substantial autonomy, are officially recognized as public institutions;

(ii) *subsidies*: the granting of statutory transfers to non-profit organizations, with no substantial control on how the funds are employed and their final destination;

(iii) *third-party payments*: the payment of a daily fee to cover the costs of non-profit agencies that provide services to clients that are recognized as state assisted;

(iv) *grants or contracts*: payments to purchase services provided by non-profit organizations and considered to be in the public interest.

These types of funding can be classified along a continuum with no substantial restraints and wide margins of discretion on how funds are used and to whom they are destined at one extreme and funding methods which encourage greater rigour in the activities of NPOs with regard to objectives in the public interest on the other.

Transfers paid without precise, explicitly stated criteria regarding either the 'deservingness' of the recipient organization or the amount of the funding are close to the first extreme. Funding is awarded by central (ministries) and local authorities that 'pour out' money to a wide range of organizations and partners. Its extremely fragmented character makes it of little use to the organizations that receive it and also emphasizes its symbolic and political value. The arbitrary manner in which politicians and state bureaucrats are able to grant this funding often transforms it into an instrument of political bargaining that is used to seek political support.

One form of payment halfway between the two extremes is the payment of daily fees on an individual client basis to cover costs incurred by non-profit organizations for service provision on behalf of the state. This is the principal method of payment to residential institutions for the elderly, minors, the disabled and drug addicts. As opposed to what happens with the most common forms of third party payments, in these cases clients are allowed neither to select the providing organizations nor to choose on the basis of price. The amount of the fees and the nature of the services are determined through direct agreements between NPOs and state authorities without any auditing of the clients concerned.

Finally, the other extreme on the continuum is funding by contracting-out. There is a specific Italian interpretation of contracting-out which has made the practice very different from what in other countries is commonly understood as a 'contract'. The main distinguishing aspects are given below.

- Government contracts are awarded mostly on the basis of private negotiations without any form of competition between different potential contractors.
- The content of contracts is decided almost exclusively through financial bargaining without any accompanying joint planning of the content and the objectives of the service funded. This is also one of the causes of the, virtually, total lack of assessment of the results obtained.
- No particular consideration is given to criteria for efficiency or keeping costs down in bargaining. Funding is mainly granted on the basis of agreeing a total price per client with no specification of the services provided.

The regulatory capacity of local authorities is very weak. The state's legal responsibility for directing and controlling non-profit organizations turns into a web of capillary administrative procedures allowing strong formal regulation, but weak financial accountability and no valid practical control. Generally, state regulation of non-profit organizations does not develop into a strong commitment on the part of local authorities to define selective goals and oblige non-profit organizations to seek them. On the contrary, it is limited to formal negative control that turns into a fragmented and particularistic regime of economic subsidy, allowing non-profit providers the autonomy to carry out their own missions. It can, thus, be stated that the practice of 'contracting out' has rarely had the effect of reducing the widespread use of discretionary powers in the relationships between the state and the third sector. In many local areas these discretionary powers have favoured the establishment of a protected social services market in which NPOs have been able to avoid competing with each other and have enjoyed preferential treatment by local authorities. On the other hand, the irreplaceable nature of the services provided by NPOs has made it very difficult for local authorities to develop effective and incisive public regulation. Both the excess of demand for social services (due to the limited supply) and the absence of competition between non-profit providers have given the latter a clear advantage when it comes to contractual bargaining. This advantage has also been favoured by a lack of qualified personnel in local authorities capable of making control and inspection effective (Ranci, 1994).

The Lack of Political Independence

Despite the important role played in implementing public policies and the considerable operational autonomy they have enjoyed, NPOs have not played an active role in the formulation of welfare policies. This is essentially due to two factors: the absence of any general frame of reference and formal recognition of the sector as a whole and the lack of political independence on the part of non-profit organizations.

As already remarked by many authors (Bassanini and Ranci, 1990; Barbetta, 1996), in Italy there is no statement of public policy that specifically deals with the regulation of the non-profit sector as a whole. This area has not yet been recognized as a field to which attention should be specifically paid when formulating government policies. Italian legislation and government regulations on this subject are extremely complex and very detailed, but they lack any overall philosophy aimed at supporting and providing guarantees for the non-profit sector.

As a result, recognition of the role of non-profit organizations as either primary or supplementary providers of social services has not been clearly defined in law and government programmes. Indeed, such recognition is very often only implicit. While recognizing the right of non-profit organizations to provide social services, former legislation has hardly given any formal recognition to the essential role these organizations play in the implementation of public policies.

There has also been no clear definition of the requirements non-profit organization must meet in order to qualify as service providers in government programmes. The terminology is at times generic, referring to the overall category of private organizations, and at other times too specific, referring to particular categories such as voluntary associations, IPABs or social cooperatives. The non-distribution constraint has rarely constituted a selection requirement for state recognition of service providers and, therefore, for access to relative state financing.

The absence of explicit recognition of the third sector has been accompanied by the very modest degree of organization and activity of civic and advocacy associations, as a consequence of the dominating role of political parties and labour unions in society. Representation of third sector interests in social services policy making has occurred mainly through the political brokerage of the Catholic Church, political parties and labour unions. This brokerage, offered in exchange for the hierarchical subordination of non-profit organizations to the political-institutional agents that guarantee their representation in the political arena, has long prevented non-profit organizations from playing a politically independent role.

Given the hierarchical and centralized structure of the mechanisms by which non-profit organizations are represented in policy making, it is clear that they have hardly ever had the recognized right to be independently consulted by government on decisions concerning legislation. Another consequence is that for a long time non-profit organizations have neither developed any significant political advocacy, nor have they played a significant role in promoting new rights to services.

Mutual Accommodation

Although the state and the third sector are heavily dependent on each other in functional terms, this has not translated into any close cooperation in setting goals and planning. This has given rise to a contradiction which seems to be particular to the Italian case: the close functional interdependence has gone with very weak government regulation of the sector and a failure to base the partnership regime on explicit criteria of what is in the public interest. Such a situation has favoured the growth of a mixed regime with two sectors involved in the supply of services without any clear lines of demarcation and very little cooperation between them.

The relations created between the state and the third sector may, therefore, be defined in terms of a 'mutual accommodation' model (Ranci et al., 1991). This mutual accommodation consists of a relationship in which there is no cooperation between state and third sector with regard to objectives and planning, but there is a strong functional interdependence between the two sectors and consequently each supports the other and tries to facilitate its work.

This historical development of relations between the state and the third sector has resulted in difficulties for local administrations to perform any guidance role and in strong tensions within the third sector pulled between the desire for greater professionalism on the one hand, and the progressive weakening of its capacity to take political initiatives, on the other. To conclude, although the mutual accommodation model has involved a price to be paid for both partners, it has nevertheless allowed many local communities to maintain an adequate level of services for several decades and in some situations to respond to new types of need and emergency situations.

Regulation of this system of mutual accommodation has been based on a fragmented and unplanned system of negotiations (Ascoli, 1993). The coordination of programmes between public and non-profit agents has been managed mainly through local concertation on particular and fragmented issues. This has resulted in political connections between politicians and non-profit organizations and the degeneration of many organizations into the private domains of individual political parties. Therefore, the considerable state financing of non-profit providers has established a mutual dependency between the state and non-profit organizations, characterized by the shift of government responsibilities outside the planning and control of the public sector, into a private domain strongly exposed to political party patronage and favouritism.

6.3. THE NEW SCENARIO OF THE WELFARE MIX
IN THE 1990s

The 1990s mark an important turning point in relationships between state and the third sector. It is the fruit of the very strong effort made by local authorities to involve the third sector in welfare policies and the consequent need to set up a general regulatory framework for financial and political relations between the two sectors. The diffusion of contracting-out at local level has, in fact, resulted in an urgent need for regulation to discipline and orient transactions that are as frequent as they are open to different and uncertain outcomes. For the first time in Italy, at least in the field of welfare policies, new regulation has grown aimed at governing relations between the actors (public and private) that crowd the social services arena (Pavolini, 2000).

The causes that have required this development are multiple. The main cause, nevertheless, consists of ever decreasing state funding to meet a welfare demand which appears to be growing rapidly. The cuts in spending required to observe the Maastricht agreement did, in fact, determine a fall in total social spending which, while it mainly affected monetary transfers to families rather than direct services, nevertheless made local authorities particularly attentive to savings.[1] The ban on public administrations taking on new employees, though an indirect effect of central government policies, was in fact very important because it made it impossible for local authorities to provide new services directly. Moreover, recent political corruption scandals brought the need for greater transparency in financial relations between local authorities and private suppliers.

An initial innovation consisted of granting NPOs official recognition by the state: as opposed to the old regulations, the new regulations fully recognized the 'mixed' nature of the welfare system and afforded NPOs equal status with state organizations. One of the first steps in this direction was the drafting of new national legislation for the third sector. Over the course of a decade, a process of *institutional regulation* of the third sector was set in motion, aimed at granting NPOs the legal status required to provide services, at granting tax concessions and at identifying forms and channels of state funding with greater precision than before. The next step was taken in the specific field of social policies, by the passing of new regional and national legislation on social services and by the imminent passing of a national law on social services. The innovation of such new legislation consisted above all in its abandonment of the traditional viewpoint in which the third sector played an exclusively *supplementary* role with respect to the state. This supplementary character of the third sector has been clearly abandoned in new legislation, which to a very large extent involves NPOs not only in service provision but also in planning processes and policy making.

At the same time, the legislation has also attempted to demarcate the characteristics of third sector organizations operating in the welfare field with greater precision. As has been said, Italy has so far lacked a uniform legal status by which non-profit organizations can be identified on the basis of inherent characteristics or the activity carried out. As a consequence, the new legislation has proceeded by identifying the various types of organizations that operate in the social services field: voluntary organizations, social cooperatives, church-related institutions, private non-profit associations, self-help groups, and trade union organizations. All these types of organization are expressly cited and explicitly recognized as primary figures in welfare policies.

The progressive institutionalization of the third sector has gone with a tendency of regional and national legislation to give support to more professionalized non-profit organizations. One particular example is given by the Region of Piedmont: its social services plan for 1997–1999 gives preferential treatment to social cooperatives in awarding contracts for service provision. The same law also obliges local authorities to allocate a proportion of their social services budget to contracts with occupational reintegration social cooperatives. The same law forbids awarding contracts to organizations made mainly by volunteers for the provision of municipal services independently of their experience and level of organization.

A crucial point that has still not been resolved by the new legislation concerns the legal status and control of IPABs, a problem on which previous attempts to reform the welfare system have run aground. The role played by IPABs in the Italian welfare system is still very considerable. They provide approximately 40 per cent of places in public and private residential care institutions. Although there is no certain data on the property and financial assets of these institutions, it is estimated that they reach quite considerable dimensions.[2] Although, from a strictly legal viewpoint, IPABs are 'public' institutions, their status is ambivalent with a mix of private and public sector elements. While on the one hand this confused status has prevented the state from imposing effective regulation, on the other hand it has also slowed down the modernization of these institutions, still often run on traditional principles. The general trend that has emerged in recent years is the gradual privatization of such institutions.

To conclude, the new legislation seems to offer the third sector full recognition of its service delivery capacity. This recognition constitutes the premise for overcoming the dualistic model according to which the state and private bodies develop distinct lines of action and converge only at an operational level. The new legislation proposes a welfare mix model in which different types of organizations are treated and valued equally and which is based on integrating different operational philosophies and principles.

Integration of the third sector into a 'mixed' welfare system is occurring through a differentiation of the forms of regulation. Voluntary organizations are mainly assigned a role of stimulation and promotion of grassroots participation, while professional organizations are assigned greater responsibility in the delivery of services (accompanied naturally by, increasingly, more funding). In this sense, the strong support given to social cooperatives and the privatization of IPABs constitute the signs of a new configuration of the Italian welfare mix in which public administrations are increasingly less involved in the direct delivery of services, which is performed by highly professional NPOs, well funded by the state, capable of exerting strong political pressure and of throwing the weight of their indispensable service provision behind contractual bargaining with local authorities.

6.4. THE MECHANISM OF THE NEW WELFARE MIX

The new trends emerging in Italian social policies have had a strong impact on the structure of the relationship between state and the third sector (Ranci, 1999). The most significant effects are the creation of new forms of coordination,

the growing split between financing and delivering functions, the introduction of market mechanisms in the delivery of social services, the shift from
grants to contracts, the introduction of service vouchers that partially transfer
the financing responsibility outside of the statutory sector. In this part we
describe the principal mechanisms that have been introduced, underlying
above all the current evolutionary process.

New Forms of Coordination

The formal recognition of the official role of the third sector is being accompanied by a massive and increasing inclusion of non-profit organizations in
planning and assessment processes for social policies (Pavolini, 2000). Large
part of the most recent legislative provisions proposes operational models
based on local concertation tables. The National law has also involved strong
pressure to introduce local procedures based on joint responsibility, including
NPOs into local social services policy planning models.

Coordination identifies a phase in which cooperation between state institutions and NPOs is not exclusively aimed at solving specific operating problems, but also to setting the general objectives of social policies. It demarcates
an area of joint decision making covering the identification of needs, the selection of priorities, the planning and assessment of operations and the allocation
of available funding.

A few points must be made concerning the meaning attributed to the
concept of coordination for further analysis of the subject. Three levels of
coordination can be identified:

- a *strategic level*, concerning values and general objectives of the policy;
- an *organizational level*, concerning specific aspects of how services are
  organized (e.g. how service quality and outcomes are assessed);
- an *operational level*, concerning the interaction between managers
  and service providers in the public and private sector in the case
  management.

An examination of local practices shows the poor effectiveness of coordination at a strategic level. This is a consequence of the limited capacity of
local authorities to develop strategic planning procedures, but other obstacles
originate with the NPOs themselves and concern their representation and
resources.[3] However, there have been partial changes in recent years. There is
a progressive narrowing of the 'culture' gap between personnel in-state institutions and those in NPOs. This has been facilitated considerably by the frequency with which individuals from the third sector have taken on political
or management responsibilities in local authorities. This constitutes a definite

change: while in the 1980s it was above all the political parties who acted as intermediaries between NPOs and the local authority management (Ranci, 1999), their role has now diminished in favour of 'trust intermediaries', often coming from the third sector itself.

Finally, a gradual process of structuration of the third sector is occurring, which at various levels is trying to build its own structures of representation by the creation of second-level organizations. This is typical of small to medium size organizations, while larger organizations often tend to maintain an independent role (CGM, 1997). These recent processes tend largely, however, to affect the organizational level of coordination, characterized by specific and circumscribed decisions, concerning organizational aspects of social policy implementation. At this level joint planning concentrates on criteria for selecting organizations for public funding. Actually intense negotiation has developed around this subject to decide how much weight to give to different elements concerning quality and price. While the selection criteria for choosing non-profit organizations for contracts has been the dominant issue in local bargaining over the last 4–5 years, quality assessment of services seems over the last 2 years to be a new table of discussion between the various parties involved. Many local authorities have recently tried to improve their ability to assess the quality of services and they have involved non-profit organizations in this process.

Finally, new modes of coordination have also developed at an operational level, where coordination between public and non-profit organizations has become widespread and has acquired great importance. This coordination tends to be useful for bringing problems concerning single aspects of services or individual clients to the surface. It takes the form of processes for evaluating services aimed at improving their management and the form they take. The effectiveness of this coordination seems to depend mainly on the quantity and quality of the state personnel involved. While these types of coordinations are widespread, their effectiveness tends to vary even within the same municipality according to the 'history' of the local situation, the presence of qualified or motivated personnel and the investment made by the public administration. In general, the capacity for operational coordination seems greater in sectors where local institutions have maintained a greater degree of direct management of services. In those sectors where in the past a complete delegation of services has occured, it is more difficult to find a sufficient number of qualified and experienced public personnel able to participate in forms of joint micro planning.

On the whole, the last few years have been characterized by a greater involvement of NPOs in planning and assessment of social policy implementation. Coordination is, nevertheless, faced with great obstacles due to lack of instruments and adequate personnel both in state institutions and in third sector organizations. These obstacles weigh above all on long-term planning, while medium to short-term planning of interaction between actors seems easier.

The chances of NPOs being included in the planning of social policies are naturally much higher where the planning activity is decentralized at a local level. It is, in fact, at this level that planning seems to be more easily extendible to organizations who traditionally are more worried about their own survival than about assuming collective responsibilities. In the majority of cases local planning already provides for a network of cooperation and mutual trust between the public and the third sector.

From Grants to Contracts

In the 1990s funding relationships between the state and the third sector are changing and the trends encountered in the previous decade have strengthened. The element of continuity with the past concerns the increase in the level of funding to non-profit organizations for direct service provision. Recent years have seen a growth in services contracted out by local authorities to non-profit organizations. This growth has occurred in two forms:

- all (or almost all) new services have been contracted out to private organizations: local authorities have hardly ever set up new departments or direct service provision;
- services which were once provided directly by local authorities and that are now contracted out to third sector organizations are on the increase.

On the whole, the third sector is assuming a priority role as an actor in the implementation of social services policies, both in sectors where traditionally there has been a state commitment (the elderly, the disabled and minors) and in new innovative sectors, often characterized by the absence of an explicit state commitment (immigrants, nomads, persons of no abode, ex-prisoners, etc.). As Table 6.2 shows, the incidence of the third sector is generally greater in innovative sectors, in which three quarters of public expenditure is transferred to NPOs. There are then some local authorities in which all, or almost all services, are provided by NPOs.

Table 6.2. The Role of the Third Sector in Local Service Provision

Sector	Percentage of State Funding to NPOs
Sectors of traditional state provision	60–90%
New sectors	80–100%

The main reasons for such a widespread adoption by local authorities are as follows:

- the presence of laws drastically limiting the power of local authorities to assume new employees has clearly hindered the growth of direct service provision;
- since the 1980s it has cost very much less to contract services out to the third sector, given the savings in labour costs and thanks to the greater flexibility; even though the savings made are gradually falling (see below), the degree of specialization of many non-profit sector providers makes it very costly to replace them;
- along with economic and legal reasons, there are certainly also political and cultural reasons: while the 1980s were the years of 'unplanned partnership' (Pasquinelli, 1993), in which services were contracted out virtually through a process of inertia, the 1990s are the period in which the need to give more space to third sector providers has been given greater consideration.

The decision to contract services out to NPOs seems to have been taken, therefore, on the joint basis of general economic considerations and of political and cultural motivations. However, it has rarely been adopted on the basis of a precise cost–benefit analysis of contracting out as an alternative to direct state provision.

A very radical change concerns the methods used by local authorities to fund NPOs. These changes have been caused by both various local necessities and the new legislation governing the system of state funding. The model of state funding inherited from the past, as has been said, left wide powers of discretion to local authorities. The latter entrusted most of service provision to NPOs, without paying particular attention to contracts. The forms of payment consisted, in fact, of the payments being made to cover the service purchased as a whole, with no specification of the content nor of the inherent requirements of the service funded. Funding was also granted by means of individual negotiation, without any competition between different potential service suppliers. It was a system which gave a large degree of independence to NPOs and at the same time freed local authorities from taking on greater planning or control responsibilities.

The 1990s constitute the period of change from the concession of huge payments to NPOs on the basis of individual negotiation to more transparent funding mechanisms (public tender in particular) and new systems of payment which introduce greater competition in awarding government contracts to NPOs. The main elements of change are as follows.

- The general practice of funding by means of grants for service provision and other activities is being replaced by contracts for the provision of specific services. An analysis of the current methods of local authority social expenditure shows that grants now represent only a small proportion of direct funding to third sector organizations: they generally do not exceed 5 per cent of total funding to the third sector, while in some municipalities the amount is nil or almost nil. What is happening in this period is an increasingly clear decision by local authorities to progressively fund only those organizations which provide services in exchange for a fee.

- Funding based on individual negotiation is becoming relatively less frequent and is being replaced by more transparent forms of provider selection, such as public and private tender. A set of factors is favouring this change: on the one hand, new EU legislation concerning government contracts and national and regional laws oblige local authorities to introduce greater competition and transparency in awarding contracts for service provision; on the other hand, the increase in the number of organizations capable of delivering the same service removes one of the conditions which made individual negotiation practically obligatory, that is the presence of only one 'contractor' capable of providing the service funded. Finally, political corruption scandals persuaded many local authorities to use more transparent procedures in awarding contracts in order to avoid the risk of incrimination.

New Contracting-out Regulation

The new legislation on the awarding of contracts marks a distinct change of route in the direction of a more transparent system based more on competition. A first step in this direction was taken in 1995 with the implementation of EU legislation on tendering in national legislation. This makes public tendering compulsory for local authorities when awarding contracts for large sums (200,000 Euros or more). From that moment the practice of awarding contracts to the lowest bidder has spread, with little attention being paid to the quality and technical/professional requirements of services. In fact, while on the one hand, the practice of awarding to the lowest bidder increased efficiency and made the relationship between NPOs and local authorities less static and accommodating, on the other hand, it has done little to encourage the growth of a 'contract culture' between the parties concerned. The practice of awarding to the lowest bidder has allowed local authorities to reduce funding without, however, this being accompanied by any serious planning (identification of priority objectives, specification of minimum standards of quality, etc.), nor by any real growth in competition between service suppliers (in the absence of quality criteria, accepting the lowest bidder has in the majority of cases translated into mere cuts in funding).

In recent years, various attempts have been made to develop state regulation capable of stemming the deteriorating quality of services caused by the practice of awarding to the lowest bidder. The most significant innovations concern:

- defining more stringent selection criteria for NPOs to participate in public tenders;
- codification of general rules for tenders and contract specifications aimed at specifying the contents of services and control procedures as precisely as possible.

First of all regulations concerning the requirements organizations must meet to obtain state funding that were more binding than in the past were introduced. Various regions set up regional registers of NPOs and listing on these is an indispensable requirement for contractors. Regional registration subjects organizations to a form of periodical control of the assets and finances of the organization, the qualifications and experience of personnel and observance of national employee contracts. It is a procedure, therefore, for surveying and selecting potential partners to work for local authorities. In the context of a general effort to regulate the qualifications of contractors on the basis of objective criteria, a tendency has nevertheless emerged to privilege certain types of organization and social cooperatives in particular. These are, in fact, considered better able to guarantee professional and efficient management of services. National law No. 381/1991, which affords them official recognition, already lays down favourable conditions for cooperatives aimed to occupational reintegration, partially exempting them from legislation concerning employment in public administrations and reserving a certain quota of contracts to them. This concession has contributed in no small measure to the impressive growth in the number of occupational reintegration cooperatives. These increased from 287 in 1993 to 705 in 1995, doubling the number of their employees (CGM, 1997). More recently, some regional legislation has strengthened this orientation granting cooperatives preferential treatment when awarding contracts.

In conclusion, the new regulation governing the access of NPOs to state contracts seems to respond to two aims: on the one hand it establishes minimum criteria of professional and management reliability for the organizations; on the other, it favours organizations that have a clearly enterprise type set-up and, therefore, seem to be able to provide better guarantees of professionalism and efficiency.

The second element of innovation is to be seen in the formulation of general rules for awarding contracts. In this field too, the legislation on social cooperatives opened up the way. Regional laws implementing the national legislation did, in fact, specify procedures and criteria for choosing contractors bidding, by imposing joint criteria of price, service quality and the reliability of the provider.

The same legislation then defined models for standard regional contracts to which all contracts between local authorities and social cooperatives had to conform. The definition of these model contracts is nothing really new from an administrative viewpoint. The innovation consists in the attention placed on how this administrative step is implemented and in the insertion of specific reference to the need for a precise definition of contents and the required quality standards of the services among the criteria of standard contracts.

On the whole, the development of this regulation shows a process of gradual structuring of the contract negotiations between public administrations and NPOs. The codification of procedures and general rules meets the requirement of local authorities to take an active role in negotiations with NPOs and to put an end to the weakness of its position on contracts which characterized its previous behaviour. Nevertheless, as we will see, this codification does not seem to completely remove the considerable margins of ambiguity and arbitrariness from contractual relations.

Attention to Quality

In the 1990s many local administrations started to change their criteria for awarding social service contracts, passing from the practice of awarding contracts to the lowest bidder able to provide the same service output at the lowest cost to criteria based on 'the economically most advantageous bid', in which bids are assessed on both cost and quality criteria. Currently, almost all local authorities in large cities adopt criteria based on price and quality when awarding contracts. One of the main consequences of this change is that the price tendered by organizations is becoming less important for winning service contracts. It is estimated that, after the introduction of quality criteria for contractor selection, price has in general accounted for no more than 50 per cent of the total points in the assessment of each bid. Furthermore, recent regulatory constraints on how prices are set considerably limit the extent to which competing organizations can use price as a means of winning contracts. After the introduction of the new legislation, for many tenders local authorities specify the qualifications of personnel delivering services and the hourly labour costs (which must conform to national industrial relations agreements) with great precision; consequently the basic price for service provision is in most cases already established. All this has the result, therefore, of a system in which prices tend to be relatively 'fixed'. In many municipalities price differences between competitors is not more than 4–5 per cent, and it is not decisive in awarding contracts. The introduction of quality among the parameters assessed for judging tenders coincides with the abandonment of policies towards the third sector aimed at containing the costs of services provided. Nevertheless, the pressure to keep welfare spending down has persisted also in recent years and has created considerable problems for local authorities. Until a few years ago a fair proportion of the burden of welfare spending cutbacks could be 'unloaded' onto NPOs by always taking the lowest bid or by awarding contracts for which the state covered only part of the cost. This strategy is now difficult to implement because of the new forms of contractor selection based less on price and by the introduction of service quality obligations which prevent price reductions below a certain level. The quantity of services that local authorities are able to purchase with a given amount of funding is tending to decrease because the unit price of services is largely fixed.

Although there are ways of getting round these restraints, greater regulation of payment mechanisms has hindered the introduction of competition mechanisms based on cost between NPOs. While the orientation of policies has been to favour competition between providers, the very characteristics of the regulation introduced at local level have in effect limited its effectiveness. The limits to the spread of competition are not, however, due exclusively to the new regulations governing tendering. They have been determined also by strategic decisions of the parties involved: local authorities and third sector organizations.

As regards local authorities, it has already been stressed that their behaviour is influenced by the new legislation strongly limiting competition based exclusively on price. Given this legal situation, local authorities have tended to defend the relationships they have established with various third sector organizations operating in their territory as much as possible. The consolidation of the public–private cooperation over the last two decades has resulted in the creation of relationships of mutual trust and of specific knowledge which local authorities are hardly willing to abandon. The motivations behind this behaviour are not just of a patronage, particularist nature; there is also an intention to safeguard service users and sets of specific services that have been established over the years.

The attempt to preserve the historical relationship established with the principal NPOs from competitive mechanisms is pursued in two principal ways:

- some local authorities give priority in the assessment of tenders to the degree of 'rootedness in the community' of an organization (generally understood as documented knowledge of the community, relationships with it, relationships with local voluntary organizations, previous work done for the local authority, etc.);
- other local authorities set aside a considerable percentage of points in tender assessment to general structuring of service provision in which

great consideration is given to relationships with state service providers, socialization with service users, the degree of innovation in the services provided; the insertion of these factors in tender assessment naturally allows more discretion in evaluation and is generally to the advantage of organizations that are already known to them.

The strategies employed by third sector organizations also try to reduce the possibility of competition. First, they often try to identify market 'niches' in which no other suppliers are present and within which they can develop such a degree of specialization that they can maintain a monopoly over the service. Secondly, they constitute 'consortiums', or 'temporary groups of organizations'. The presence and consolidation of these 'networks' of organizations seems to offer the chance for many small to medium size organizations to continue providing services even in a more competitive market, improving their operating capacities and potentially their professionalism with the experience. Often consortiums handle administrative duties of individual organizations such as relationships with public administrations and/or bookkeeping and accounting. It can be hypothesized, therefore, that the growth of these second-level organizations in Italy has prevented the introduction of competition from increasing the size of NPOs, favouring the survival of small to medium size organizations and raising their level of professionalism.

The Progressive Introduction of Managed Competition

A further innovation in recent years consists of the gradual reorganization of methods of funding based on the payment of a fee per client by public administrations who act as a 'third party payer' of the service provided by non-profit organizations to eligible individuals. As has already been said, the payment of client fees is the most frequently used method of public funding for residential and home care and does not involve any procedure for the choice and selection of the provider (neither by public administrations nor by clients).

Even though state funding of the more costly and demanding services (e.g. home and residential care) still occurs by traditional means, many municipalities are beginning to experiment the introduction of 'managed competition' forms of funding for support or recreational type services (transport for the disabled, holidays for underprivileged children, etc.). The national law on social services currently being drafted provides for the gradual passage from a contract based system (i.e. the public administration pays for a service provided by a non-profit provider) to a system of 'accreditation', in which the amount of state funding is fixed by choices made by clients.

The principal features of this system in Italy were established by a set of regulations which have recently radically transformed funding of hospitals and health services (France and Arcangeli, 1996). The basic principles are as follows: (a) providers are paid on the basis of rates set by the region or municipality; (b) the amount of funding is dependent on the ability of the providers to attract more customers: 'the money goes where the customers go'; (c) in order to be authorized to operate, providers must obtain 'accreditation' by the relevant public administration.

Accreditation seems, therefore, to respond more decisively than the new contracting out regulations to the demand for a clear distinction between the funding function and actual service provision. Public administrations are responsible for the defining criteria and professional and technical standards for accreditation (which must guarantee minimum quality standards for services), while providers (both state and private) are called upon to compete against each other in the sale of their services to the public.

There remain, however, many questions over how managed competition will actually work once it is applied to a field of services less easily standardized than those in the health field and in which the ability of clients to choose is in any case considerably limited. Managed competition does in fact assume, in its most *laissez-faire* version, that control over the quality of services is exercised by clients themselves through their power to choose. In the social services field, this power to choose appears rather problematic, since it is difficult to imagine that public administrations will limit themselves to funding decisions taken by the clients of services.

The main problem, therefore, concerns the extent of the regulatory powers exercised by public administrations. Managed competition may involve a different regulatory role for the public institution controlling the funding. This could range from a system heavily dependent on market forces in which local authorities are limited to the role of 'third party payers' who fund decisions taken by private individuals (or their agents) and have virtually no regulatory power, to a system in which local authorities use the accreditation procedure to select the most reliable providers or to plan services with accredited providers setting an overall maximum spending limit as well as limits on spending for each specific service.

While the introduction of managed competition responds to the demand to separate funding from actual service provision and to introduce elements of competition in the relationship between state and the third sector, it cannot translate into a well established 'social care market'. Such an outcome is hampered by several factors connected both with the regulatory role that local authorities intend to maintain and by the possibility that behind the 'modern' image of managed competition, a network of collaboration between state institutions and NPOs is established hostile to the introduction of mechanisms that are too competitive. It is, therefore, more likely that the progressive introduction of managed competition will contribute in the short term to guaranteeing standards of quality and professionalism often ignored with the contracting-out practice.

6.5. THE NEW SHAPE OF THE THIRD SECTOR

While there is a great heterogeneity of the organizations that make up the Italian third sector, the dominant trend is now the growing polarization between volunteer-based organizations and more professional organizations. At one extreme we find organizations based exclusively on voluntary work while at the other there are organizations which operate with paid personnel. Organizations at these two extremes have very little in common. However, if we look along the continuum, we come across voluntary organizations capable of providing highly specialized services as well as organizations where paid workers are assisted by substantial groups of volunteers providing quality services.

We assume a classification which tends in general to distinguish between organizations capable of 'operating at a not very specialized level in the provision of services that do not require a quantity of work and technical qualifications greater than that which can be mobilized by volunteers' and other organizations which are 'totally or predominantly professional, capable of providing services that require a high level of financial investment as well as specific professional and management capabilities' (Ranci and Ascoli, 1997, p. 220).

Organizations composed only of volunteers 'to all effects and purposes constitute an organizational structure which often seems capable of guaranteeing stable and continuous operation' (Ranci and Ascoli, 1997, p. 220). In 1997, it is estimated that 12,556 organizations that were operating in Italy composed predominantly or exclusively of volunteers that met the following criteria: they consisted of at least five interacting people, a minimum organizational structure (a person in charge, a definite name and an address), self-governing, permanent operation (operating for at least one year) and the presence of an operational unit at least (Frisanco and Ranci, 1999).

The services provided suggest a tendency of these organizations to specialize in services that require little financial investment and a limited contribution by qualified personnel. The most frequent services are in fact counselling, accompanying people, moral and religious assistance, home visits, education and training.

The overall picture that emerges shows the extraordinary importance of these organizations, genuine 'social welfare infrastructures' which help to enervate the fabric of relationships on society, enabling participation and involvement in person, bringing people together and above all strengthening the capacities of the less privileged.

In a context characterized by the growing polarization between volunteer-based organizations and professional organizations, a particular new type of professional non-profit organization, the social cooperative has recently become widespread. These organizations resort mainly to paid employees, but the workers are at the same time members of the cooperative which is governed by a board elected directly by an assembly of the members. It is, therefore, a professional organization based on association.

In 1996 there were almost 3,857 social cooperatives according to the Ministry of Labour and 2,320 according to the 'Centrali Cooperative'. Even if the second figure is used for a cautious estimate, these cooperatives increased by more than a quarter (+27 per cent) between 1993 and 1996. Here too, as for voluntary organizations, the organizations are on average small in size.

As provided for by Law No. 381/1991, there are two types of social welfare cooperatives: type A provide direct social services, while type B specialize in occupational reintegration of the underprivileged. The cooperatives that provide social services, 'in the great majority of cases provide services for the elderly, minors and the disabled and then to a lesser extent for drug addicts and psychiatric patients and finally for persons of no abode and immigrants... The most commonly provided service, and the most widespread in absolute terms is residential care. It is the service used most for minors, drug addicts and psychiatric patients, followed by care in the home, above all for the elderly' (CGM, 1997, p. 52–53).

It must be pointed out that both these types of cooperatives, direct service provision and reintegration of the underprivileged, tend to specialize in highly professional services, where financial investment of a certain size is required.

The social cooperative is not the only form of organizational structure professional non-profit organizations may assume in Italy. On the whole the current phase is characterized by the development of new types of organization and by their progressive specialization, which is helping to increase the general level of structuring in the Italian third sector.

In 1990, a law reforming the public sector area of the Italian banking system set in motion a gradual distinction between the actual management of certain banks (the 'Casse di Risparmio') and the foundations which owned them. The latter were given the priority tasks of pursuing philanthropic aims and of supporting the local community, the purposes for which they were originally formed. At the same time, mention must be made of the very considerable number of ordinary foundations. A study photographed the situation in 1995, identifying the existence of 536 foundations. More than half had obtained legal recognition since 1986. The types of foundations are quite different from those found in other countries (e.g. the United States or Germany). Around four-fifths of Italian foundations were founded by individuals, suggesting 'a predominantly individual and family origin' (Ranci and Barbetta, 1996, p. 22) of these organizations. Their size, however, is quite modest: 58 per cent have assets of less than one billion Lire, while 11 per cent have assets exceeding 10 billion and 3 per cent over 50 billion Lire.

As opposed to what happens elsewhere, most foundations in Italy are operating, while only a minority (approximately 25 per cent) are grant making. They employ around ten thousand persons (9,478), a very large proportion of which are female (two-thirds), constituting a solid source of employment with 2,683 volunteers and 398 on transfer with special leave.

The presence of many new professionalized non-profit organizations confers very different meanings on the third sector. The growth and legitimization of the sector is creating the terms for an organizational 'challenge' with regard to the state: new models for regulating third and public sector relations are now needed. The vast majority of the third sector appears to be committed to an attempt at innovation intended to increase capacities for 'integration' and 'social inclusion'.

In this perspective two current processes seem important: the diffusion of higher level organizations and the increase in the capacity to influence policy making. On the one hand consortiums, federations and national associations are on the increase. This facilitates the transfer of welfare technologies from the most 'advanced' to the most 'backward' organizations and, therefore, has important side effects for local development in terms of welfare and cultural innovation. Local service provision systems are, in fact, opened up to innovative processes: debates start up between the most significant forces in society, public and third sector workers start to learn together, prejudices and stereotypes are swept away and a common culture is formed, there are experiments with networks which also involve private individuals and encourage social cohesion. On the other hand, in the political arena Italian third sector organizations are forging alliances and processes of association that are not temporary and which is very significantly increasing their capacity to influence welfare policy decision making. New collective protagonists are, therefore, coming forward, highly representative of their members, to sit at negotiating tables at national and local level.

On the whole, the changes introduced to the third sector in recent years have considerably changed the features of the sector itself: it has become more structured internally, organizations have a stronger bargaining position when seeking state funding, and the specialization of organization is a process that is acquiring greater and greater force.

6.6. POLICY ORIENTATIONS AND DILEMMAS FOR THE FUTURE

Beyond the Model of Mutual Accommodation?

The overall outcome of the phenomena discussed in the previous sections of this chapter is characterized by a uncertain situation with dilemmas and problems the solution to which is neither easily predictable nor to be taken for granted. These dilemmas can be better framed in the Italian context, if we synthesize some of the information used in the preceding sections. Analysing the changes in the public/private relationships from the 1980s until now, it is possible to identify three periods, which are characterized by regulatory models different in terms of: (a) actors involved in the public policy making process; (b) public sector's mechanisms to select private providers; (c) public sector's financial and control mechanisms of third sector providers.

Table 6.3 shows the main characteristics of the regulatory models in these phases. If the model in the first phase, called Mutual Accommodation, as it has been described earlier in this chapter, can be considered the starting point for almost all the experiences, the shift to the second one and even more to the third one has not necessarily happened everywhere. There is a sort of a 'patchwork situation', where different regulatory models co-exist in similar contexts. The evolutionary three phases model presented here is not, therefore, applicable to every local authority, but it seems more adequate to describe and explain the more innovative contexts and often medium—big size local authorities, which are usually more concerned with more pluralistic

Table 6.3. The Changes in the Italian Welfare Mix

	The 1980s	The Beginning of the 1990s	The Second Part of the 1990s
Actors involved in the Public Policy Making Process	Statutory actors	Statutory actors	Statutory/Private actors
Public Sector's Mechanisms to select Private Providers	Private agreements	Economic competition	Accreditation-vouchers; Relational Contracts
Public Sector's Financial and Control Mechanisms	Grants No controls	Contracts Financial controls	Contracts Final and process controls
Regulatory Model	Mutual Accommodation	Competitive Market	Joint Managed Competition

and effective ways to regulate the interaction with private or non-profit providers.

The public/private regulatory model of the 1980s applied usually to new third sector organizations, founded beginning from the 1970s, the traditional regulatory model used in the previous decades towards the traditional non-profit organizations (IPABs, Church organizations, etc.), which had delivered social services. What has happened in the 1990s allows us to change, at least partially, this viewpoint. For the first time in Italy, there has been a growth of regulation specifically aimed at providing a background of stability and homogeneity to relations between state and the third sector. By putting an end to established practices based on mutual accommodation, this new regulation marks an attempt to give more transparency and general principles of behaviour to a system of relationships which until recently has been heavily characterized by discretionary powers and local bargaining, sometimes with no regard to the public interest. Hence the attempt to provide more detailed regulation of contractual and financial relations between local government and service providers.

A second, but no less important innovation consisted of giving NPOs recognized status within the welfare system: as opposed to the previous one, the new regulation that is emerging fully recognises the 'mixed' nature of the welfare system and gives NPOs an equal status of public institutions.

A third important element of innovation is represented by the strengthening and the increased structuring of the third sector, especially its more entrepreneurial components, through either a growth in size or the creation of umbrella organizations, strategies which have allowed many organizations to be more effective and representative at the policy making and lobbying process with public sector authorities.

To conclude, there have been and there are two parallel processes in progress during this decade: the strengthening of state responsibility for social policies and the strengthening of the institutional role of the third sector. Therefore, the greater role in policy making assumed by the third sector is a result not of the reduction in state regulation, but it is occurring thanks to its increase, concentrated on coordination, on the definition of the rules of inter-action between the various actors, on inspection and verification of results.

This nevertheless has introduced an element of new tension in the processes of defining the new regulation. The new regulation has, in fact, gradually introduced the dynamics of competition into a field traditionally dominated by a philosophy of local concertation. Therefore, the 1990s can be seen as a period of potential change compared to the regulatory logic of the 1980s, period which is anyway characterized by an increasing tension between the growth of both collaboration and participation in policy making and competition for obtaining public funds.

The New Enabling Role of the State

At the beginning of the 1990 there is a first new regulatory model which often replaces the mutual accommodation one and might be defined as 'competitive market'. This model is characterized in the first place by the introduction of mechanisms for the private providers' selection and control based on economic competition and its main focus is economic efficiency and costs reduction, instead of the traditional model based on negotiated concertation. The controls used by local authorities are mainly focused on costs and other financial issues, taking into little account forms of evaluation related to the services production process and the quality of the latter.

Moreover, even if the national legislation at the beginning of the 1990 recognized third sector organizations' public importance, their involvement in public decision making remained limited due to different factors: the use of 'traditional' informal networks between public and third sector actors, the slowness to introduce at the local level national innovative legislation, the plurality of NPOs and their limited capability to cooperate, the difficulties to coordinate joint working groups between public and non-profit actors.

In general the introduction of competition mechanisms seems to have partially monopolized the contents of the discussions and the interactions between public and third sector actors, creating an atmosphere of partial distrust and suspicion. Economic issues have often been the main concern of the interaction instead of more general policy issues.

The relationships between organizations and local authorities at the beginning of the 1990 are, therefore, characterized by an increase in conflicts, due on one hand to the introduction of competition mechanisms, mainly based on efficiency and costs savings, on the other to the limited development of third sector/statutory collaboration mechanisms in the policy making process.

On one hand, due to budget and transparency needs, local authorities became more strict in the way they managed the relationship, increasing the level of formalization and the 'distance' with their third sector counterparts. On the other hand the latter, which had grown in size and importance, also thanks to the legislative public recognition, felt that it was exposed to a too harsh competition and its participation to the public decision making process was often strongly limited. The fragmentation and the 'distance' between the central government and local authorities, typical of the Italian situation, produced a model characterized by a formal legal recognition at the national level, often without any effective change in the forms of third sector involvement in the public policy making process in many local authorities.

Starting with the second part of the 1990s it seems that the relationship in some contexts changes again with the introduction of a new model of 'joint managed competition'. There is an increase in joint planning activities between statutory and third sector organizations, thanks to a series of factors: the higher level of third sector structuring, with an increasing role played by umbrella organizations (e.g. consortia) able to represent many NPOs, and an increased attention to NPOs' involvement by local administrations, partly due to the implementation of the regional and national legislation. The greater use of joint planning facilitates, therefore, the setting of forms of collaboration also in the evaluation and control phase, where there is a shift from just financial control to process based controls. Also the statutory providers' selection mechanisms tend to shift towards different directions. There is an introduction of third party payments systems in the form of accreditation and vouchers for those services where it seems reasonable to believe that users or carers can make their own decisions and choices.

In all other services, where it seems more difficult for the users to judge the service quality by themselves, there has been the introduction of competition mechanisms not just price-based, but also based on structural and quality indicators, trying in this way to manage together at the same time efficiency with effectiveness.

The use of providers' selection mechanisms based not just on price but also on other more qualitative indicators has the indirect effect of introducing again elements of discretionality in local authorities decisions in relation to whom should win the contract and receive public funds. Discretionality was relatively absent in the former model, where the only element taken into consideration was the price offered for the contract by single organizations. The decision to shift from a price-based selection mechanism to a more complex one has been influenced by many factors.

As it has been already underlined, at the macro level there has been the introduction of legislation which dealt with the determination of evaluation parameters for contracts, parameters not just based on price (in particular the regional legislation which derives from the law 381/91), or of minimum wages standards for NPOs' workers. This legislation has become the framework inside which Local Authorities had to take decisions in terms of regulatory model to utilize.

At the micro level, the most careful local authorities have realized the risks and also the (transaction) costs that a model based on price competition and no joint planning bears. If local authorities want to maintain or reach a satisfactory level of services in terms of quality, an only cost-based providers' selection mechanism requests, for many complex social services, an increase in monitoring costs, due to the fact that the price itself is not a sufficient source of information (Bartlett et al., 1998).

This last model of selecting and controlling providers is proper, according to Dore (1983), of 'relational contracts', contracts between two parties in which the service funder tries to establish a medium- to long-term cooperative relationship with the service provider as long as the latter guarantees a proper and effective commitment. The existence of a potential market to which the funder may resort to seek other suppliers remains the condition that maintains the efficiency and effectiveness of the service at a satisfactory level. The main principle at the base of this kind of relationship between (public) purchasers and private (non-profit) providers is that, if the aim of a purchaser is to obtain a better efficiency and quality, it must build long-term relationships with providers. In this way the trust that has been built in the reiterated interaction limits the necessity to utilize strict controls, often too expensive. The fact that it is always possible to change providers and there is a contestable market should push the providers towards increasing efficiency and quality. Altogether this model of joint managed competition is spreading in different contexts.

Dilemmas

The model of relations that seems to best define the Italian situation is based on consensus and incrementalism in the decision making processes. There is a limited number of potential suppliers, and they are in any case pre-selected either formally or informally by the local authority, thereby greatly reducing the competition. The capacity of local authorities to identify the specific characteristics of the service remains limited, favouring a process of negotiation to reach mutual agreement on the main aspects. The negotiation, however is not so much over general policies, as it is over individual projects and their assessment and the definition of general guidelines for funding in a context of progressive agreement on basic principles. The relationship increasingly tends to take the shape of an agreement between equals in which either party can threaten to withdraw, being aware, however, of the negative consequences of such a decision. This greater equality in the relationship is ensured by the local authority's motivation to reduce possible information gaps and by the fact that LAs in any case provide the funding and by the increased capacity of NPOs to aggregate and, therefore, to exert pressure and play a more active role.

If this model of joint managed competition seems potentially altogether the most satisfactory, in comparison with the former ones, in terms of ensuring better quality and efficiency, user choice, participation to the public policy making process, it has anyhow some elements of risks. In particular, joint planning in public policy making presents some problems, even if it opens up new ways and possibilities of pluralistic and democratic participation by citizens, users and civic society organizations. The two main problems are related to: (a) the potential 'conflict of interests' for those organizations which both provide services and participate to decide which policies should be implemented and how the financial resources allocated; (b) the criteria used by local authorities to decide which non-profit organizations should take part at the policy making process. The main risk in Italy now is that it will be the more entrepreneurial and professionalized organizations will be involved in this process, while the other ones will have more problems to participate due to the lack of time, knowledge and influence. The increasing polarization among third sector organizations might also have a strong impact in terms of non-profit sector representation at the policy making process.

It musts be underlined that this 'representation' problem was also present in former regulatory models, where, if there were any non-profit involvement in the public policy making by local authorities, it happened through informal networks. Therefore, in comparative terms, it seems that the joint managed competition model is not resolving a traditional problem of regulatory systems, more than creating a new one.

It is also problematic in this latter model, the fact that there is an introduction again in the providers' selection mechanisms of discretionality in the decisions taken by local authorities, which have to judge the possible providers on the base, not only, of cost parameters but also of quality/structural standards. There is a serious risk that the actual model might turn itself into a more formalized version of the 'mutual accommodation' one, with, in comparison to the former one, NPOs and statutory authorities collaborating and interacting in more transparent and formalized ways, but within a logic of resources exchange, which is profitable for them and not necessarily for the users and the tax payers.

Bearing in mind that social markets systems will probably have a relatively limited increase, due to the factors above underlined, the introduction of market mechanisms like competition, even in the form of relational contracts, seems to demonstrate that these mechanisms are not necessarily sufficient by themselves to ensure better efficiency, effectiveness and users' choice. There should be other mechanisms and institutions, some of which operating outside the relationship between non-profit providers and local authorities purchasers, able to carry out the role played by the market for the production and exchange of goods and services between private enterprises.

From this point of view, the same kind of problems might arise in social markets, if the public accreditation model would work just in terms of control of formal requirements. In conclusion, the model of joint managed competition needs some specific institutions which can make it function, avoiding collusion, opportunism and clientelism; risks that might originate from a close and 'cosy' relationship between local authorities and non-profit providers. As it is already said, a process of institution building is currently occurring in Italy. However, such process is still incomplete.

The statutory control mechanisms, based on public regional or national organizations, able to make accountable local authorities and their relationships models, are still limited. The statutory capability to monitor relationships at the local level seems poorly effective: regions, for example, have not been so far able to undertake planning and control policies in this direction (Ranci and Vanoli, 1994), even if some of them have recently taken some steps towards it (e.g. the regional legislation on contracts and social cooperatives).

Also users' organizations have still a limited role in terms of fostering accountability: as it has been shown in these pages, a regulatory model based mainly on the relationship between local authorities and the more profession-alized and entrepreneurial NPOs can mean a 'marginalization' from public decision making processes of many of those third sector organizations, among which there are also users groups and associations, that have usually a limited role in the provision of services. Even from a more general point of view, it can be noticed that compared to other western European countries, such as for example the UK, the issue of consumerism and users' empowerment seems less central in the Italian debate and in public policy decisions.

Therefore, the 'success' of the joint managed competition model in terms of efficient and effective public/private partnerships seems, probably, more related to the limited presence of opportunistic behaviours and the goodwill to improve the local welfare system by the two main actors (local authorities and third sector providers), than the contemporary presence of mechanisms and institutions able to prevent deviations towards clientelism and opportunism.

The building of this model is still an open-ended process. Its main effect has so far been the creation of a more institutionalized, less fragmented rela-tionship between state and the third sector. The introduction of competitive mechanisms has favoured, in an unplanned system largely exposed to discre-tionality and political patronage, the growth of more transparency and more regulatory capacity on the part of the state. Whether or not this process will definitively take the Italian welfare mix away from the mutual accommoda-tion model, is a matter of the future.

Notes

1. State expenditure on social assistance fell from 4.88 per cent of GNP in 1990 to 4.16 per cent in 1994 (Commission for the investigation on poverty, 1997).
2. According to a recent research (Ranci and Costa, 1999), there are a total of 4,200 IPABs operating in Italy with around 80,000 employees.
3. In many local authorities, setting up joint planning is hindered by the difficulty in coor-dinating a large number of small organizations in meetings with state institutions. The problem of resources, on the other hand, concerns the fact that only big organizations have planning capacities and time available to intervene effectively at discussion tables, while organizations with fewer resources play only a marginal role.

Chapter 7

Answers without Questions? The Changing Contract Culture in Germany and the Future of a Mixed Welfare System

ADALBERT EVERS AND CHRISTOPH STRÜNCK*

7.1. INTRODUCTION: THE CHALLENGES BEHIND CONTRACT MAKING AND THE MAIN ARGUMENTS AND OBSERVATIONS OF THE COUNTRY STUDY

Changes in the relationships between public authorities and service providers express themselves in changing forms and contents of contract making. The contract culture can therefore be understood as a reflection of what is going on in matters of welfare in the social service field, where besides state-public and commercial providers different forms of not-for-profit providing organizations play an important role (Evers, 1997). Even if one deals mostly with not-for-profit organizations as contract partners, as in the following article, there is a broad variety of questions about social welfare services and their provision which can be taken up by thematizing contracts. They cover economic and social, managerial and professional, financial and political aspects of welfare.

* ADALBERT EVERS • Justus-Liebig-Universität Giessen FB 9, Bismarckstr. 37, D 35390 Giessen, Germany.   CHRISTOPH STRÜNCK • Department for Political Sciences at the Heinrich Heine Universität, Düsseldorf, Universitätsstr. 1, D 40225 Düsseldorf.

The following report, concerning the situation and trends in Germany, will throughout be based on a differentiation between two problem dimensions which are affected and influence contract making and which have usually been discussed without further differentiation (see e.g. for England: Knapp and Wistow, 1994; for the US: Kramer, 1994; Salamon, 1995): a more narrow technical and economic dimension and a wider social and political one. The emphasis of this article will be put on giving a better visibility to the latter, showing that there are, in Germany, a number of largely unresolved social and political questions behind contract making, answered by management experts without having been posed in their own right. Let us first of all briefly mention some of these basic questions.

First of all, service-contracts reflect a certain understanding with respect to the basic roles and tasks of public authorities and not-for-profit providers; in modern democratic welfare states there is a long history of debates concerning these issues, stating, for example, that social service tasks should be basically state public, with a mere pioneering and lobbying role of civic organizations, or stating that they should just extend and complement what state institutions guarantee; contrary to that, there have as well been claims, that the provision of such services should be primarily a matter of social concern within the society and that the respective charities and voluntary organizations should handle it 'freely', without both state support and state patronizing. Obviously, there are more positions than the ones just mentioned. They all have an impact on the idea of the mutual roles and responsibilities of both sides which is behind any form of a contract.

Furthermore, what is of much influence is the idea of the nature of the services, their scope, availability and professionality, and the concept of rights and responsibilities of the individuals and groups addressed. Obviously, much is left to the public, local concerns and the respective civic organizations themselves when and where the public authorities have decided to contain to a kind of generalized support for each and every civic initiative which acts on behalf of solidaristic purposes; in this case, the public authorities just follow general lines concerning grants for such organizations, tax reductions, etc. In many areas the public authorities have however taken a more extended type of responsibility, by guaranteeing firmly the availability or the reimbursement of certain kinds of personal help and services independently from local variations of resources; provision by not-for-profits is then often the start of a creeping process of increasing public responsibility; this can be studied impressively over more than a hundred years in areas like education and health. However, it is questionable whether in the future all services and rights linked with them will or should have such a highly state-based status, so much uniformity and comprehensiveness—maybe they will be more patchy, more dependent on what is added by local solidarities to their scope and quality. Obviously, different perspectives on that will have an impact on contracts and on what they say about the mutual rights and obligations of both sides, the public authorities and the social actors represented by a not-for-profit organization as service provider.

Finally contracts reflect, however, as well a more technical and limited purpose concerning economic and financial efficiency. This is a problem which is often confused with the broader challenge of governance problems, to the degree, the very concept of policy making and governing gets reduced to effective management (PUMA, 1995). The public institutions which give support have for example, in any case a legitimate concern to check whether the respective measures are suited to reach the intended goals for which they give their support. Furthermore, especially at times social tasks are seen as being of lesser importance and when public finance is under pressure there can be additional incentives to try to get more services for the given public spending and therefore, to intervene into the way the providers organize their services and use the public funds. The thinking in managerial terms can, and will perhaps dominate to the degree the fundamental questions about the sharing of sociopolitical responsibilities, the nature of the service to be provided, etc. are settled. This means, on the other hand, that to the degree new social challenges are not compatible with organizational and professional routines developed so far, *concepts which focus on managerial questions are insufficient for tackling this wider problem field, or get 'loaded' with conceptional problems and conflicts not debated in their own right and terms.*

Reflecting the sometimes hidden aspects of contract culture the following contribution concentrates on four central points:

(1) The present changes in the contracts between public authorities and public funding institutions like the social insurances on the one hand and not-for-profit providers on the other are predominantly articulated in terms of managerial concerns with efficiency, getting 'value for money' and avoiding the shortcomings of traditional corporatist arrangements.

(2) They mirror as well a widespread lack of willingness and/or capability for good governance of the public authorities in dealing with the respective problems, then passing them over to third sector organizations.

(3) The capability for strategic political action of both sides, public authorities and third sector organizations depends on finding a consented interplay and division of responsibilities in a largely 'mixed' welfare system. One can find a relative strong impact of a quasi-market model with the public authorities as financing and regulating a field of competition between all sorts of providers.

(4) Another basic problem mostly hidden in contract making is concerning the future design of services, be it on behalf of such social

policy challenges like dealing with innovation or finding the right balance between uniformity and plurality in service provision.

(5) What seems especially remarkable for Germany is the fact that these problems and trends are showing differently in different service fields;

   (a) only in the sector of services for elderly care can one find a clear overall concept of a quasi market, strong standardization and tight regulations;

   (b) contract making in other mainstream services in the social field, like child care, reflects a somewhat lesser degree of centralized rules following long-time established traditions of (local) corporatism;

   (c) diversity, but as well insecurity and inclarity, concerning the ways and content of future contracting are especially high where services are for weaker groups, tackle new problems and are situated in fields where rights and responsibilities are low and/or unclear.

Summing up, one can say that in Germany, central and local governments as well as the big financing institutions of the social insurances and even most of the voluntary providers presently concentrate very much on what is calculable and feasible in managerial terms. When it comes to the relations of local governments and third sector organizations providing social services, so far, the question 'Who needs whom—why and what for?' (Deakin and Gaster, 1998) can only be answered in an empirical description of what has been built up in the past; answers are largely unclear, when it comes to the future. The changing contract culture in Germany is a reflection of unresolved questions concerning the future of a mixed welfare system. In order to develop this message accurately, three steps will be taken:

- the first step will be to summarize the peculiarities of the German system of state—third sector interrelations in order to understand better, which fields and paths of traditions actors today have to make their moves in; this chapter refers to studies and literature available;
- the second step will be to illustrate hallmarks of the changing contract culture in Germany; for that purpose a number of small case studies has been set up; on the one hand they show, to what degree the problems take different forms in different service fields, on the other hand they have been selected with an eye on showing what could be seen as most illustrative cases concerning present barriers and potentials for change; all six case studies are based on interviews of the authors and/or research they presently undertake in these sectors;
- finally, a third step will consist in drawing conclusions, which debate more extensivly what has been indicated above as the central insight to be offered by this country study.

7.2. PECULIARITIES OF THE GERMAN SYSTEM OF STATE—THIRD SECTOR INTERRELATIONS

Historical Aspects

A central point of departure for the German system of state—third sector interrelations has been the flourishing of manifold charities and self-help organizations in the second half of last century—organized by local citizens concerned, in the context of one of the Catholic or Protestant churches and in the context of the organized forms of labour movement (Evers, 1995). Central organizations mainly followed tasks and problems instead of ideological camps and only at the end of the last century, the predecessors of the present big voluntary organizations, like Caritas and Diakonie were founded. It was already before the end of the last century, that in many German cities the provision of social services developed in the framework of a corporate system, with municipal representatives on the boards of the local (not-for-profit) welfare organizations and sensitive mechanisms of adapting mutually the priorities of municipalities in the social field and the concerns of the voluntary organizations pioneering services and looking for municipal support (Sachsse, 1993).

The way from a rich diversity of initiatives toward an organized landscape of some big organizations was paved mainly in the Weimar Republic (Tennstedt, 1992). The new democratic state developed as a central partner for issues of social help and services alike, by installing the ministry for work. Its legislation and political culture of central bargaining like in industrial relations favoured central bargaining throughout as well as centralized umbrella organizations to communicate with. However, the initiative to organize on a central level was speeded up especially by the voluntary bodies in the camps of the two big churches—the Diakonie (Protestant) and the Caritas (Catholic), alongside with the smaller Jewish agency and a 'Fifth Welfare Association' (today: the Deutscher Paritätischer Wohlfahrtsverband, DPWV).

They felt threatened by the strong social-democratic/state ambitions toward transforming the dual structure which had grown within the municipalities cooperating with voluntary bodies toward a 'municipal socialism', with services to be run by the public authorities themselves. In fact, the real legislation process in social welfare reinforced the 'dual system' of public purchasing and private providing which had already developed.

The third sector organizations, therefore, developed a strong position both by their national organization and its joint 'Liga' (national association) as well as by stepwise building up their role as primary partners alongside with the development of social services on the local level. The 'Arbeiterwohlfahrt' (the voluntary organization associated with the social-democratic camp) had to join the national 'Liga' in the late 1920s and to cooperate within the given culture of state third sector relationships. This was marked first of all by an increasing role of the municipalities and the health insurances as financing bodies, taking parts in negotiations about concepts and standards. Secondly it was marked by the fact that the established not-for-profit organizations became acknowledged as being the privileged partners when it came to carrying out and providing a service (Kaiser, 1993).

After the deformation under the Nazi rule (with its forced *etatization* of the organizations) the new Federal Republic took up again and continued the road which had already been paved in the interwar period. In a number of social laws (concerning social assistance, services for the youth and in the area of help and care) voluntary organizations were given a special public status and a privileged role as service providers; they had to be contracted in first whenever a public funded new social service or institution had to be built up. Given the strong influence of the (catholic) church, the dual system was often interpreted as the practical realization of the principle of subsidiarity (Sachsse, 1995). Summing up, two peculiarities should be underlined.

First of all, Germany belongs to that group of welfare states, where— different to England with much of the ordinary social services being provided by the municipalities and in contrast to Sweden with the role of civic organizations largely reduced to advocacy and campaigning—voluntary organizations are firm pillars of the institutional system of welfare provision; they always had the difficult task of cooperating closely with public authorities in the provision of standardized mainstream services and being simultaneously responsible for new needs to be answered and services to be provided; the result has been a strong prevalence of their first role which always helped in consolidating and developing.

Secondly, in Germany therefore corporatist arrangements have a long tradition: (a) on the central level and in the respective policy sectors (health, social assistance, youth policy including child care services) when it comes to negotiating standards for social services and institutions and centrally prescribed levels of remuneration for services rendered; here the big five voluntary bodies usually took part (the ones already mentioned and the Red Cross); (b) on the local level of daily municipal policies concerning social services (mainly: services for the elderly, for youth and family help and child care); here the representatives of the voluntary bodies take part in planning the type and levels of public provision as members of the local committees linked with the local parliaments (e.g. in the committees which are obligatory in the area of planning facilities for children and youth); given the tight relationships between the representatives of the municipalities, the political parties, the social insurances and the voluntary organizations and their boards, it was no wonder that the system of accountance was similar to the public cameralistic system and that trust and negotiation play a big role in governing the mutual relationships. However, some events in the last 25 years made this system increasingly less coherent.

The cultural changes of the late 1960s brought about a number of local initiatives, associations and self-help groups which either did not join one of the big voluntary associations or just loosely organized in the DVPW—the one which is less powerful, but much more open to take a modest role as a mere umbrella organization. As a result in Germany one can find something like 'two cultures' of a traditional and a new generation of associations and service providing organizations. Meanwhile, the new ones have often been practising more than 25 years as well. In some sectors—like in the area of child care facilities organized by the parents—they received to get the same status concerning contracts on economic support as the other older providers. In other sectors—especially where the service concepts gave innovative answers to conflictive issues not easy to harmonize with the culture of the majorities, like many services for drug addicted people, for women under pressure etc.—it became much more difficult to get the same reliable and considerable level of public support traditional voluntary organizations get.

Furthermore, in old and new areas of social services—in the field of child and elderly care but as well of health and 'wellness' new commercial providers took their chance; the willingness of people to finance commercial suppliers has been growing and partly these providers managed to become new additional contract partners for the public authorities and the health and care insurances.

Finally, professionalization, the task of administrating general services open for every citizen and the tight interrelations with the public authorities and the financing organizations created the well-known 'institutional isomorphism' (Powell and diMaggio, 1991). The cultural and ideological roots of the traditional voluntary bodies weakened considerably and this again had an impact on their character as organizations which mobilized solidarity by volunteering or donations. Alongside with the German reunification, their role as service providers in corporate arrangements with local and central policy makers, the professionals in the fields and the representatives of the refunding organizations (see the role of the health and care insurances) has been reinforced further. In the former GDR, where a parastate organization (the Volkssolidarität) had controlled the field, the organizations were implanted top-down without even the reminders of a religious or social-democratic culture existing. Here they started with the role they had assumed over time in the former FRG—as kinds of 'welfare trusts' (Angerhausen et al., 1995).

With an eye on that it can be easily understood why the movement of New Public Management does comprise in Germany the organizational structures of the voluntary organizations at once: they are a complementary part of the public system of provision (Wollmann, 1997). However, some scandals about dilettantism ('voluntary failure'; Salamon, 1987a) in operating with public funds had speeded up this orientation towards installing a new managerialism and a more consumerist organization.

Main Features of the Present Situation in Germany

In order to understand better the peculiar role of the German voluntary bodies as central and mainstream providers of (health and) social services, the following indicators might be useful (BAGFW, 1997). In 1997, they employed around 940,000 persons; the biggest organization is Caritas with about 400,000, followed by the Diakonie with about 330,000 employees (the biggest German employer, Daimler Benz has about 240,000); main growth happened in the 1970s up to the late 1980s where the number of employees doubled. In the church organizations the role of the clerical which formed the majority in the 1950s has become insignificant (4 per cent of employees). For years the organizations have been declaring that they work with about 1.5 million volunteers. However, studies indicate that this is by far overrated. In the health sector the organizations run about 40 per cent of all hospitals, 40 per cent of all home care services, 50 per cent of all (homes for the) elderly and nursing homes and about 60 per cent of all kindergartens.

The small-scale local initiatives and asssociations which developed after the late 1960s are difficult to measure; it is estimated that there existed around 50,000 local groups in the old FRG in 1991, with nearly 2 million cooperating members; however, only less than 10 per cent of these groups employed (usually more than one) professionals. To the degree these groups are offering services to others, they are engaged in problem areas, like in help for especially disadvantaged groups; usually the commitment of public authorities is low here and there are less routinized systems of public support and reimbursement for what the associations are doing in such areas.

In contrast to the second wave made up by small local associations, the organizational features of the big voluntary associations are more complex. The five national organizations mentioned are organized according to a double ratio.

- On the one hand, they understand themselves as organizations which represent a specific system of societal goals and values, defending the interests of underprivileged and weak groups; accordingly the formal command structures are led by persons which do this work as volunteers, coming from the realms of church or other related organizations.
- On the other hand, they never established themselves as member organizations (except the 'Arbeiterwohlfhahrt' / 'workers welfare'), but as organizations made up by the membership of the service and help providing (local) associations. If they are concerned with the problems of the groups they work for, they are not committed to them by organizational relationships.

The Contract Culture

In order to understand the role of contractual relationships in the past and future a look toward the financing structure of the national voluntary organizations is instructive. Here one has however to rely on estimates since most of the voluntary organizations do not publish coherent figures. According to a frequently quoted estimation by Goll (1991) about 11 per cent of all resources are public subsidies, while about 80 per cent of the total of 46 billion DM turnover are made up by reimbursements for services rendered; nearly 5 per cent come from donations and membership fees and 4 per cent from the churches.

- *Subsidies* can come from all levels of the state; they take mostly, (a) the form of a one time initial *investment* of a ministry of one of the 'Laender' (the federal units below the central state) or of a district or a municipality in the construction of a child care or an elderly care centre which is then run by the respective voluntary body; or it can, (b) mean to subsidize the operating institution; this happens often in the framework of a special time limited public programme or by a grant paid from the budgets of the municipality; for subsidies it is typical, that there is no clear relationship with a reverse commitment of the receiver for giving a certain level of services etc.
- *Reimbursements* are clearly related to designated numbers and types of services rendered, they can for minor parts come as fees from the clients themselves; the vast majority however comes from the social insurances (health and care insurance) the social assistance agencies and in case there is a clear contractual relationship with service-performance from (municipal) public budgets; negotiated and fixed sums per service rendered or per day/place/hospital bed are payed for care rendered in nursing homes, shelter, etc. The negotiations about the terms and levels of reimbursement for care rendered have therefore by tradition been the most important topic for the vast majorities of the institutions and services run by the voluntary bodies, and it was quite important that the voluntary bodies and providers were able to take part in these negotiations.

There is quite a variety of forms of subsidies and reimbursement. Some reflect local traditions, others mirror the peculiarities of a specific administrative and policy field; for example, some service providers are paid nearly entirely from the local funds for social assistance, others get the bulk of their resources from municipal grants which have to be (re)stated every year, and still others get their money overwhelmingly from the health and care insurances.

What makes it even more complicated is the fact that many service providers rely on budgets which represent a resource-mix of subsidies and reimbursements from different sources. Therefore, there is neither a coherent way of changes of these kinds of resource arrangements nor of the contractual conditions linked to them. There are, however, three factors which are important throughout the social service sectors:

- The fact that the public money, coming from social assistance, social insurances and public households is getting scarce is most central; this creates more rivalry, but as well attempts for adapting to the new situation in one or the other way; new types of contract making are one of these features.
- The developments within the big voluntary associations and the service providers which are members in these associations are presently most interesting regarding concepts for managerial modernization: new trends are towards implementing controlling, 'profit centres', internal quality control etc. (Heinze et al., 1997). There are however only rare signs of linkages of this kind of managerial modernization with an intended and conceptionally grounded rethinking of ones own role in a changing environment.
- If there is after all a conceptional vision, enabling the voluntary providers to create a concept which links managerial modernization, the need for new service concepts and a redefinition of their relation to the public authorities and financing organization, it is the rise of the market liberal paradigm. Compared with the past of a friendly and for a long time quite comfortable social corporatism, it offers a much more economistic idea of the whole 'business' of welfare provision—of the ways to define needs, services, consumers and the architecture of a system which according to this paradigm should switch from a partnership in public service to participation in a public-managed competitive system, where the other side is a business partner (Wistow et al., 1996). When it comes to contract making, in theory this means for the public authorities, that it would be the best way to make public subscriptions, to take the provider which offers the best value for money, etc.; in practice the continuing traditions of bureaucratic regulations cannot be abolished at once and neither can the system of exclusive corporatist relationships simply given up, which offers flexibility and compromises based on mutual trust as developed in years of cooperation.

With reference to our tasks of analysing the changing contract culture in the fragmented and differentiated field of social services it is suggested here to separate three fields with different contract regimes; (they are enumerated here under (1) and (2a) and (2b), due to the fact that the major difference is to be found between (1) and (2)).

(1) In the area of *health services*, there is a contract regime, where the founding and continuing investments and costs of buildings and equipment (e.g. hospitals) are paid from public budgets, while their contractual relationships with the health insurances (and sometimes the social assistance departments) are about the reimbursement of the services rendered; this can be done—as for example, in hospitals—in terms of consented prices for clinical surgery or for practicioners in accordance to a detailed list of priced medical items. The providing organizations are the partners of the insurances while the social welfare organizations as umbrella organizations have only a consultancy role. What is important when debating the contract culture in the field of social services is that in Germany the care reform of 1994 introduced these rules with some modifications to the field of care services. Thus, the Bismarckian principles have been transfered to this once less institutionalized field (Munday and Ely 1996). The first case study in the following third chapter will illustrate this.

(2a) The second contract regime is found in the field of other social services, especially when it comes to well established social services and items corresponding to clear-cut rights of the users and citizens (services for youngsters, day care for children, services for people with disabilities a.o.). The costs of the services are covered either by tax money from the public budget of ministries and/or districts and municipalities. In case the services address means tested groups out of social assistance budgets it will be financed mainly by the municipalities. For the level of reimbursements (besides the minor grants and subsidies) a kind of fixed price for example, per day and bed is consented. Usually, this price becomes resettled and changed (not drastically) every year. What is important concerning this traditional contracts on reimbursement is that, there was and is still the possibility to get a financial minus made over the year (e.g. by an unforeseen rate of empty beds) covered by an *ex post* grant. In the framework of such traditional 'cameralistic' contracts each and every item of the service provider had to be notified for final reimbursement; if less became spent than foreseen, less became repaid. This means that for providing not-for-profits saving money does not pay off in such a system, while likewise spending (a bit) too much does not worry them. The bureaucratic but guaranteeing character of the traditional contract protects them from risks, but likewise does not encourage them to take one. And obviously, the *ex-post* reimbursement can only be understood if one takes into account that there was and is a basic trust that the providers, because they operate not-for-profit (and not for egoistic reasons but in the name of the public good) can keep an intrinsic motivaton to do the best they can with the money negotiated initially.

(2b) A third contract regime is found mostly between the municipalities or respective ministries on the level of the central state or the 'Laender' and initiatives and organizations which provide innovative types of help and services whose offer is not consolidated as a right of the users and citizens. Very often this is done by small local associations for such services as, for example, drug-consultancy, social work in community development or help for homeless people. The providers get a yearly grant from the municipality to be politically restated every year or they get subsidies in the framework of a (time limited) model project. In times of financial distress such voluntary grants and programme funds, usually contracted for just a year, are extremely shaky; here traditionally gaps were filled *ex post* after the end of a year, too; so far (2a) and (2b) differed mainly with respect to the fact that, whether a medium/long-term and stable, and or a very short-term and shaky relationship of support and refunding was prevailing. The regime of precarious funding we have just sketched is typical and central for many small-scale organizations. It is estimated that such types of funding only make up for about 5 per cent of the income of corporate members of the big voluntary organizations; the more they orient themselves simply toward their organizational stability and growth, the less they will be ready to take the risk of engaging in difficult fields with unstable contracts.

In both sectors sketched under (2a) and (2b), there is a managerial modernization under way with ministries and municipalities reshaping their contractual relationships with the providers; instead of deciding yearly about (in the care area mostly invariant) sums of subsidies for local services like a youth centre, a shelter etc., they increasingly install new types of contracts which on the one hand are laid down for some years and give global sums, while on the other hand they entail some clear statements about the scope of services to be rendered. This could put those associations which run mainly on year to year subsidies in a better position in terms of safety, while it makes the situation less comfortable for the big voluntary agencies. This development has triggered off a debate among social policy experts, to what degree this switch is completly undermining the old local corporatism which built a closed shop of providing voluntary organizations or mainly changing the rules of the game within the same bunch of participants (Heinze a.o. vs Olk).

7.3. ILLUSTRATING HALLMARKS OF THE CHANGING CONTRACT CULTURE—SIX CASE STUDIES

The following case studies have been selected with reference to the main points of concern of our contribution as explained in the introduction. Five of them try to capture the different situation in areas with rather well-established and widespread 'mainstream' services and in other subsectors of social service provision with a more limited and experimental character. Case six puts emphasis on the global challenges for not-for-profit organizations concerning all their tasks and dimensions which go beyond service provision. The cases are partly based on knowledge derived from research projects and studies of the authors, partly on findings from other research and partly on interviews done in the course of the preparation of this paper.

Mainstream Services—Installing a System of Contractual Relations in the Care Service Sector

Care services, used overwhelmingly by frail elderly people, are the most important social service system besides day care for children. And in Germany they are characterized by a new system of contracting which is different from the contract culture in all other social service sectors (for more details see: Evers, 1998).

The foundations for the new system have been laid in 1995, when being in need of care became a socially insured risk like pensions, accidents and health. Now for care, as well there is a conscriptive social insurance solution; the insurers are the existing health insurances, but the new branch is formally independent; each health insurance has now an additional care insurance branch (Alber, 1996).

So far the providers of institutional and home care services (municipal, not-for-profit associations and commercial ones) received their reimbursements either from the care-dependent persons themselves or, in case these were dependent from social assistance, in the framework of contracts with the municipal social assistance offices; besides that the municipal and not-for-profit organizations got additional grants mainly for investments and maintenance; the commercial providers had ususally to run without such money (Garms-Homolova, 1994).

There were two main reasons for introducing an insurance-based solution. On the one hand, it was seen as unfair, that so many people had to take resort to social assistance in case of care dependency, especially in institutional care, with its high costs around 6,000 DM/month and more than 80 per cent of all people to be paid or helped by social assistance. On the other hand, the municipalities which have to bear the bulk of social assistance costs (which made up for two thirds of all social assistance payments) were eager to get rid of them by installing an insurance solution.

The most important element in the new reform with respect to the issue of contract culture is the introduction of a quasi-market system with very restricted rights and incentives for political intervention of public authorities in the future. Legislators have been 'courageous' (Schulin 1994, p. 303) insofar as they have removed the ancient special and favourite conditions for not-for-profit providers. Much more than in the health sector, a system of competitive tendering has been installed. Every provider which fullfills some professional premises has to be allowed to offer institutional or home care as a provider licensed for insurance reimbursement; commercial providers are now explicitly put on equal footing with providers which work in the framework of the big voluntary agencies (as corporate members and not-for-profits); municipal-based organizations are to be transferred into a quasi-commercial or not-for-profit status; in order to safeguard equal conditions for each competing provider, public authorities are not allowed anymore to give continuous grants to a special group of providers (the not-for-profits).

With the 'Laender' and the municipalities having nearly no saying in terms of planning and the number and distribution of service offers developing now in a market style, the care insurances become the central partners for establishing contracts about the services to be offered and the reimbursement rules with the providers of institutional and home care services. And it is at this point that the tight neighbourhood between health insurers with their personal and care insurers, between health and care professions and between the ministry for labour and social affairs and the insurance system and logic in general (Goetting et al., 1994) has lead to a contract system which is in various ways a kind of copy of the rules and regulations in the health system.

What has been copied from the health field is first of all the high degree of uniformization of contract making. There is anything but a lose system where the single different insurances would negotiate special contracts with the providers, for example, with different types and levels of reimbursement. Instead the rules for reimbursement are the same between the various insurances and not locally agreed but negotiated on the level of the 'Laender'. The first step is a contract about becoming licensed as a provider. Second, the federal state associations of the insurances make a general agreement/contract with a delegation representing the interests of all providers and their associations in that 'Land'; these contracts contain agreements about the type of remuneration, professional standards and other general conditions for reimbursement. Finally, in a third step in recurrent negotiations on the same level with the same partners agreements are made about the level of reimbursement for the care provided. The care insurances representing their interests altogether create a kind of 'unified insurance' (Eisen and Sloan, 1996), but the providers as well, as different as they are (big or small commercial or not-for-profit) have to develop consent for negotiation, for example, concerning the type of reimbursement, the differentiation and ranking of care tasks, the spectre of services to be offered, etc. The two main effects are uniformization, a far reaching suppression of diversity and a strong position of the insurances as a unified contract partner.

In order to be aware of the degree and type of this consented administrative uniformization that characterizes this system of provision (which formally builds to a large degree on third sector and commercial provision and could allow for encouraging competition between different styles of caring and helping) one has to know a bit more about the reimbursement system now agreed upon between the insurances and organizations of the providers in nearly all 'Laender'. Care is divided up into hundreds of single tasks and these tasks get lumped together again into modul-packages, with an agreed price for reimbursement of the package and a clear rating of each and every element of the package (with usually low ratings for social tasks and higher ones for medical tasks). Within such a system of contracts about refunding, there is nearly no room for diversity and competition on quality, but an enormous incentive for competition in terms of performing care faster and in a more streamlined way in the framework of a general 'leitbild' of care which is a fairly technical and medical one (Meyer, 1997).

Finally, what is quite remarkable is the fact that the municipalities and the 'Laender', which have after the reform less possibilities to intervene into the care field, rather feel freed from obligations than robbed of rights and responsibilities. They are glad to be able to restrict their part toward a minimum (e.g. additional social assistance payments) and to point at the responsibility of a self regulating system of financers and providers where seemingly no politics at all are needed, because in the new law even the total care budgets are capped—altogether the insurances are not allowed to spend more than what comes in by a fixed unchangeable 2.75 per cent contribution of the insured.

Mainstream Services—Modernizing the Contract Culture in the Area of Institutional Care for Children and Adolescents

The following example is about the contract regime as described in (2b) in Chapter 1.3, with services which have been evolving and routinized for decades. The example deals with care for children without families or which had to be taken from their families and to be cared for and looked after in separate homes. The departments for youth help of the municipalities or districts (representing smaller municipalities) are the partners in negotiating the financing of such homes which in their majority are carried by not-for-profits, but sometimes by commercial partners or the municipality itself. The fact that these services are routinized, shown by the convened standard formulas about the square metres, technical qualities and number of professionals per child— items which can be controlled by a special agency on the level of the 'Land'. In fact, over years the real services had reached a level well above these minimal standards. As it had already been described in the general introduction, the traditional contracts about reimbursement worked with two magic formulas. One was the 'Pflegesatz', that is, the per client care-expenses, defined as the total costs of the institution divided by the number of clients. The other central formula was an *ex-post* cost-coverage obligation. In case the per capita care expenses after a year were higher than one had thought before the deficit became covered by the financing institutions *ex post*. This classical protective type of reimbursement contracts obviously presupposed the idea of a trust-based relationship, where the financing institution trusted that the service providing institution cared for not intentionally causing any additional costs.

In such areas of routinized and mainstream social services the angle point for reforms is the idea, (a) to structure single elements of the services as prized products, comparable with the prices of other potentially competing service-offering organizations, and (b) to come to a contract where costs to be reimbursed and services are *ex ante* defined. Consequently, if the service providing institution does a clever management it can keep savings for reinvestment; losses are a risk which has likewise to be beared by the organization. The general idea behind the overall trend of introducing such 'performance-contracts' should be rather clear—it is about imitating market mechanisms for getting more transparency of cost-performance relationships, more incentives for improvement and more incentives for a kind of entrepreneurial behaviour on the side of the service-providing organization. The main practical problems with this new concept are at present as follows:

- municipal contract partners try to buy just those 'products' which are undeniable; in the course of negotiations the service provider sometimes needed the help of the quality control agency, testifying that for example, a certain ratio of clients/personal suggested for the contract by the representative of the municipality was below the limits;
- the effects of a more entrepreneurial and competetive approach vary; in fact many relationships between municipal financers and service providers have built up over years and in no ways this is substituted

by a system of an open subscription with the competitors offering the best value for money winning the contest; so what one finds is a mix of elements of corporatism and trust-based relations and of economic elements meant to work in an impersonal and 'neutral way'.

In fact, so far there are little signs, that the representatives of the municipalities are able and/or interested, to negotiate for savings by innovations concerning the design of the services and the ways they are institutionalized; negotiatons are mostly for savings for the financing side through slimming the traditional services by only contracting in the undeniable product packages. In all cases it is positive for the financing side that it has not to bear financial risks which are in the new contract system shifted entirely to the providers.

Innovative Service Providers in Marginal Sectors of the Social Service System—Contracting for a Year to Year Survival

In order to understand better some of the problems of small-scale organizations pioneering new services (the contract regime sketched under (2b) in Chapter 1.3) we have chosen the example of an association which started in the end of the 1970s by developing help and advice in psychosocial affairs linked with drug problems. They did it in the country side of Hessen and they were backed by a threefold support: the general concern with the rather new drug problem, the idea in the social ministry to develop a network of advice centres throughout Hessen and the advocacy of university experts. Founding an association for running such a centre needed social entrepreneurs who are a cornerstone for each social initiative which has a weak institutional position. In this case, like in other similar cases, about half of the money came from a model programme of the 'Land' and the other half from the local district and its municipalities. And like in many similar cases, too, the type of contractual arrangement was at the same time generous and pedantic. On the one hand, the money was given as a kind of grant, independent from the number of people helped or assisted; naturally, a yearly report had to be made but no link between the amount of cases performed and grant giving existed. On the other hand, it was typical as well that the grant contract had to be renewed every year, something one could never be shure of. At the same time the rules for the use of funds and the accountance were very bureaucratized; at the end of each year, costs had to be laid for every pencil used and there were tight limits, for example, for shifting money between different sectors, e.g. from expenses for working materials to costs for stuff.

Under the pressure of tight budgets a new system is in the course of preparation. Presently, grants are frozen till the end of 1999 which gives at last some security in scarcity. The shape of the new mode of contracting which is presently prepared so far looks as follows: probably only one-third of the funds will be a grant type support for the institution; about 40 per cent shall be reimbursements for priced types of single items (like counselling) and another third for the delivery of performance packages (like a campaign in local schools against drug use). The associations in the field have mixed feelings; especially the little ones never had the overhead to pay someone for managerial items, which will get more importance in the new contracting system. Already, presently, the social ministry prefers to negotiate with bigger organizations, having experts/social workers as general managers, that were more successful in becoming big, professionalized and differentiated.

The structure of the work and services rendered is more open than ever. What is done and wanted by the ministry, develops without any influence from parliamentary politics. Moreover, what happens in the ministry is not the outcome of a consented strategy, but depends much more on the degree of success of committed individual bureaucrats within the ministry. For the future of the service and its provider, the central point then is, whether there are people who do not just think about how to reduce funding, but as well how to support future oriented trends in the respective service field. The impact of contracts beyond their role for managerial reform depends on clientilistic and personalized relationships with key persons and not on a political controversies or a consented policy.

The missing of a public policy, however, opens up a broad space for the development of private strategies of the initiatives concerned, which can take a more or less political character. There is a growing need for the entrepreneurs in the associations to look for local support and funding which compensates the tightened funds from the ministry and the district. In the case interviewed, a local support club of engaged citizens has been set up with the help of the local mayor; the association seeks for enterprises willing to pay for an anti-drug service and counselling and more emphasis is put on types of help and advice for which one can get reimbursement, for example, from the health insurance. So the new contracts are part of a situation, where there is not anymore the (central ministry-led) idea of building up a fixed reliable service network, perhaps modelled like already existing provision structures, but the idea of supporting (with more control of the funding) a structure which is multidependent and needs to be much more oriented to the demand not of individual clients, but of the institutions and power structures in their local and regional environment.

Building up New Services for New Needs of Special Groups—The Example of AIDSHelp Cologne

Strategies and policies which try to formulate answers toward the AIDS-problem are a good field of example concerning the difficulties to find a consented and contracted place for new initiatives. Many municipalities have created posts of an 'AIDS-Coordinator' networking the many different initiatives, projects and service points and charged with creating a municipal concept; the 'Laender' gives extra money for installing such a post.

Besides what is done in the framework of additional services given by the already established social welfare organizations, new initiatives have emerged, which concentrate exclusively on the challenges of AIDS. These local AIDSHelp organizations have, for example, organized a joint nation-wide emergency call number and belong to federal organizations on the 'Laender' and central state level. Besides, they are as well members in that nation wide social welfare association which is operating as an umbrella organization for all kinds of social associations and initiatives—the DPWV (see 1.1). Germany's biggest local AIDSHelp organization is to be found in Cologne. It is characterized by a considerable pool of volunteers and—besides counselling persons with AIDS and helping them to get service flats—the organization emphasises its role in campaigning and lobbying. For their 120 volunteers they have created special training programmes with a professional coordi-nator. At special weekend sessions potential volunteers are checked first and in case they become accepted, they get a formal contract and a clear job description for their specific task as volunteer.

The organization has financed itself so far by a mix of donations, funding from the local labour office related to work and integration programmes, grants from the municipality and special reimbursement from a social assistance title which allows to repay for counselling special problem groups even if single persons are not means tested.

Getting among other resources municipal grants is advantageous, because one can dispose flexibly on some money which, for example, can be used for overhead costs, not covered by the other programme related sources. The grant comes, however, from the municipal health office which—besides subsidizing local initiatives—has developed own concepts and services in the field of prevention and counselling, too.

Yet, both sides, AIDSHelp and the municipality think it would be better to switch from grants to contracts which specify the tasks to be publicly reimbursed and/or supported. Obviously, AIDSHelp hopes to come to contracts which give a more significant profile and more acknowledgement to those priorities standards and practices it has pioneered by itself. Therefore, it is eager to step into kinds of negotiations which are not only about money and formal conditions, but about concepts and priorities of a local AIDS policy. At the same time AIDSHelp wants to have a contract which is flexible when it comes to the relative weight and share of public money which the consented activities finally get in practice.

However, the municipal AIDS-coordinator has developed likewise a detailed concept and obviously would like to come to change the yearly

300,000 DM from a grant into a number of separate contracts which would secure, that AIDSHelp Cologne has to operate alongside his ideas. He would like to see that implemented by operating solely with programme related funds, where all municipal reimbursements and/or subsidies are clearly linked with seperated time limited programmes. AIDSHelp would then have a multiplicity of single contracts with the municipality.

One of the main problems with such a concept would be the total loss of the 'grant'—dimension allowing for supporting an institution with overhead costs and non-specialized professionals and members. A further problem would be the fact that new activities and programmes could not be started unless they are agreed with the respective representative(s) of the municipality. AIDSHelp Cologne, for example, plans to install a special health agency with another local organization, specialized for AIDS related care services in order to broaden the activities, develop new contact points with the municipality and to get refunding as well from the health insurances. AIDSHelp Cologne would then become more stable and independent by more interdependency with a variety of funds and sources. However, this would be difficult to the degree this has an impact on existing or ought-to-be contracts with the municipality which do not foresee such possibilities.

Negotiations would be furthermore complicated because there are as well other organizations besides the local AIDSHelp which offer AIDS-related concepts and services—drug initiatives, specialized home care services etc. However, each organization has a different spectrum, differing standards and a different organizational context wherein to place measures concerning AIDS. Therefore, it might be both unfair to contract just with one partner, while making an open subscription for a detailed programme would be very challenging for the municipal health office.

However, a major reason for the present stagnation of a potential process of modifying contractual relationships is the absence of democratic politics. The city parliament has not yet come to an AIDS policy-concept; for years local politicians have been avoiding clear statements about what should be done in matters of AIDS, because for them with a broad electorate it is either a highly critical or a not so important question. And therefore, both the detailed concepts of the municipal AIDS coordinator and of AIDSHelp cannot be negotiated and get a real political impact.

Contracting Innovation—How to Safeguard at once Autonomy and Accountability?

At the margins of the highly regulated area of health and care services it is quite well possible to strive for service innovations; because such services for people in high need without insurance based rights are paid from the social assistance funds of the municipalities. Presupposed, one can give a credible promise to the local financing institutions that these innovations will result in savings within a rather short time there is room for experiments and innovations. In order to illustrate how this can work in the social service field a look at another model project in the City of Frankfurt is instructive. It is settled in the area of home care for people who need a lot of time-intensive help and care and are living without family support: people who are demented, live with substance abuse or are for various reasons strongly deso-cialized. Here, the fact to be noted first is that on the one hand institutionaliz-ing them is enormously costly (on the average about 8,000 DM per month), yet on the other hand a German city in contrast to the US perhaps cannot let such citizens go totally unhelped. In case they are not rated as clients with a right on help reimbursed by the new care insurance, the municipality pays services for them from its social assistance funds. However, caring for such people needing very much time to be looked after at home can be more expensive than institutionalizing them; they are legally well-protected against becoming institutionalized against their will and so the city has sometimes to pay sums for service and guarding arrangements in their homes, that are above the costs for institutional care. At the same time, however, the quality provided was so far very meager; no professional concepts and standards had been developed for such type of intensive home care; often, a considerable amount of social assistance funding goes to a commercial service provider for little service quality; it gets paid simply for getting a lay person to stay day and night with the client.

Now two not-for-profit providers have associated and engaged in devel-oping a quality service for such people in need, which entails flexibility of professional help (e.g. no constant supervision but intense help in crisis situ-ations), the activation of their own resources and of informal help; they hope that after some time the clients can do better with less help.

The contract set up between the department for social assistance of the city of Frankfurt and the providing institutions, Caritas and Contact, gives on the one hand some guarantees to the city. The providers promise to develop a quality service for a group of about fifty people which presently cost about 5,000–7,500 DM/month at a per capita price of 6,000 DM, which is an enor-mous sum, but still below the present costs of alternative institutional care. This way, financial safety and a certain degree of savings is contracted in for the city. On the other hand the providers are allowed to use a case manage-ment approach in order to decide for themselves how to distribute over time the total budget they dispose of (as a sum of the individual budgets for the members of the group) in a flexible way between the individual people; sav-ings made by a (temporary) bettering status of some clients can be used in order to compensate for additional or unforeseen costs caused by others.

The problematic aspect of such arrangements which try to combine security/accountability and a sharing of the cost reductions that result from new and more responsive and productive service concepts could be described as follows: it needs either detailed control by the municipality or a very much trust-based relationship between municipality, providers and clients in order to avoid a situation, where the respective clients have just 'chances', but no guaranteed minimal rights (except for being kept out of an institution) for a better treatment. Providers who are not trustful, could, in the framework of the arrangements described before, well work for their own good at the cost of their clients, by caring less for the money received. In the innovation presented here, the kind and level of service the individual client is about to get, remains uncertain and beyond all control. Productivity gains and contracts as just described would perhaps not be possible in a simple quasi market context and even in the example described a lot is left to do, for example, building up independent advocacy for the service users and their rights and concerns as one possible type of quality and resource control.

Surviving as a Not-for-profit and Voluntary Organization in an Environment of Subcontracting and Competition—The Example of the CARITAS in Frankfurt

So far it has been illustrated, what different ways of contracting could mean for service providing organizations; but not-for-profits are about more:

- advocacy for or self-organization and empowering of a specific group;
- a strive for innovation in the framework of a strong idea of the public good;
- professional ethics and the concerns of the users and coproducers.

How can such elements of their identity survive under conditions as described above? With respect to that, one can find two different types of answers. What is presently prevailing is in a way copying what the public administrations are frequently doing. They as well like to substitute the broader challenge of modernizing welfare policies by the one dimension of modernizing the logics of management. Another more rare answer insists on the fact that managerial and political modernization should not be confused but separated. Becoming a modern enterprise is seen as unavoidable, but as affecting just one dimension of one's identity as a civil association.

It is interesting to sketch an example, where a local welfare agency, the Frankfurt Caritas has tried to develop its own idea of how to sharpen its profile as in intermediate institution, intertwining and balancing different tasks and logics (Evers, 1995): (a) the role as a service providing institution, (b) the role as an organization which is stirred by its values toward innovating and pioneering new services for new needs and problems, and (c) the role as an organization which defends the interest of disadvantaged citizens and groups in the light of the social and moral values defended by the catholic church and movement.

Not that Caritas would not always have claimed to do that, but till recently everything was mixed up: economic deals were made with moral arguments and vice versa. This pictured in the financing structure as well. A majority of the Caritas undertakings had a mixed resource structure. The most important part usually comes from public institutions like the municipality or the health or care insurance. Often, various funds from insurers merged with church taxes and sometimes as well with the small sums that come from donations and fund raising. In 1995 with a new director, the Caritas took a clear reform initiative trying to separate the different faces of its 'multiple' identity.

First of all, it has tried since 1995 to enlarge that part of its activities, where the costs of the services which Caritas provides (care for frail elderly people, homes for children and youngsters, kindergartens etc.) are completely covered by the reimbursements agreed in the respective contracts, coming from the social assistance funds, the public budgets or the budgets of the insurances. In established fields of service provision with clear reimburse-ment rules Caritas tries to behave as a competitive provider and subcontrac-tor, arguing for more value for money and the need to manage creatively limited funding instead of going the route of resignative saving strategies.

Secondly, besides the dominating sector of activities where Caritas operates exlusivly on the grounds of public state and insurance funding, the resources which come from church taxes, donations and fund raising are concentrated on self-financed innovative projects, where Caritas feels the need to break new grounds. This happens, for example, by investing in a new concept of commu-nity development or in a concept alternative to meals on wheels: helping as much people as possible to take their meal in a local restaurant. For such and similar activities it tries to use the contact with the local catholic parishes and their readiness for voluntary work and cooperation. People who give money to Caritas can be shown where their money goes. It is naturally hoped that such innovation areas affect the priorities of the local social administration.

A third initiative of Caritas was to set up a local umbrella organization, bringing in a lose way all catholic organizations that work in Frankfurt in the social field, like family associations, associations for specific social purposes etc. together; the aim is to strengthen in Frankfurt a voice and lobby for 'Caritas' not as an organization, but as a purpose to be upgraded and renewed.

Obviously, this lose portrait sketched with a little sympathy just gives an idea about a concept and 'Leitbild'. The problems are manifold. First of all, it might be questionable to separate totally commercial and social areas instead of trying to renew a concept of a kind of intermeshing social and economic rationales in order to reconstruct a 'solidaristic' service economy (Laville, 1994) to (in contrast to charities and voluntary organizations which never had an own economic concept). While the Caritas is confronted with the enormous dominance of the first area, where it understands itself as a 'normal' service provider; there could be well the danger that the other areas of activity will not do more than some 'window-dressing' for this core area.

7.4. CONCLUSIONS

What was to be demonstrated by the six short but illustrative case studies has already been indicated in the introduction and it can be taken up now again in more detail.

Behind the Changes in the Contract Culture—Open Questions Concerning the Future Concept for Services in a Mixed Welfare System

Questions concerning the services to be provided have played a role throughout all the cases portrayed before; the contract making must either reflect a shared service concept or give some room for experimenting specific and situation related types of provision:

- for example, in case 1, concerning the new regime in elderly care, a clear hierarchical service concept has been introduced in favour of items of medical care and at the costs of questions of social help and care;
- in case 2 the traditional service concept was not touched; the struggle was solely about the degree a defined service can be meagered;
- in the cases 3, 4 and 5 however, the special problem has been the development of innovative service concepts; on the one hand the problem is that they are still on the way to take a clearer shape and position; on the other hand their design and funding structure seems—differently to traditional public mainstream services—to develop toward a more 'destandardized', 'localized' and 'mixed' structure; this calls for a wider room and more tasks for negotiating contracts (like in cases 3 and 4) and/or for setting up type of contracts that do not prescribe very much the tasks to be fullfilled, but just set the financial limits (like in case 5);

- for the reorganization of the CARITAS in Frakfurt the differentiation between already established and routinized services on the one and new services to be developed and pioneered on the other hand is a fundamental point of departure.

Summing up one can say that once one conceives public social services as a standard model, the perspectives will differ very much from a perspective where generalized support for innovation or a public contribution which solely secures some basic standards are requested.

A Prevalence of Managerial Concerns and a Quasi-market Model for Regulating State–Third Sector Relationships

As we have stated in the beginning, changes in contract making can be linked with wider questions concerning the future of social services and mixed welfare provision as well as with the more narrow questions of striving for more managerial efficiency. Such managerial concerns are clearly a driving force which is present all over the three areas of social services that we have differentiated. This should not be a surprise and meet with what has been described in various studies. It is driven, too, by a new generation of experts within the non-for-profit organizations; they turn out to be less commited to the corporate creed and often have an economic understanding of their work. The general trend is towards a weaker role of grants for organizations and institutions and a more enlarged role of performance-linked contracts. All the six case studies in Chapter 2 tell this story. There are however different accents in two of them:

- the CARITAS in Frankfurt (case 6) accepts such a system for those areas, where it is acting as a subcontracted organization for the municipality or the refunding health and care insurance; it does not accept it, where it pioneers projects that get support from different sides and where tasks and challenges cannot be easily classified and broken down in quantifyable items; subcontracting marks a part— indeed the most important—but not all of its reality as a voluntary organization;
- the innovative project for intensive home care for persons in high need (case 5) has like wise achieved a considerable autonomy by global budget regulations that save financial and bureaucratic costs for the public authorities; however, a quality oriented control concerning the right use of such client budgets seems to be left here as a task so far untackled.

Summing up, one can say, that there is a shift from a traditional culture of corporatist, often trust based cooperation between providing and financing organizations toward relationships that accentuate a managerial and entrepreneurial role of providers and types of contractual relationships that give less backing in terms of institutional support and more in terms of reimbursements for specified service performances.

This fits rather well with the given prevalence of what might be called a 'quasi-market model' for regulating the relationships between public authorities and service providers in the field of social services (for the early stages of this concept see: Taylor and Hoggett, 1993). This means, that the public authorities and/or the social insurances finance the major part of the services to be delivered and thereby set the grounds for providers of all sorts to engage in this field. Commercial and not-for-profit providers are treated alike as competitors. So far only in the area of elderly care (see case 1) this model has taken clear shape in practice. However, it plays a role as an implicit or explicit point of reference when experts and administrators today think about reforms in other areas of social service organization.

Yet, the reality is still quite different from the assumptions and perspectives of such a model and it can be doubted whether it will pass there unchanged. In the cases 3, 4 and 5, both sides, the public and the third sector operate without a very clear concept of their own role and of that of their partner; for example, in case 4, both sides, the AIDSHelp Cologne and its respective partner in the local administration know what they want to achieve in material terms; but they do not dispose of an outspoken concept, concerning e.g. a fair overall relationship between third sector providers and public authorities. There are three basic problems with taking over the quasi-market model as a general model for regulating public–private relationships in the fields of social services:

- First of all, outside the fields of established social services meant for the mainstream of the population, like child care or elderly care, the challenge is usually to build up or maintain a kind of public help for a special group very much in need; wherever it comes to help special highly needy groups or to pioneer something for new needs, 'competition' and 'user choice' have little impact; a service market can sometimes develop later on, but at the very start, the field itself has to be developed.
- Second, the economic concept of building up a purchaser–provider split governed by the rule of competition has as well only restricted room with respect to practices of open subscription, etc., of the financing public side. Competition can be limited to the interior of established policy networks and corporatisms; competition rests very limited so far partly because of the transaction costs of switching to a new model.

- third aspect is concerning the 'infrastructure' needed by the competing commercial and not-for-profit organizations. While the commercials can usually dispose on a well-developed infrastructure in a market society, this is much more questionable when it comes to third sector organizations; they need a specific civic infrastructure (of private and public commitment) and perhaps solid general public support as civic associations in order to be able to stay competitive in their role as service providers, without their broader role as a civic association being distorted; the future of civic associations acting as service providers on quasi markets will be shaped by the fact whether they can rely on a supportive structure of social capital.

The Freedom of Third Sector Providers as a Result of a Missing Political Commitment of Public Authorities

As it has already been pointed out, in many areas of social services one seems to step into a situation which is marked by a rather low level of purposeful political initiative (in terms of intervention, developing frameworks and concepts) of the public authorities. Very much depends on whether social entrepreneurs, representing social reform ambitions, can be found. The cases 3–6 represented such active and entrepreneurial third sector organizations. Quite often their public partners in the parliaments, administrations or social insurances are however not likewise active political forces, but rather passive. To the degree the public institutions represent potential resources, but no own concepts and priorities, they are regarded by the social entrepreneurs as mere potential 'hosts' for bottom-up social projects. The social initiatives have to be eager to identify and meet certain expectations of the respective authorities (e.g. for savings without much political noise) or to make a proactive link with groups or persons in the 'hosting' administration that are likewise engaged and motivated.

This trend—as illustrated especially in the case studies 3 and 4—however, leads toward changes in the process of political dialogue and negotiation that are questionable: it is then not about finding a compromise between partners with different socio-political concepts and priorities, but about the development of a clever political opportunism, helping each initiative to get individually as much as possible from the political market constitued by their public counterparts.

The public authorities may be just concerned with getting rid of a political and social responsibility at lowest possible costs. In face of partners, which have just such a reduced concern, those social initiatives will win, which serve this interest most sucessfully. Therefore, most negotiations are not about service concepts but about meagering, reducing and streamlining the existing services.

Quite often it seems, as if public policies have lost the ability or even the ambition to monitor processes of opinion building towards shared, viable and reliable visions and concepts ('Leitbilder') for services, to be concretized through mid-term strategies and concepts. In such a situation much depends on informal relationships and alliances with reform minded persons or groups within an administration. However, such type of 'political partner' can give resources and incentives for reform practices but not a reliable social policy framework.

With respect to the service providing (third sector) organizations one can say, that under such conditions, 'social reform entrepreneurs' are central and undeniable; but obviously the 'negative freedom' created by the absence of a public policy restricts their possibilities.

Variations According to the Different Sectors of the Landscape of Social Services

As it has been shown the changes in the contract culture, even though they express themselves very much in managerial terms, are shaped by the different historical backgrounds and contexts in the subsectors of social services:

- in the first subsector, the area of care services, the recent comprehensive reform has created a rather coherent corporatist system of shared government and a quasi market. The consented rules and conditions for reimbursement represent a kind of 'mega-contract'.
- a second different sector is constituted by all those social services like, for example, child care, which are mainstream services with considerable rights assured to the citizens and possible users; here the ideas of creating kind of quasi markets, introducing more open competition where there was traditionally a rather closed shop system have its impact; in that context the ways seem to be paved toward refined systems of political negotiation with a lot of local variations.
- a third subsector, portrayed by us in the case studies 3, 4 and 5 is about services for special problem or 'target' groups, about issues which may be more controversial than mainstream provision and about needs public authorities may be less concerned with; here funding is less stable, routines are often missing and quasi market concepts make little sense.

The overall reluctance of the public authorities to take political responsibility can show differently in all the three fields. In the field of care services an initial investment of the political system now pays off by better chances for local politicians to refrain from former responsabilities; a kind of 'self regulatory system' has been set up. As far as the other social service fields are concerned, policy makers and administrators can restrict themselves to a mere pragmatism of 'muddling through', safeguarding themselves by the contracts made against unforeseen financial results of rights given or actions of service providers allowed, without caring very much about the concepts and quality.

The Nature and Values of Third Sector Organizations

In a way the situations of these organizations can be described as the challenge of at once rebuilding their boat and finding a suitable course on an open sea. The problem with the changing contract culture, is, that often only a managerial language is spoken while in fact all the three dimensions of the roles and identities of voluntary organizations are concerned and get negotiated again. Besides their role as service providers, their roles as value-based interest organizations and as pioneers for new, first of all minoric, social policy and service concepts are concerned. In most cases the development of simple coping strategies to keep up with financial distress overshadows the tasks of rebuilding one's identity as a third sector organization. The paper has presented a number of attempts to step out of this situation on different levels of conceptional clarity: movements like AIDSHelp Cologne (case 4) try rather 'instinctively' to keep autonomy; initiatives like the drug consultancy (case 3), try very much to escape a one sided state-dependency by becoming interdependent with a multiplicity of (societal and local) solidarities; but during our interviews no sign was given that this process of 'learning by doing' is echoed and supported by a wider debate. Finally, the concept of the Caritas in Frankfurt, which tries to separate and possibly reintegrate the different aspects of what makes up for the identity of an 'intermediate' and 'polyvalent' (Evers, 1995) organization seems to express a likewise very developed level of strategic orientation (see for this as a generalized perspective for voluntary organizations: Knight 1993). But our interviews showed that this was more the outcome of the cleverness and experience of its leader at that time than of a broader public reform debate.

On Perspectives

In fact, a theoretical analysis cannot substitute for a so far missing political debate and controversy about the blueprints of a future division of roles and responsabilities in a system of mixed service provision. But it can at least help to disentangle the different questions and challenges which are often confounded or confused when it comes to debate changing ways of contract making between public and third sector partners.

Our analysis suggested that broader social policy questions about contracting and a more narrow concern with modernising contracts as an organizational and managerial instrument should not be confused; wherever the latter is used as a substitute for the former, this will create in one or the other way social and political by effects. However, on this more basic level today in Germany managerial answers seem to be given to questions not even posed (Bönker and Wollmann, 1996).

- The very concept of rights and qualities of future social services remains quite unclear; to what degree should they all develop like the school and hospital system formerly did—into a rather uniform, comprehensive and standardised system? Or does one have to search for a new balance between reliable rights and flexibility, giving services by additional commitments of different social partners (the users, social sponsors, etc.) a much more 'local' flavour, using contracts, which long for such a diversity and taking into account that such an approach will result in more territorial inequalities?
- A consequence concerning the nature of the future partnership between public authorities and third sector providers is partly flowing from that; the degree they should engage themselves as subcontracted providers of public services depends very much on the concept of a public service; it then makes a difference, whether these services are merely part of a centralized provisional system or part of a network, which is simultaneously shaped by the locally different degrees of social solidarities and commitments. In the latter case, third sector providers as intermediate bodies (Evers, 1995) with their ambiguity (Lewis, 1996) which results from the fact that they operate between the world of universal public decisions and a diversity of special communities are kind of 'natural partners'; because then, they can maintain a degree of autonomy by multidependency; basing themselves not exclusively on public funding, but as well on a variety of social capital resources as, for example, public and local support, voluntary commitment and donations is then a specific strength for such an open definition of what a public service should be;
- What are the right institutional answers for taking into account the difference between those service areas where the task is administering routine and evolution and those other service areas, where it comes to develop innovative answers and possibly new rights? Obviously, in both cases different types of contracts are needed.

Different concepts about the nature of a future welfare mix and about future service networks legitimize different types of contract making. And furthermore, the different traditions in various service sectors have to be taken into account as well. What is needed therefore, is the coexistence of different situation-oriented types of contracts—in some cases very complex ones supposing a high level of responsibilities and political dialogue on both sides, and in other cases—for example, wherever it comes to initiate nonconformist service projects—much more lose and 'relaxed' contractual relationships. Perhaps the problem with the present contract culture is not so much rooted in the limited knowledge about instruments and technology, but much more in missing political concern, commitment and finally clarity about the relative impact of different criteria in a given case.

Chapter 8

Spain: Steps Towards Partnership and Marketization*

SEBASTIÁN SARASA AND GUIDA OBRADOR**

8.1. INTRODUCTION

Evaluating institutional reforms in the Spanish social services is not easy. Political decentralization and the paucity of homogeneous systematic data about what and how organizations are doing, makes it difficult to get information about the nascent reforms that were implemented in the 1990s. We have chosen one *Comunidad Autónoma*—Catalonia—because of the availability of data. Nevertheless, a general overview of Spanish social services and the role of the third sector in it, is offered for a better understanding of the institutional and social background.

Catalonia, like the other 17 Autonomous Communities, enjoys full legal competence in social services. Like in many other Communities the social services system is the domain of public responsibility and the initiative of the third sector must be included in the Authorities' planning and be coordinated by the latter. In order to achieve this objective, Catalan social services legislation allows the third sector organizations to participate in decision making as representatives of collective interests. Third sector organizations have operative autonomy

*This work has been possible thanks to the funding of the Ministry of Education and Culture of a more vast research project on 'The Last Resort' (*La última red de protección social en España*, SEC97-1377). Much of this chapter owes its contents to the previous contributions to the project by Elisabet Almeda, Dolors Obiols and Carolina Costa.

**SEBASTIÁN SARASA • Universitat Pompeu Fabra, Dpt. Ciencies Politiques I Socials, Ramon Trias Fargas, 25, 08005 Barcelona, Spain. GUIDA OBRADOR • CRID-Diputació de Barcelona, Salvador Mundi, 6, 08017 Barcelona, Spain.

and are considered now as one of the instruments of decentralization in public services provision. Moreover, the Catalan social services legislation is one of the few in Spain where collaboration with commercial firms is explicitly recognized.

Catalan social services are characterized by the strong presence of the third sector, which in certain fields of action is overwhelming. It caters to almost a half (48.2 per cent) of the entire battery of social services in Catalonia, which are highly heterogeneous, albeit concentrated. A third of these services falls on the Red Cross, the Catholic Church and the Savings Banks. The presence of for-profit organizations is less outstanding, 17 per cent of the places, mainly concentrated where profitable demand can be found, as is the case of old people's homes. Public subsidies to private centres represent a considerable portion of the expenditures of *Generalitat de Catalunya*'s Social Welfare Department. These funds are the result of a policy of subsidies and agreements that over recent years has been complemented by the transfer of the management of some large public agencies to private initiative. This political option has enabled the consolidation and growth of the third sector and the emergence of a new private economy linked to the social services.

In order to get an in-depth knowledge of the effects of the reform we have focused our attention on three fields of services; the programmes for the elderly and for the handicapped and a new programme for long-standing unemployed people which was started in the early 1990s. The first two were established some time ago and are well embedded in the relations with public administrations developed before reform began. The third will probably be institutionalized without the weight of the past. The survey has consisted of several interviews to selected representatives of peak associations of service providers, some individual organizations, and politicians and civil servants of the Catalan government and the Barcelona's City Council. The findings have been complemented by a documentary analysis of legislation, tendering conditions and official statistical data.

8.2. HISTORICAL LEGACY

The background of the Spanish Welfare State[1] is highly conditioned by what was, and was not, done under Franco's regime. Under his dictatorship a meagre, authoritarian social protection scheme was set up inspired to conservative corporatist principles which granted access to social protection only upon prior contributions to Social Security. Within this welfare regime, the few governmental social services provided, were highly centralized and mostly subsidiary to private organizations and family prevention schemes.

Spain's peculiar path to modernization and the lack of democratic freedom during the 40 years of Franco's dictatorship have also conditioned the development of civil society, as well as the relations between the third sector and the

State. In social care, the relations between public authorities and TSOs have been characterized by political patronage, the third sector's financial dependence on government funding and the hegemony of the Catholic Church in social services provision. (Sarasa, 1993; 1995). A historical view of social services in Spain also shows the leading role played by religious organizations within the third sector in the pre-constitutional era, even if, during the transition to democracy, other organizations made their appearance mainly promoted by associative non-confessional movements and headed and run by professionals, families and user groups (Montraveta and Vilà, 1995). After the promulgation of the Constitution and the acknowledgement of the Social State and Rule of Law, a process leading towards greater State initiative was begun. Governmental services greatly increased in importance and throughout the 1980s public opinion assigned a secondary role to third sector organizations. At the same time, profit-making business initiatives were starting, particularly in the services for the elderly (Montraveta and Vilà, 1995). This did not prevent the third sector's consolidation, mainly thanks to its provision of specialized services, although third sector organizations were also authorized to provide primary care services.

Since 1977 the democratic governments have endeavoured to extend coverage of already existing social policies (mainly in health, education, non-contributory pensions and unemployment benefits) but means tested assistance still prevails over universalism. These innovations, particularly in social care, have been a challenge above all for regional and local authorities as law making and social services provision were defined by the Constitution as the competence of the *Comunidades Autónomas* governments.

The results of this evolution have not been very different from those reached in other Southern European countries. Some common features can be identified:

1. *Insufficient provision of services.* The level of both publicly and privately financed resources for residential services, day centres and home care is lower than the European Union (EU) average (Anttonen and Sipilä, 1997). Women, whose employment rate is also lower than the EU average, provide the bulk of social care inside the family.

2. *Means tested services.* Public social services are means tested, thus favouring for-profit provision in residential care and children's care above all. Due to the absence of universal public provision, voluntary organizations have been and still are the main providers for those who are not poor enough to deserve government attention, but are poor enough to be excluded from market provision.

3. *Regional inequalities* both quantitative and qualitative, and different management styles of the services (Room, 1991), are the consequence of high regional decentralization of public services and also differences in modernization and wealth between regions.

4. *Insufficient coordination of policies* between public and private sectors their relationship being largely based on particularism and political patronage (Sarasa, 1995).

8.3. THIRD SECTOR AND SERVICES PROVISION: ACTORS, TARGETS AND RESOURCES

Two kinds of organizations can be found among third sector providers of social services. On the one hand, those that could be defined outsized in terms of resources and social relevance; the most important are the Red Cross, Caritas, some saving banks and the Spanish National Organization for the Blind (ONCE—*Organización Nacional de Ciegos Española*). Each of them is partially specialized in terms of users, and competition between them is relatively weak. On the other hand, there is a variety of medium and small organizations, mainly locally or regionally rooted. As we will see, apart from the biggest, most third sector organizations are financed basically from government funds and the services they provide are complementary to statutory ones. This makes it necessary to clarify who the main public actors are.

Actors

The Spanish Constitution guarantees the decentralization of social services to the *Comunidades Autónomas* (Regional Governments), but the decentralization process has been uneven in terms of speed. The so-called 'historical communities' (Catalonia, Basque Country and Galicia) were the first to be allowed to provide social services. All the others had to wait until 1992, although many of them had their own legislation ready before that time. The legislation on social services initially enacted by *Comunidades Autónomas* in the 1980s gave priority to statutory services and considered the services offered by the third sector as complementary and residual. However, the lack of resources and the need to develop a network of primary care which would regulate the access to the system contributed to the maintenance of the inherited *status quo*, with the bulk of specialized services in the hands of the third sector. The legislative reforms introduced by some *Comunidades Autónomas* in the second half of the 1990s recognized this reality and explicitly abandoned the pretension to take direct responsibility for services provided by civil society.

While *Comunidades Autónomas* are responsible for social services, local governments in municipalities with more than 20,000 inhabitants are responsible for primary care, whereas specialized care is mainly provided by regional and supra-municipal governments. Another important actor has been the Central Government, which together with *Comunidades Autónomas* and municipalities has built a network of primary care services all around the country. The creation of the Ministry of Social Affairs in 1988 represented a landmark in the effort to extend coverage. This Ministry, as well as local and autonomous governments, gave an impulse to mutual agreement plans that would help to consolidate the statutory social services network in those municipalities and regions which could not develop it due to insufficient financial resources and inadequate political instruments.[2] Furthermore, the third sector also benefited from Central Government's funds made available by the 0.52 per cent of the income tax that tax payers decided not to transfer to the Catholic Church.

Sharing Targets

The social services structure of the third sector in Spain is by and large very similar to that of the public sector with respect to target groups. Children, elderly and handicapped people are the bulk of users in both sectors.[3] The proportion of total human resources and money spent by the third sector and public organizations in social services for drug-addicts, AIDS victims and ethnic minorities is relatively small in both sectors. That does not mean that specialized voluntary organizations do not exist. In fact, some of these organizations take care of people that would otherwise be excluded from services provision due to their reluctance to use it. However, civil society as a whole does not seem to be more concerned about these people than public administrations are. This is something likely to happen in a democratic political regime where civil society and political power are interlinked. It becomes more difficult to understand if one accepts the hypothesis according to which the third sector develops where the State fails. This approach tries to explain the existence of the third sector arguing that government tends to provide services for the middle voter neglecting the needs of minorities and, therefore, leaving space to private organizations (Weisbrod, 1988). This could be right in isolated cases in Spain, but it is not a powerful argument explaining the third sector's existence and functions.

There is, however, some kind of division of labour between government and the third sector, the former providing primary care, which is the gateway to entry in the social services system, and the latter providing specialized services to which people can be referred from primary care. Table 8.1 shows the minor role played by the public sector in specialized services for handicapped and elderly people.

The share of specialized services provided by civil society, however, is not the same all over Spain. Generally speaking, it is greater in the North than in the South. Furthermore, the area of the *Comunidades Autónomas* along the Ebro River (Catalonia, Basque Country, Aragon, La Rioja and specially Navarra) stands out against the rest of the *Comunidades*. As Table 8.2 shows, the GDP per capita of each *Comunidad Autónoma* and its capacity to create employment positively correlates with civil society's capacity to produce social services. This means that territorial inequality in services delivery has not been corrected by public intervention, as one can see from the low and statistically

Table 8.1. Places in Specialized Services for Handicapped and Elderly People

Comunidad Autónoma	Handicapped Occupational Centres (Places per 10,000 inhabitants)[a]			Handicapped sheltered workshops Therapy (Places per 10,000 inhabitants)[a]			Elderly Nursing Homes (Places per 100 inhabitants older than 65)[b]		
	Total	Non-profit	Public	Total	Non-profit	Public	For-profit	Private	Public
Andalucía	10.06	7.88	2.18	1.92	0.00	1.74	0.17	1.58	0.76
Aragón	13.40	12.96	0.44	6.82	0.00	6.56	0.26	2.38	1.40
Asturias	7.75	4.72	3.02	6.72	1.15	5.38	0.18	1.77	1.18
Baleares	10.77	10.38	0.39	3.79	0.21	3.38	0.20	1.20	1.94
Canarias	9.03	5.30	3.72	1.09	0.00	0.62	0.47	1.31	0.97
Cantabria	5.46	5.44	0.02	4.30	1.38	2.92	0.00	2.37	0.83
Castilla-León	12.58	8.92	3.66	1.89	0.00	1.07	0.82	2.86	1.45
Castilla-Mancha	8.91	6.25	2.66	0.51	0.15	0.10	0.27	2.36	0.97
Cataluña	10.67	9.71	0.96	9.33	0.36	7.58	1.39	2.75	0.82
Com. Valenciana	6.82	3.99	2.82	1.56	0.00	0.98	0.58	1.43	0.62
Extremadura	11.27	8.96	2.31	3.91	0.39	2.41	1.10	1.28	1.18
Galicia	6.88	6.78	0.10	1.06	0.00	0.48	0.58	1.09	0.43
Madrid	10.81	8.43	2.38	3.69	0.00	3.13	0.55	1.39	0.88
Murcia	10.59	7.20	3.39	1.41	0.27	0.52	0.62	1.17	0.78
Navarra	26.68	24.24	2.44	56.57	27.20	3.77	25.61	3.40	0.77
País Vasco	15.12	11.92	3.20	13.54	3.22	9.16	1.16	1.84	1.18
Rioja	11.51	10.00	1.51	2.38	0.00	1.62	0.75	3.14	1.26

Source: Own elaboration from *Proyección de la Población Española*, 1994. Madrid: Instituto de Demografía, CSIC.

[a] *Guía de centros: relación de centros ocupacionales y especiales de empleo* (1997). Madrid: Escuela Libre Editorial y Fundación ONCE.

[b] Madrid: INSERSO, 1995.

Table 8.2. Correlation Coefficients between Third Sector Provision and Economic Indicators

	GDP per Capita	Available Family Income per Capita	Gini Index of Family Spending	Poverty Rate (below 50% of Average Income)	Older than 65 Rate	Unemployment Rate
Total OTPC places	0.446	0.195	−0.174	−0.331	0.117	−0.449
per inhabitant	0.073	0.452	0.504	0.195	0.655	0.071
Non-profit OTPC places	0.522*	0.305	−0.119	−0.382	0.205	−0.531*
per inhabitant	0.031	0.233	0.649	0.131	0.431	0.028
Public OTPC places	−0.260	−0.395	−0.211	0.170	−0.318	0.279
per inhabitant	0.314	0.117	0.416	0.513	0.214	0.278
Total PJC places	0.415	0.221	−0.272	−0.481	0.113	−0.447
per inhabitant	0.098	0.393	0.290	0.050	0.665	0.072
Public PJC places	0.314	0.136	−0.282	−0.412	0.082	−0.418
per inhabitant	0.220	0.602	0.273	0.100	0.754	0.095
Non-profit PJC places	0.590*	0.412	−0.084	−0.517*	0.165	−0.211
per inhabitant	0.013	0.100	0.747	0.034	0.527	0.417
For-profit PJC places	0.302	0.152	−0.250	−0.372	0.084	−0.429
per inhabitant	0.238	0.561	0.332	0.141	0.748	0.086
Private ENH places per	0.368	0.294	0.026	−0.294	0.588*	−0.496*
inhabitant older than 65	0.146	0.251	0.921	0.251	0.013	0.043
Public ENH places per	0.371	0.287	−0.100	−0.015	0.244	−0.317
inhabitant older than 65	0.142	0.264	0.704	0.953	0.345	0.215
Cáritas spending	0.401	0.137	−0.261	−0.250	0.263	−0.451
per inhabitant	0.110	0.599	0.312	0.334	0.308	0.069

Statistical significance in the second row of each item* Correlation is statistically significant at 0.05 level (Two-tail).

OTPC (Occupational Therapy Centres for Handicapped people).
PJC (Sheltered workshops for Handicapped people).
ENH (Nursing Homes for the Elderly).
Own elaboration from: Fundación FOESSA, *V Informe Sociológico sobre la situación social en España*. Madrid: 1994; Instituto de Demografía, *Proyección de la población española*. Madrid, 1994; Instituto Nacional de Estadística, *Contabilidad Regional de España. Serie 1991–1995*, 1997.

insignificant ratios between number of public places per capita and any other variable. It is beyond the scope of this paper to decide whether economic modernization is the main factor explaining such territorial differences in the third sector provision of social services or whether, as Putnam et al. (1993) suggest, civic community development can explain both economic modernization and institutional performance. We simply confirm the association between third sector provision and economic development, as well as the fact that the public sector does not seem to balance the territorial inequalities derived from it.

Another key element concerning distributive justice is the role played by government and the third sector in reducing inequalities between rich and poor people inside each *Comunidad Autónoma*. It is possible to argue that the third sector shows a different interest from statutory services in richer and poorer people, even though both provide services for the same people. A survey shows that only 50 per cent of the poorest families are users of social services (Rodriguez Cabrero, 1993), a half provided by public agencies and a half by voluntary organizations, the latter being only slightly more oriented towards emarginated people than public ones. Therefore, one can not affirm there is a significant difference between public and private intervention in meeting the needs of the poor.

Third Sector Resources

Public transfers are the main source of third sector funding,[4] exception made for the largest organizations like Caritas, Red Cross and ONCE. The last two derive most of their resources from lottery privileges granted by the State. It is not surprising then, that the economic contribution of Spanish civil society to social services financing is very low. Table 8.3 shows that the biggest and

Table 8.3. Public and Third Sector Shares of Total Spending on Social Services in 1987

Sector	Millions of Pesetas	%
Total public sector	*314.551.9*	*85.85*
Regional governments	71.495.8	19.51
County councils	37.396.8	10.21
Municipalities	19.611.2	5.35
Central government	186.048.1	50.78
Total third sector	*51.836.5*	*14.15*
ONCE[a]	42.416.0	11.58
Savings banks	8.433.0	2.30
Red Cross[b]	987.5	0.27
Total	366.388.4	100.00

Source: Own elaboration from Rodriguez Cabrero (1990).

[a] Lottery spending has not been included.
[b] Red Cross spending is for 1985.

more autonomous organizations' contributions in 1987 (Saving Banks, Red Cross and ONCE) did not exceed 14 per cent of the overall spending on social services, although it should be noted that the contribution of volunteers' unpaid work is not counted.

8.4. HETEROGENEOUS MIXING OF ADVOCACY AND SERVICES PROVISION

Third sector activities are regarded, sometimes in a very naïve way, as a valuable contribution to welfare through their economic and political functions: services provision and advocacy. However, both contributions are frequently assigned to the overall sector and no details are given about how and when they mix in the same organizations, and their effects on organizational behaviour. Our intention is to distinguish between those two organizational goals in order to see whether the mixing of advocacy and provision functions in the same organizations can be associated to a larger role of the market in social services. To this purpose we will analyse three different niches of social services in Catalonia.

Services for Handicapped People

As far as services for the handicapped are concerned, the third sector certainly takes the lion's share. The public sector is important in the provision of residential care and specialized care centres, but in no case does it exceed a fourth of the entire offer (see Tables 8.4 and 8.5). The only service which is totally statutory is the Observation and Assessment Teams, which is obvious if one bears in mind that it is by them that a person's degree of disability is measured, and hence he/she becomes entitled to social care.

Table 8.4. Places in Residential Accomodation and Day Centres for Handicapped People

Centres for the Handicapped	Total places	Third Sector	%	Profit-making	%	Public Sector	%
Occupational centres	6.759	5.950	88	—	—	809	12
Handicapped people's homes	1.765	1.589	90	40	2.3	136	7.7
Specialized care centres	1.127	845	75	—	—	282	25
Nursing homes	2.608	1.480	56	450	17.3	678	26
Total	12.259	9.864	80	490	4.0	1.905	16

Source: Map of the social services in Catalonia, Department of Social Welfare, 1996.

Table 8.5. Other Service Equipments for Handicapped People

Kind of Services	Total Number of Equipments	Third Sector		Public Sector	
			%		%
Early stimulation	57	39	68.4	18	31.6
Occupational integration services	84	74	88.1	10	11.9
Observation and assessment equipments	13	—	—	13	100.0
Total	154	113	73.4	41	26.6

Source: Map of the social services in Catalonia, Department of Social Welfare, 1996.

Compared to other groups of social services users, the handicapped are the best organized self-help group. Services have mainly been in the hands of non-profit organizations due to the inadequate provision offered by public authorities and the market. During the last years of Francoism, some families with handicapped members decided to take the initiative to fight the initial inertia. This action was later complemented by innovations introduced by professionals trained by the organizations themselves who took on leadership in the sector. In the case of mental illness, for example, the period of highest creative growth in terms of technical equipment was between 1974 and 1982, coinciding with the years of the country's transition to democracy. It was during those years that more than half of the facilities existing today were first set up. Despite its relative dynamism, this initiative has shown insufficient growth capacity to absorb the entire potential demand, despite the fact that the handicapped people's organizations have achieved a relatively high degree of federation and coordination in comparison with other groups (Sarasa and Martinez, 1996).

A different matter altogether is the situation of the blind. Organized under the protection of the National Organization for the Blind (ONCE) the State granted them the privilege of running a lottery that has enabled the ONCE to become an extremely powerful organization controlling all services for the blind as a monopoly.[5]

Services for the Elderly

At the end of the francoist regime, the development of community social services for the elderly was scarce and there were practically no home care services at all. Consequently, the care of the elderly fell above all on their families and, to a lesser degree, on for-profit and charitable nursing homes. Later on, the local and autonomous authorities gave an impulse to the development of centres in the larger towns and cities. Nevertheless, the insignificant initial provision meant that the shortage of residential and community services for the elderly is still acute, above all if we bear in mind that most of the people living in these homes are destitutes, especially women. Many private residential homes lack the necessary conditions of hygiene and habitability, and the number of places available is still insufficient as provision only covers 2 per cent of the population over 65 years of age.

As one can see from Table 8.6, nowadays, services for the elderly are provided in a somewhat equal proportion by public authorities, the third sector and profit-making organizations, the last mainly concentrating on residential care, whereas public initiative is more relevant in home care and leisure clubs. As for the organizational structure of the third sector organizations, leisure clubs are run by associations created during the last 10 years with the support of town halls and savings banks, whereas residential care is supported by foundations and traditional religious institutions (Vidal, 1992). Both have a very low degree of coordination and federation, which affects their ability to directly influence policy making.

According to estimates made by Vidal (1992), in the field of the elderly and old people's homes and leisure clubs between 60 and 70 per cent of the current spending comes from self-financing. It must be underlined that the largest part (60 per cent) of the financial resources contributed by the Catalan civil society to welfare services is concentrated on old people's homes. The case of the leisure clubs is different. The premises are usually provided by the Town Halls, but the Savings Banks contribute some 40 per cent of the expenses. Hence, the leisure clubs cover their expenses with private money, but the equipment and investments are statutory.

One peculiarity worth noticing about third sector organizations is the radical distinction between associations run by the elderly themselves and non-profit organizations that provide services. Different from what happens with the Handicapped, it is unusual for the organizations providing social services to be set up and run by associations of the elderly as such. Furthermore, the degree of viability and political capacity of elderly associations is inferior to

Table 8.6. Supply of Social Services for the Elderly

Centres for the Elderly	Total Places	Third Sector	%	Profit-making	%	Public Sector	%
Day care centres	2.351	877	37.3	201	8.5	1273	54.2
Residential care	35.855	11.017	30.7	14.245	39.7	10.593	29.6
Leisure clubs	689	357	51.8	—	—	332	48.2
Total	38.895	12.251	31.0	14.446	37.1	12.198	31.9

Source: Map of the social services in Catalonia, Department of Social Welfare, 1996.

that of the organizations of the handicapped. The political power of elderly people comes from their weight in terms of vote, but not from their capacity to organize themselves, provide services, and make policy proposals.

Inter-departmental Minimum Income Programme: A New Last Safety Net

In 1990, a minimum income programme was set up for the first time in Catalonia. One year before, a similar programme had been started in the Autonomous Community of the Basque Country, and little by little all the Autonomous Communities in Spain have adopted it. The programme known in Catalonia as the 'Interdepartmental Program of Minimum Income' (*Programa Interdepartamental de la Renda Mínima d'Inserció*, PIRMI) is the latest government policy aimed at providing financial help to people who have lost or never had, a right to contributory social security pensions. This programme is organized jointly with the government's de Catalunya's Departments of Labour and of Social Welfare. Its object is to ensure a minimum income to people in a situation of extreme poverty who, in exchange, commit themselves formally to an individualized plan of social and occupational integration drawn up by social workers and experts. Therefore, it is not a form of social benefit of the kind existing in some European countries. It is rather an attempt to offer economic assistance—once the need is recognized—in exchange for allowing social workers to make a close follow-up of the beneficiary family, whose members are asked to make certain efforts deemed essential to a better social integration.

Close collaboration between Public Authorities and the third sector organizations in managing services is another feature of the 'PIRMI' in Catalonia. This collaboration concentrates, above all, on the specialized services of the social–occupational programme. As regards collaboration in intake services, TSOs only followed up 5 per cent of the total number of applications. This limited participation, however, is very important because it makes access to the programme possible for some groups, like the homeless and gipsy communities that traditionally have remained outside statutory social services. The Generalitat's intention is to build a public network able to identify the needy and follow up the applications for minimum income, granting private initiative a complementary role in social and occupational programmes.[6]

The typical users of this programme are people excluded from the regular labour market, amongst whom we frequently find people with serious health problems, drug addiction and emarginated people without social and family ties. Single women with relatives to look after and unemployed men are the bulk beneficiaries, plus many who work sporadically in the black economy with little social acknowledgement.[7] Hence, this is a group of very poor people who have little capacity to organize themselves and make their voice heard by public opinion. Their advocates have been social and religious groups, especially Caritas. This Catholic organization was a pioneer in sociological studies on poverty in Spain and one of the main services providers for people excluded from governmental social services.

This programme was the result of several factors. (a) First of all, the imitation of other European countries which had raised the issue of social exclusion and started a debate leading to experiences such as the French REMI, which greatly influenced Spain. (b) Secondly, the studies on poverty made by Caritas, which aroused controversy on a problem that both politicians and public opinion prefer to forget. (c) Last but not least, the General Strike called by the main trade unions in 1988 against the unequal distribution of costs and benefits in the economic restructuring.

The Generalitat de Catalunya set up this programme as a result of trade unions' pressure following hard negotiations with different organizations specialized in services for the destitute. In short, this brief background of the minimum income programme shows it owes little to the users' capacity of civil pressure but a lot to the influence of foreign experiences and the intervention of trade unions and philanthropic organizations.

Summary

As a result of the analysis of these three niches of social services one can conclude that the third sector plays a crucial role in the provision of social services. However, services provision should be distinguished from advocacy. Sometimes these functions go together in the same organization, sometimes they do not. Trade Unions have played an important role in promoting the regional minimum income placement programme, but their role as social service providers is insignificant. In the same niche, civic and religious organizations merge provision and advocacy but they can not be considered the direct representatives of destitute people, and neither can the unions. A different case is that of the organizations for the elderly. There is here a sharp division between service providers, both for profit and non-profit organizations and the associations which try to defend the interests of the elderly in general, but which play a minor role in service delivery. A different case is that of the organizations for the disabled, where advocacy and services provision activities are usually mixed and where users, their families and professionals sit on the boards of the organizations.

8.5. INSTITUTIONAL REFORMS IN PROGRESS: DELEGATION OF POWERS OR SHARED GOVERNMENT?

Institutional reforms concerning the relationships between the State and Civil Society are seen from a different perspective depending on the observer's ideological sympathies. Radical liberals and conservatives argue in favour of a reduction in public expenditures and an increase in civil society responsibilities through the extension of the social services market and private philanthropic action. Leftist observers show little confidence in the reforms that they identify with the anti-Welfare State right-wing proposals. In the middle, the centre–right and centre–left positions see reforms as a means to save the Welfare State, increasing its efficiency by decentralization procedures. So one can identify two possible results of the reforms depending on the observer's point of view. One, shared by radicals both from the left and the right, emphasizes that reforms go, or should go, depending on the political bias, towards public delegation of responsibilities in Civil Society and competition among market actors. The more centrist view announces a process of relative privatization but in a context of state-regulated markets and shared government between the State and Civil Society.

Are reforms in Spain triggering a process of 'delegation of powers' or of 'shared government'? It is difficult to answer these questions without clarifying such concepts as 'delegation' and 'sharing'. Delegation of public responsibilities should mean a reduction in public expenditure and privatization of public services provision. Shared government implies coordination between public and private sectors without any reduction in the planning, financing and regulating functions of public administrations. Available data do not yet allow a clear evaluation, but they continue to be the object of our analysis.

Public Expenditure and Privatization Trends

Public expenditure in social services constantly increased through the 1980s. The social services share of the whole Generalitat de Catalunya budget rose from 2.23 per cent in 1982 to 2.68 per cent in 1988.[8] Social services expenditures grew at an average annual rate of 12 per cent, almost twice the average rate of expenditure growth in the years 1992–1995.[9] Statutory social service expansion began to decline in 1992 and has continued to this day. Initially, this decline coincided with a period of economic depression but it is not correct to say that budget restrictions are only due to economic slumps. In fact, the early 1980s saw a fast increase in social services expenditure, in spite of the recession.[10] Political factors also influence budget cuts. One cannot forget the pressures for the reduction of public deficit made by the European unification process that imposed restraints on public expenditure and a privatization policy aimed at balancing the budget. Can this be regarded as a delegation of public responsibilities? There is no doubt that, at least in terms of expenditure, public responsibilities have grown more slowly in the 1990s than in the 1980s. The question now is whether these public expenditure constraints are an ad hoc solution to enter the EU or whether it signals the beginning of a new scenario of massive delegation of public responsibilities. At the moment, no political coalition in government is explicitly announcing a radical cut in welfare budgets.

With respect to the privatization process one can identify several options. (a) Privatizing services management but maintaining their ownership public. In this case privatization means a new way of promoting efficiency but without a delegation of responsibilities. (b) Privatizing the ownership of services. In such a case the delegation of power is acute and can only be partially compensated by a strong public regulation of services provision. There exists, though, another way of reducing the influence of the public sector in welfare without privatizing the existing services; limiting public growth while promoting new private services, in such a way that in the long term the balance between public and private sectors will change in favour of the latter. This strategy is easier to implement in residual welfare states, like the Spanish one, where public services are fewer than in more institutionalized ones.

With the statistical information available at the moment, it is not easy to support these options with quantitative data. But our survey suggests that, what is being implemented, at least by regional and local Catalan governments, is the privatization of public services management, with public authorities keeping their legal ownership. The public administration has built a kind of quasi-market by accepting tenders from for-profit and third sector organizations.

At the same time, new public programmes have been institutionalized— as is the case of the PIRMI already described—and the Department of Social Welfare's Action Plan for the next few years announces the integration of organizations from the third sector into the governmental social services network. This integration could be interpreted as a greater statutory regulation over the third sector and the maintenance of public subsidies. But, at the moment, some experts criticize public subsidies for not covering the total cost of the services provided by third sector organizations. These analysts also consider that subsidies to the third sector should be restricted to a given, limited number of activities and not become the main form of financing social services. In this latter scenario, it is argued, grants degenerate into an instrument by which public authorities can transform citizens' rights into an optional and contingent offer that the government can change at will (Vilà, 1997).

Steps Towards Shared Government

The Social Services Bill has made it compulsory to create new Participation Councils, of an advisory nature, with the participation of representatives of the third sector, political representatives, and public authorities experts. Even so, the third sector representatives are always a minority when it comes to voting. This means that the power of third sector in these advisory councils to influence public programmes is limited. However, the role of these Councils, mainly composed by people from the political world, is that to provide information about its actions and promote welfare values and cooperation between the state and the third sector. The function of the Councils is uneven, depending on factors such as the ideology of the governing party and the degree of enthusiasm and leadership skills of politicians. There are Councils whose function is purely ritual whereas others, such as that of Barcelona's City Council, which is governed by a centre–left political coalition, are seriously committed to citizens' participation.

As for the third sector's role, it depends to a large degree on the level of social recognition of its organizations and their political influence. Social groups with needs that go beyond class boundaries, such as the handicapped and the elderly, have more power than poverty stricken groups. The handicapped have shown great ability in creating their own services, and that has encouraged Public Authorities to promote forms of close collaboration. The elderly have created associations to defend their interests, but only a few to provide services which are the domain of the third sector organizations and private firms. The poor have done neither of these things; their interests are indirectly represented by trade unions and religious/non-religious organizations delivering services for the long-term unemployed.

Summary

Public social expenditure keeps growing, but at a slower rate. This slow growth is affecting both citizens' rights and the solvency of some of smaller voluntary organizations, which are trying to obtain resources from the bigger ones.[11] At the same time, privatization processes are limited to the management of public services, and regulation seems to grow hand in hand with a slow and uncertain growth of citizens' participation Councils. These changes can be understood, at the moment, as a way to improve the efficiency of the public sector and to promote coordination of services providers more than as a way to reduce its deficiencies. However, the development of the Councils is still too limited to speak of shared government. Furthermore, keeping or increasing the budget restrictions on social services might mean that in the future the State gives up responsibility, leaving Civil Society to care for itself, regardless of its capacity to do so.

8.6. THE EFFECTS OF GREATER PARTNERSHIP AND MARKETS

Sociological literature on organizational isomorphism argues that in consequence of the pressure of the State and the market, third sector organizations tend to become more alike, sharing bureaucratic procedures, administrative means–end rationality and a narrow value-base. As a consequence altruism, on which the third sector is grounded, can decay along with the comparative advantages it brings about.

There is no doubt that the role of the market in social services and cooperation between third sector organizations and public administrations have grown since the end of the dictatorship. Whether these pessimistic hypotheses have come true or not is an empirical question that is hard to answer due to the lack of data. What our research can offer are the actors' views and how they evaluate the process and its consequences. Obviously, we do not assume the interviewed have perfect information to properly evaluate the good and bad consequences, but they are relatively well informed given their position as professional staffers and representatives in public and third sector organizations. Furthermore, through them one can grasp a few things which are a key to understanding what sort of climate can fuel or resist reforms in one direction or another.

Some preliminary words must be said about the hypotheses that warn about the dangers threatening third sector. A considerable proportion of the scientific literature sees third sector organizations as more efficient in producing welfare for economic and political reasons. Economically, third sector organizations deliver services that state and market fail to provide and they do so in a less costly, more flexible and innovative way. Politically, third sector organizations are the backbone of democratic regimes. They allow political and cultural options to be channelled, contributing to influencing public opinion and policy-makers' agenda.[12] Some sociologists, Etzioni (1973) among them, consider third sector organizations as an alternative to the market and the state combining advantages from both without their disadvantages. Third sector organizations, like firms, are supposed to be flexible, innovative and non-bureaucratized. At the same time, they do not pursue profit maximization.

The third sector is supposed to be ruled by an organizational logic different from both state logic and market logic. Third sector organizations are characterized by high levels of informality, altruism and solidarity in the relations among their members and supporters (Powell and Friedkin, 1987). Their goals are not simple and unique, but heterogeneous and even conflicting among them. In fact, they would be governed more by values than by means–end rationality. This would imply third sector organizations are less subject to criteria of efficiency in providing services and explains their enormous capacity to survive over time.[13]

With this organizational logic at the core of the third sector, the pressures to modify it by the state and/or the market could have catastrophic consequences. There is a long tradition in social sciences of studying conflicts of value vs. means–end rationality, bureaucratic against informal relationships and, finally, altruism against self-interest. Titmuss' seminal work on blood donations stressed this confrontation in social policy alternatives, asserting that the market corrodes altruism, the last being more efficient.[14]

Since privatization strategies and quasi-markets have become a common feature in the social policies of many countries, many arguments have been added to deny the corrosive effects of the market logic on altruism. Ware (1990) has argued that third sector organizations are copying organizational styles from business firms in order to obtain resources from them. The consequence of isomorphism could be to deter volunteers, who would feel unattracted to the hierarchical and bureaucratic forms characterizing big organizations. Along the same lines, Wuthnow (1991) suggests that privatization processes have generated more centralized control over third sector organizations and radical ideologies have changed their goals and objectives. The increased cooperation between third sector organizations and the state and the market has brought about more bureaucracy and centralization, whose consequences are often inefficient and ineffective policies and a total lack of creativity so that the voice of new interests and ideas can not emerge except through alternative movements. Technocratic criteria of efficiency only evaluating a form of output easy to measure and instrumental rationality have blurred the borders between third sector organizations, public agencies and for-profit firms. This transformation is deterring people from collaborating altruistically with third sector organizations and represents the main threat to the third sector. Volunteers are not looking for efficiency but for a kind of human relationship that professional life and bureaucracies deny them.

These supposed dangers of quasi-markets for the third sector are fuelling the debate about whether privatization should seek to promote cooperation or competition between voluntary organizations. Many sociologists think that the third sector should resist the pro-competitive forces of public contracting, while many economists recommend competition.

In order to be able to evaluate the reforms made by the main actors, we will focus on a few aspects. Each of them can be summarized in one question. First, is market logic growing in the sector? If so, are cooperation and coordination among actors being eroded by competition? Third, are partnership and/or competition relationships reducing the quality of services in favour of cost reduction in a context of public expenditure restrictions? Fourth, are stronger links between third sector organizations and public agencies producing more bureaucracy and professionalism? Fifth, if this happens, does it really mean a loss of the identity of third sector organizations, a deterrence of volunteers and a reduction of the comparative advantages of third sector organizations? The people interviewed seem to think that the market and competition are growing in social care but they only affect the third sector in a very selective way. At the same time, bureaucratization is increasing, along with identity conflicts inside organizations. Notwithstanding this, it seems that altruism is not affected, at least as long as voluntary organizations are successful in implementing strategies aimed at promoting it.

Selective Progress of Markets and Competition

The market can influence public social services in two ways. First, by increasing individual and family demand and second getting the State to become the main purchaser of services through tendering processes. Both ways need a great deal of support from public agencies. In the first case, public funds must be transferred to families to increase their purchasing power and/ or to providers in order to reduce the costs they have to bear. In the second, public administrations delegate management to private bodies which, together with governmental agencies, manage tenders for public services. Both ways are being followed in Spain, but selectively.

Tendering causes quasi-markets to grow in social care, independent of the political ideology of local governments. This means giving better opportunities for cooperatives of professionals and for-profit firms to deliver state-subsidized services. But competitive tendering is not the only way in which non-profit organizations get funds from public administrations. Interest associations are financed mainly by grants, while non-profit providers enter into a partnership with the public sector with the purpose to obtain funds through agreements on joint programme development. These agreements are judged unsatisfactory by voluntary organizations due to the uncertainty of the income and the financial precariousness derived from the systematic delays in the transfer of public funds.

Third sector attitudes to quasi-markets vary depending on the nature of the organization. Associations for the elderly show little interest in and knowledge of the subject while handicapped associations and cooperatives collaborating in the Minimum Income Programme are better informed and more concerned with the problem. The latter group is more involved in delivering services, and the selective use of several kinds of public transfers explains their different concern. The selective use of grants, partnerships and quasi-markets seems to depend on the kind of services and above all on the structure and nature of providers. In the case of the elderly, for example, it is not common to find interest associations delivering residential services as happens with the handicapped organizations, where in many cases the borders between services provision and advocacy are blurred. Third sector organizations mainly consist of handicapped people, their families and professionals, therefore partnership relationships and grants are more common than tendering due to the political costs government should have to bear if it denied funds to an organization providing services to its own members. Something similar happens when organizations have deep social roots and are value-oriented, as in the case of Caritas. It seems that the less the third sector organizations are based on values and advocacy, the more common tendering becomes, unless tendering becomes a rhetorical formalism to hide trust and political patronage. Given the situation it is not surprising that quasi-markets and for-profit firms have grown up in the provision of statutory services but the former have been less successful in establishing a relationship with public administrations. It is also not surprising that the associations for the elderly have been less concerned with management reforms.[15]

The development of markets through the promotion of individual demand is also going on in a selective way, although there are signals announcing it is becoming more and more common. In some programmes, especially those for elderly people, allowances are granted to families that can decide where to get the social services they need. Furthermore, some local governments and the Ministry of Labour and Social Affairs are considering the introduction of vouchers as a way to promote employment and face the emergence of jobs in the black economy.

The reaction of the third sector in the face of this new trend towards markets is ambiguous. On the one hand, many organizations would like to change the current methods of financing based on discretionary annual subsidies, and they would like to be more involved in the public services network via pacts with public authorities. However, some organizations fear greater integration will mean a loss of autonomy. On the other hand, certain interviewees believe subcontracting via tender and direct grants to families can also be an alternative to the current situation as they trust the quality of their own services and know for sure the supply is insufficient. Nevertheless, there are certain fears that this strategy could open the way to mercantile enterprises. Private firms are viewed with some apprehension due to their ability to force costs down and the risk of greater discrimination against non-profitable users. Apparently, there has been insufficient debate on the issue and the third sector is still lacking a consistent opinion, possibly due to the fact that it is still a rather novel experience, not extended throughout the country. But everything seems to indicate that the use of selective market procedures will increase as no strong opposition to them has been detected.

Is the growing use of the market logic increasing competition and eroding cooperation among agents? In order to answer this question it is necessary to clarify the concepts of competition and coordination. It is assumed that partnership is the realm of cooperation and the market is that of competition, but such a sharp distinction does not seem to be correct. The fact that relationships between the third sector and public administrations are mainly based on subsidies and not on market mechanisms does not prevent the various organizations from competing for resources. But this competition is based on the ability to wield political influence and develop personal relationships with civil servants and senior staff in the public sector. In the interviews, the leaders in the sector frequently recognized that political affinity with the governing political coalition is very important when it comes to obtaining resources. Some highlighted the importance of offering new services that nobody else is offering. This is an incentive to innovation that arises out of market processes.

Growing Bureaucratization

Closer collaboration between the third sector and public administrations is resulting in greater demand for efficiency, accountability and professionalism, but it is not clear how services quality is being affected. Management economics is often mentioned by political leaders talking about cutting down expenses and reducing public deficit. One of the general goals of the Generalitat de Catalunya's Social Services Plan for the period 1997–2001 is the efficacy and efficiency of resources, and certain policies to ensure this are being implemented in the field of services for the elderly and the handicapped.

Apart from the content of the projects, tendering processes require that certain administrative objectives are reached, the most significant of these being the supervision of access criteria and certification. The latter refers to inscription in the Register, which is subject to the inspection of the autonomous government and has the function of controlling a level of 'minimum quality'. The certification confirms that the conditions of the infrastructures comply with the regulations in force. Furthermore, it requires that the applicant provides its activity programme, indicating its objectives as well as its internal regime, a financial-economic study of the viability of the service and information on the staff, including job contracts, working hours, category and qualifications. In subsidizing private initiative through tenders governments use these requisites as 'quality assurance' methods. Similarly, financing through homogeneous modules (the amount of which has been 'frozen' in recent years) irrespective of the performance of the service means there is little incentive for quality. It could be said that quality is something taken for granted or impossible to measure rather than a goal to be achieved. This interpretation is suggested by the fact that inspection and control of social services mainly regard the condition of the facilities and the respect of the rights and duties of the users. This explains why some interviewees who receive subsidies say that the authorities are not very interested in the quality of the services provided and the data requested to assess the quality of the performance mainly concern quantifiable aspects. Moreover, they think that the demand for quality is incompatible with government's intention to cut subsidies.

All that has been said does not imply qualitative aspects are entirely neglected in the authorities' decisions. Government officials at Barcelona's City Council said that in a contracting out procedure quality is a fundamental parameter, especially as regards the number of hours dedicated to the public. In the case of the Minimum Income Programme, the government has begun to implement a strategy of occupational placement according to which tenders are run among social placement programme-associated organizations for rehabilitation financed by the public sector. In these tenders, all the organizations competing for the programme are supposed to present a budget of the same amount. In this way there is no risk of the tender being won by the providers making the cheapest bid. As all of them make the same price, the quality of the project is what really matters. Something similar occurs in subcontracting services for the handicapped. Some organizations, although running services contracted by public authorities, are not compelled to compete with others but are pre-selected on grounds of quality or their affinities with the governing team, irrespective of costs. At times they do have to compete, but this does not mean that the provider quoting the lowest price is always the one to be selected.

Obviously costs are important. Indeed, budgetary limitations condition which services can be offered and which cannot, and also affects the quality of the welfare services delivered by third sector organizations. Many of them are unable to develop all the services they consider necessary, as they cannot find the necessary funds. Moreover, in certain fields of services a set sum per user is granted. This happens with social–occupational placement organizations in the 'PIRMI'. This form of subsidy can have negative effects, as the quality of the service provided is not taken into account. Hence, whereas for some voluntary organizations this may be an advantage if they spend their subsidies on low-cost activities, for others who would like to offer higher quality services the amount is insufficient.

In short, budgetary restrictions and difficulties in measuring the output of the services tend to make the issue of quality secondary, but this cannot be said to be the result of market procedures. There are sufficient indications that when these procedures are applied, the purchaser's trust in the provider is a factor as important as the cost of the service offered or even more important. The quality of services is supposed to be guaranteed mainly through input control due to difficulty measuring output. The result is an increase in professionalism and bureaucratization. Albeit with unequal development depending on the type of service involved, legislation in force has promoted the professionalism of the personnel in charge of the social services. Professionalism is measured on the basis of the qualifications demanded and the proportion of paid personnel in the different types of services while little emphasis is put on forms of assistance and orientations in the work itself. Residential services and those concerning the occupational integration of the handicapped are the ones which require more specialization as workers have to perform many tasks that usually involve health caring. In short, from a formal viewpoint, the government is pressing for more professionalized human resources in social services, irrespective of their qualifications.

Identity Conflicts and Growing Volunteering

Efforts made in producing services and negotiating public transfers reduce energies for advocacy and threaten the identity of organizations. On the other hand, organizations highly committed to certain causes and created with the purpose of delivering services to the needy, with little or no ability to organize themselves, are becoming the defenders of the interests of these people as their own financial resources and social relevance increase. In this sense it should be noted that collaboration in the management of public services provides resources which are indispensable to influence public opinion, and advantage some organizations as long as they remain committed to their values. The question then is whether closer collaboration with public administrations and access to public transfers empower organizations and help them to get resources that they did not get before. In general, bigger organizations are supposed to have greater capacity for public opinion mobilization than smaller ones.

In the case of organizations providing services to the handicapped, the threat of losing identity is deeply felt by board members. When asked about the emergence of conflicts between their role of defender of the group's interests and specialization in services co-financed by the authorities, the interviewees immediately replied the conflict did indeed exist. Several factors were brought forth to explain how the relationship with the authorities, and above all the issue of financial dependency, was undermining the identity of third sector organizations, by which they meant their capacity to express the needs of the group they represented.

The organizations dedicate a large part of their time to negotiations with different government representatives. Financing is the core of the deals. Budgetary allowances, the amount of the modules and the granting of funds to the organizations for different concepts are fertile grounds for disagreements between the representatives of the government and those of the third sector as well as within the latter.

Furthermore, the conditions imposed by the authorities on access to funds make professional management increasingly important. Tasks like accounting, accountability, working out statistics and indicators on the users, drawing up reports, preliminary drafts and documentary accreditation all take up a lot of the more specialized managers' time. On the other hand, planning and organizational strategies are often neglected as the staff are absorbed in everyday matters.

Another administrative aspect decisive for defining the role of third sector organizations as defenders of particular interests, is the criterion on which subsidy allocation is based, above all with regard to the needs of the handicapped. The organizations for the handicapped are compelled to renounce projects, objectives and methodologies that do not suit the government. They have to adapt to criteria they do not always share, sometimes giving up what they consider the group's needs. The priorities of the group they represent become secondary with the subsequent weakening of their role in presenting proposals and requests.

Finally, the changing role of third sector organizations has a lot to do with their difficulty to express freely, the conflicts within the sector and, especially, those with public authorities. They fear governmental funds could be reduced if their voice became too critical. Furthermore, some representatives of third sector organizations think that if direct payments to users become more common, organizations will be less and less able to make their voice heard, and their struggle to assert the group's rights will certainly become less successful.

In the case of the PIRMI, the social placement programme organizations run the risk of losing their identity as defenders of the poor and the unemployed and of becoming providers of profit making services. However, according to public administration experts, the advantage is for third sector organizations a better and more realistic view of the problem. This is already happening in some organizations working on the implementation of the programme that are abandoning their advocacy role. Many even agree that it would be advisable to adopt market mechanisms in collaborating with the public sector, as they consider themselves very efficient and do not want to depend on discretionary annual grants. Apparently, losing identity is not a problem with large organizations with a strong ideological commitment like Caritas, some of which refuse to collaborate through subcontracting mechanisms as they prefer to maintain their autonomy and consider subcontracting a strategy for the State to delegate its responsibilities. In short, it seems that a closer collaboration with the State, although unavoidable due to the lack of their own resources, is seen by non-profit organizations more as a serious threat to their identity than as a neutral source of income.

The commitment to values also seems to be a necessary condition to keep volunteers on track, and a certain sociological literature warns us that rising bureaucratization threatens volunteering. But how serious is this danger? One of the government's policies, over recent years, has been to encourage voluntary work in social services. These policies have coincided with campaigns launched by different bodies to attract volunteers, and volunteerism is still one of the main resources for many third sector activities. Whatever the case, one of the most evident effects of the many campaigns carried out is that lately volunteerism has become a subject for public debate.

In the current setting of unemployment and increasing precariousness of the labour market, it is not always easy to distinguish between voluntary dedication to a service and occupational placement strategies. The presence of students and unemployed professionals with hardly any experience among the volunteers attending to the handicapped has generated tensions concerning the recognition of their work. Being aware that they are, in fact, providing personal services such as those which are the domain of the new professions some volunteers have asked for a job contract. The problem is made worse by the growing participation of profit-making firms in the scenario of subcontracted public services. In this sense, the College of Social Workers (El País, 28th December 1997) denounces the occupational precariousness in which these workers find themselves, as well as professional quackery and the lack of professionalism of many 'volunteers' staffing jobs involving a high degree of responsibility.

This problem is tackled differently by different organizations. In the field of the handicapped the problem is greater and third sector organizations have emerged as a real employment option for some volunteers with particular profiles. This orientation is discouraged by such organizations as Caritas, according to which volunteering should be more altruistic and committed to certain ideals and have a Catholic identity, something that has not prevented the number of volunteers from increasing since 1983. In Caritas they are aware of the risk of deterring volunteers with excessive bureaucracy and, to avoid this, they have adopted a strategy based on the decentralization of decision making and the institutionalization of parish assemblies where professionals come to discuss issues with the volunteers and exchange experiences. Other voluntary organizations with far fewer economic resources do not have many possibilities to be professionalized and their activities are mainly based on volunteerism. At times, these volunteers are requested to comply to norms similar to those that professionals have to follow in terms of standards, hierarchy and division of labour.[16] The ability to keep up motivation and identification with common values among professionals and volunteers appears to be a crucial element in overcoming organizational conflicts between these two parties. On the other hand, whenever services require high professional levels either due to the demand of the public authorities or to the features of the users, some third sector organizations have preferred to define tasks by using separate juridical figures. Here, the original third sector organization is maintained as a body based on volunteerism while a new organization is created, usually profit-making or commercial, mainly composed by professionals. This enables them to access bank credit more easily, as banks tend to mistrust the solvency of third sector organizations. The idea is that the more professional an organization or a service is the easier it becomes to obtain funds. A portion of these funds is then used to pay the coordinators of activities largely depending on volunteers committed to the organization's values.[17]

In this situation, there is some concern about the juridical problems that can arise when volunteers are able to prove that their relationship with the organization, in terms of labour legislation, involved their being subject to conditions typical of ordinary employment. We may conclude this section asserting that, despite trends towards higher professionalism, there are indeed many organizations that claim they have increased their number of volunteers. The theory according to which increased professionalism and bureaucracy irretrievably discourage volunteers does not seem to be well grounded. In large, bureaucratic organizations such as the Red Cross and Caritas, professionals have been given the task of organizing and supervising the volunteers, with remarkable success. It is, nevertheless, true that another type of volunteer expressing his commitment in an organized regulated setting is replacing the traditional type that used to be far more informal and common.

8.7. CONCLUSIONS

Forty years of conservative dictatorship and the delay in the modernization process kept Spain at a distance from the general European trends in social care. At the beginning of the democratic regime, in spite of the underdevelopment of public services, third sector providers were economically weak, formally uncoordinated, unequally distributed across the territory and very dependent on personal and political patronage. Twenty years later, social services provision has grown following the increase in public spending, and the relationships between public administrations and third sector have become closer and more formalized. This closer cooperation has generated more bureaucratization and conflicts of identity for third sector organizations, but at the moment it cannot be predicted whether it will deter volunteering, as some sociologists think. During the 1990s, the wave of institutional reforms throughout the EU has also reached Spain. New forms of public management and quasi-markets are extending in social services smothering the institutional culture of the third sector. The cases studied have shown how difficult or fast it can be to introduce market mechanisms into the relationships between public administrations and the third sector. The new institutional culture is extending selectively in social services depending on the social context where institutions are embedded.

Markets are growing faster in fields satisfying two conditions:

(a) The users' and providers' organizations are clearly differentiated. This is the case of the services provided directly by the public sector in general, or of the services for the elderly, which are not generally provided by self-help associations.
(b) There is no lack of individual demand and purchasing capacity for the services offered. The Minimum Income Programme does not satisfy this condition. Providers and users are different and this satisfies

condition (a); but the users' perception of needs is different from the perception of experts and authorities.

On the other hand, partnership relations tend to survive better in fields where the boundaries between advocacy and provision are more blurred because:

(a) users' associations are involved in direct provision, or
(b) there are strong, independent organizations with a clear value orientation.

In these cases, the risk of the political costs involved in refusing a tender can be high enough to dissuade the authorities from generalizing the system. This problem could be solved if government opted for individual choice through vouchers or similar kinds of allowances. But it is not clear whether this option will meet the resistance of many organizations that fear for-profit competitors.

Notes

1. For a description of the characteristics of the Welfare State in Spain, see Moreno and Sarasa (1993) and Rodríguez Cabrero (1993).
2. This Ministry was eliminated when the new conservative government won the elections in 1996. Its functions were transferred to the Ministry of Labour and Social Security.
3. See Rodriguez Cabrero (1990) for public services and Rodriguez Cabrero and Montserrat (1996) for the third sector.
4. Rodriguez Cabrero and Montserrat (1996) estimate that, apart from the biggest organizations, the most of voluntary organizations derive 67 per cent of their resources from public transfers. Aguiar and Pérez-Yruela (1995) estimate that 50 per cent of voluntary organizations in Andalusia got nearly 60 per cent of their resources from the Andalusian Welfare Department in 1992.
5. For an analysis of this nation-wide organization for the blind, see the work of Garvía (1992).
6. It should be noted that the participation of the third sector in the programmes of social–occupational integration for long-term unemployed people is included in the autonomous government's policy to delegate to private agencies the matter of occupational training financed through EU cohesion funds.
7. On the profile of the users of the Minimum Income Programme in Catalonia and Spain in general, see: Generalitat de Catalunya *Conclusions from the Evaluation of the Interdepartamental Programme of Minimum Income Entitlement*. Barcelona, 1994 and Aguilar et al. (1995).
8. The calculation has been made using the Catalan Institute of Social Services budget published by Crespo and Rimbau (1998, p. 741).
9. Calculated on the expenditure on services made by the Social Welfare Department that absorbed the Catalan Institute of Social Services previously integrated in the Department of Health. The budget, excluding pensions, grew from 257.5 to 308.5 million ECUs (Crespo and Rimbau, 1998, p. 741).

10. From 1975 to 1985 the amount of employed people constantly decreased. The trend was interrupted during the second half of the 1980s but in 1991 a new period of employment reduction began again (Toharia, 1994, pp. 1279–1286).
11. Some managers of big voluntary organizations interviewed, stated that there was, in fact, a cut in public subsidies that obliged small organizations, to ask the bigger organizations for financial help.
12. Douglas (1987) has summarized these arguments.
13. For an introduction to this debate, see Anheier and Seibel (1990) and Perry 6 (1993).
14. This hypothesis is partially accepted by some economists but not in such a radical formulation. Arrow (1975), recognizes that in the case of some goods, their quality is not easily evaluated by consumers who may prefer non-profit providers to avoid being exploited. But that does not mean markets corrode altruism and social order as Titmuss wrote.
15. It should be stressed that dissatisfaction with subsidies and interest in alternative methods of financing are lower in those organizations essentially dedicated to the representation of specific interests, as is the case of the Elderly People's Associations. The more specialized the organization is in a given type of service and the more dependent it is on public resources, the greater is its interest in financial stability and market procedures. In the interviews, it was found that third sector organizations with financial autonomy and a firm ideological commitment and solid values are not eager to accept the market logic. Such reticence also emerged at organizations which, due to their limited financial resources, cannot afford to pay professionals and rely almost entirely on voluntary work. These organizations do not consider themselves capable of competing with profit-making enterprises.
16. One such case is that of *Amics de la Gent Gran* (Friends of the Elderly), a volunteer association helping the most fragile of the elderly. Of the eight people under contract working in the association, two of them deal with selecting, training and supporting some 600 highly motivated volunteers who, according to the association's managers, work almost like professionals.
17. This statement contradicts the complaints of some organizations which declare that the costs of services provision are higher than the funds they receive from the public authorities. This could mean that the situation must vary depending on the type of service involved and the varying degree of management efficiency within the TSOs themselves.

Chapter 9

Changes in the Welfare Mix: The European Path

Ugo Ascoli and Costanzo Ranci*

9.1. THE NEED FOR CHANGE

Between the end of the 1980s and the beginning of the 1990s a clear change occurred in the orientation of social care policies in almost all the countries of Western Europe. The change arose from the perception of a structural crisis in the previously established mixed model. The main cause of the crisis was identified, in the political rhetoric of the time, in the 'failure of the state' to ensure a system of social care adequate to a situation in which social needs were rapidly changing. The crisis was identified at two levels: (1) a financial crisis due to the difficulty in economically sustaining public care programmes in the face of a growing expansion of the demand;[1] (2) an organizational crisis, caused by the bureaucratic rigidity and constraints to which public care programmes were subject. Of these two aspects, the first was the most valued: keeping costs down had in fact become the main objective of reform policies of social care systems. Furthermore, the pursuit of this objective seemed to depend inextricably on the possibility of reducing the role and commitment of the state.

An *ex post* analysis of the changes introduced in social care systems during the 1990s, nevertheless, does not confirm the idea that they were characterized by drastic cuts in public spending, or by a massive retreat of the state. It was more a reduction in the rate of growth in social spending or, in some

* Ugo Ascoli • Universita di Ancona, Facolta di economia, Piazzale Martelli, 8, 60121 Ancona, Italy.   Costanzo Ranci • Politecnico di Milano, DIAP, Via Bonardi 3, 20133 Milano, Italy.

countries, a freeze on increases in spending, which, nevertheless, was already absorbing a residual proportion of total welfare expenditures in all the European countries (Rostgaard and Fridberg, 1998).

In the second place, the state did not withdraw, but maintained a crucial role in funding and regulating social care systems, even if the decade of the 1990s saw further moves towards the construction of a more mixed organization of the provision system.

Rather, the crucial problem that the new policies sought to solve was another: not so much reducing public intervention, as *expanding the supply and improving the quality of the services* without putting excessive pressure on costs and, at the same time, being able to respond to the growing need for care in the population.

The reorganization of national social care systems that took place in the last decade was determined to a large extent by the fact that the new social risks typical of post-Fordist society (Esping-Andersen, 1999) require more the development of a system of social services than the maintenance of a system based on direct insurance and income intervention by the state (Rostgaard and Fridberg, 1998).

The requirement to expand and improve national social care systems conflicted, on the other hand, with the fiscal limits on the expansion of public intervention and with the inertia of the welfare mix model inherited from the past. The task faced by the new policies was, therefore, to find a new organizational set-up that would allow expansion and accurate targeting of social care systems and not their reduction.

In the light of the changed social and institutional context in which social care policies were moving, the demands which most strongly led to a reorganization were as follows:

(i)   the first demand was *for a reduction in operating costs through more efficient and effective use of the funds available.* This was the strongest need in all the countries considered in this study and it was this which gave most legitimacy to reorganization. It translated above all into a process pushing towards efficiency and monitoring. Clear signals of attempts to apply the guidelines of 'new managerialism' were seen in almost all the countries and they translated into the use of new procedures for the assessment of costs and results, taken from management models employed in private enterprises. This occurred in both the public sector and in non-profit organizations that provided social care services. In Norway, for example, the growing introduction and implementation of Management by Objectives (MBO) was observed, which translated into procedures aimed at the introduction of quantitative result indicators and the establishment of effectiveness measurements in a field—like social care—traditionally dominated by qualitative assessment of results. Management by Objectives is indicated by Eikås and Selle as a good example of the penetration of the use of instruments of the market into public sector; the introduction of procedures to monitor costs and results did not necessarily involve, and in Norway did not imply, privatization of the system of provision, so much as a change in the principles and forms of state regulation.

(ii) The second demand was *to increase the financial resource destined for the production of social services.* In some countries this demand led to the creation of new systems of finance which allowed the beneficiaries of services to contribute to the costs, as well as the creation of a private social care market for clients with greater purchasing power; measures were introduced to involve and provide incentives for specialist market operators (insurance companies, for-profit firms providing home care, etc.) to provide services that were charged for (totally or partially). More generally, there was a change towards what Taylor in her chapter defines as 'the privatization of finance'. The demand to mobilize private finance had caused a progressive erosion of the principle of universalism and was encouraging more targeting in the public provision.

(iii) The third demand was *to make the supply of social services as well as the availability of funding for service provision less discretionary.* In many countries the network of social care services constituted a marginal element in a welfare system basically hinged on pension and income maintenance programmes at the end of the 1980s. A large part of care rested on the shoulders of the family, above all in the countries of continental and southern Europe, while public programmes (including minimum income programmes in southern European countries) were of modest dimensions and left to the discretion of local administrations. As a result, expansion of these services required the introduction of automatic mechanisms to trigger provision, the definition of compulsory standards for the volume and quality of the services provided and the recognition of clear entitlements based on a precise assessment of need.

The last decade of the twentieth century and the first years of the new century have, therefore, seen the structuring of a new policy field, which previously constituted a residual area of European welfare systems. Social care policies are therefore destined to constitute an increasingly crucial and recognized area of welfare policies (Alber, 1995). On the one hand, this area seems destined to expand greatly for demographic and social reasons (correlated with growth of the elderly population and social exclusion induced by changes in the labour market and families), while, on the other, it will become increasingly more complex due to the plurality of the actors and of their principles, and due to the increasing variety of different needs and, therefore, of the services that must be provided to satisfy them.

The scenario in which the transformations of the last decade occurred was one of growth and change in the general organization of welfare systems and not merely a reduction of public intervention induced by increased pressure on costs. They originated from a variety of contradictory demands at the base of which lay the fundamental need to introduce new ways of organizing service provision as well as relationships between funders, service providers, final beneficiaries and regulators, in a policy field that appears more crucial and destined to expand and become increasingly complex.

9.2. WHICH POLICIES/WHICH MEASURES

The development of new policies, aimed at transforming the overall organization of service provision, sought to meet this set of demands. Adoption of the policies also involved a radical definition of the instruments and forms of public regulation. These measures did not correspond to a uniform and detailed plan to reform the system, but were rather a process of gradual adaptation to problems that were slowly coming on to the agendas of policy makers as requiring a solution. Despite this, a coherent line of *incremental reform* of social care systems emerged from the solutions that were adopted. We will seek here to outline its general framework.

One of the first changes introduced was a shift in the balance between public, private and the third sectors: there was a relative reduction in direct state provision and a progressive increase in provision by private or non-profit agencies. All the countries considered showed the same tendency, even if to differing extents and with the accent on different aspects. In the case of the UK, the new orientation is more explicit than in the other countries: under the 1990 NHS and Community Care Act, 85 per cent of the money transferred from central government to local authorities was required to be spent in the third or private sector. One consequence of this law was the substantial public funding of third sector organizations (above all in the area of services for the handicapped, for minors and for young people), as well as the growth of provision by for-profit organizations (in the field of residential services and generally where there was greater competition between providers).

In other countries, public programmes were not really cut as such, but there was an increase in direct provision of services by non-profit organizations or by private agencies on behalf of the state. In Italy, a shift of balance can be seen during the 1990s: since the 1980s any increase in the volume of social services was effected by involving non-profit organizations and for-profit agencies in service provision. The overall result is that now the relative proportion of services provided by the third sector has grown, although the state has not given up responsibility for direct provision. Spain and France show the same trend: there have been no significant cuts in public intervention, but, nevertheless, the new services that have been provided are run entirely by private or non-profit organizations. For example, in recent years in France, the state has strongly encouraged, through generous tax incentives, the involvement of private firms in the area of home services. In Norway too, a growing tendency to outsource services to reduce costs has been reported.

One inevitable consequence of this increase in the private or non-profit component of provision is that the third sector has taken on a primary (not a supplementary) role in the provision of social care services. This has occurred above all in the more innovative and less structured provision (aimed at new types of beneficiaries such as immigrants, the homeless, HIV sufferers, etc.,) where the third sector is the dominating sector and is able to combine public sector funding with a considerable degree of autonomy in taking initiatives. This increased importance of the third sector has also been accompanied by a generalized increase in funding to non-profit organizations and a transfer of public responsibility from state to the third sector.

In parallel to public funding of outside providers, public administrations have also encouraged the growth of private agencies interested in winning public contracts. In Great Britain, the for-profit private sector for the provision of residential services has increased enormously, while in Germany the large private insurance companies, already active in the health field, have been massively involved in the new long-term care insurance scheme launched in 1995. In France too, private agencies have gained more space in home care, challenging the non-profit organization monopoly. It is only in Italy, Spain and Norway, that for various reasons, the role of the for-profit sector still appears to be very limited.

The relative increase in the size of the third sector and the for-profit sector in social service provision does not coincide, apart from the particular case of Great Britain, with a significant fall in the absolute level of direct public sector provision, nor with significant cuts in welfare spending. On the contrary, in some countries the shift of balance between sectors has coincided with an increase in public sector commitment and with a general extension of social care programmes to a wider population. In these countries the growth of the third sector has, in fact, coincided with the start up of new welfare programmes supported by the state or with the extension of existing public programmes. The most significant cases of new welfare programmes are the recent introduction of minimum income schemes in Spain (1990), their experimentation in Italy (1998) and the new Italian law for personal social services (2000), which involve both increases in public welfare spending and closer involvement of non-profit organizations in social and job integration programmes. Another case is the long-term care programme in Germany, which has extended the right to social care services on a universalistic basis within a compulsory public scheme for the first time. Again, in Germany, the Child Care Act of 1996 recognized the right of all children over the age of three years to child care (Anttonen and Sipilä, 1996).

To summarize, in the course of a decade there has been a parallel change that involves various European countries: on the one hand, public responsibility for the provision of social care services has increased to cover wider sectors of the population, even to the point of universalistic programmes, and on the other hand, the third sector and for-profit agencies have been involved more and more in the setting up of new programmes and the extension of traditional programmes. The two phenomena are closely correlated and confirm the idea that there is no competition between public and private or non-profit sector in the social care field, but an increasing interdependence of roles and responsibilities.

In addition to the increase in the relative importance of the third sector, there has been another change of equal import. This concerns the *partial introduction of market mechanisms for regulating relations between providers and payers/beneficiaries of social services*. The term 'privatization' is not proper to a description of this case to the extent that, rather than a transfer of the ownership of service provision organizations, there has been a process of marketization, that is, a gradual introduction of competitive rules to govern relationships between the various public and private or non-profit actors operating within the mixed economy of social care services.

Various measures have been adopted in different countries which signal greater marketization of the social care system. In general two different paths can be identified, already discussed in the introduction to this book (cf. Chapter 1): on the one hand, *a supply-driven marketization*, which establishes greater competition and monitoring of efficiency in relations between the state that provides funding and the private or non-profit providers of services, and on the other hand, *demand-driven marketization*, which introduces competition and monitoring of the results by the final beneficiaries of services.

The first path involves the introduction of systems for monitoring costs and results typical of agencies that operate on the market. Management by Objectives is employed in Norway, France and Germany, both in public administrations and in the relations between these and private or non-profit providers. In the second case, the tendency is towards new performance contracts in which: (i) the individual components of a service are considered as specific products with a price comparable to that quoted by other competing providers; (ii) costs are reimbursed and services are provided according to strict cirteria established *ex ante*, which also includes procedures for assessing results. The general idea that lies behind the introduction of MbO principles is to imitate market mechanisms in order to obtain more transparency in the comparative assessment of costs and results, as well as to encourage business type behaviour by non-profit providers. *The development of MbO procedures involves a change in the way non-profit organizations are recognized: they are more and more considered as real 'enterprises'.*

Another supply-driven model of marketization, widespread in all the countries considered, concerns the change from grants to contracts as means of state funding. In some countries, such as Great Britain, this change is written into the legislation (e.g. the NHS and Community Care Act of 1990), which makes the regulation of financial relations by means of contracts compulsory. In other countries the change *from global rather discretionary grants to special financing based on contracts* is common: it is found in France, Italy and Spain. In Germany, the trend is to increase the pressure for greater efficiency in contract arrangements. Even in Norway, a change has been observed from basic to project grants, which are more time-limited and involve more public supervision and control, even though the government does not intend to abolish the grant system but wishes to establish the principle that not all the present use of grants is in accordance with the government's expectations and purposes.

Resort to contracting-out spread in parallel with the introduction of tendering for state funding of services by private or non-profit providers. European Union legislation encouraged this development by setting monetary thresholds above which tendering becomes compulsory for awarding government contracts. The practice of tendering, according to those who propose it, should increase transparency and efficiency in procedures for selecting and controlling private or non-profit sector providers. Nevertheless, this assumes that a plurality of competing providers exists. But even when competition between providers occurs, resorting to tendering does not always guarantee the expected results if public administrations fail to monitor costs and the quality of the results purchased from private or non-profit providers.

These and other difficulties have prompted many countries to develop new welfare programmes by setting up quasi-markets (LeGrand, 1990). The most well known case is the long-term insurance in Germany, which allows all private or non-profit providers that meet various minimum professional standards to compete in the supply of residential or domiciliary services covered by the compulsory insurance system. Other important examples are also to be found in France and Italy. In France, a variety of different methods, such as vouchers and tax credits, have been adopted to contribute in the purchase of private care services. In Italy, various local authorities have adopted a voucher system or care allowances to move purchase decisions as close as possible to the final beneficiary. In Great Britain too, there is strong emphasis on consumer rights and this has led to the adoption of measures like Direct Payments, which give disabled people and the elderly the right to put together their own packages and purchase their own care.

Taken together, these measures signal a new season of social care policies based on the idea that market rules, once they have been adapted to the particular product of social care, allow services to expand without an excessive increase in costs for public administrations. Marketization, then, is the theme that unifies these different programmes, even if different meanings have been attributed, to this term.

One step is common to all the measures, whether supply-driven oriented or demand-driven oriented marketization: in both cases, an increasingly clear split is made between funding and regulatory functions (which remain the responsibility of the state or are transferred directly to the beneficiaries) and operational functions (increasingly contracted-out to private or non-profit suppliers). If the mixed model that emerged historically in the social care field was characterized by close interpenetration by the state and the third sector, in the era of marketization there is a clearer distinction, than in the past, between the state, the third sector and the individual beneficiaries. State responsibilities are distinct and relations between sectors are based more on contracts defined in terms of an exchange of money for services, where quantity and quality are proportional to the costs incurred.

As we will see, one widespread effect of this split between funding and provision is that the position of privileged partner enjoyed by non-profit organizations has become weaker, while there are more incentives for the entrance of more business-like organizations and for-profit agencies into the new social care market. In a competitive environment, the privileged position of the third sector is in fact weaker, even if state funding increases.

Marketization also changes the system of established relations between state and third sector in another sense. The underlying idea behind the practice of contracting-out and quasi-markets is that it is preferable to define relations between funders and providers so that it is the purchaser (whether it is the state or the final beneficiary) who establishes the terms and conditions of provision. This makes a substantial change in the relations between state and third sector: while the grant system constituted an investment by government in the activities of non-profit organizations and in their capacity to act autonomously, now relations between the sectors take the shape of 'contracts' in which more of the content is specified by the purchaser. As a consequence, many non-profit organizations have seen a reduction in their autonomy and ability, widely guaranteed in the past, to benefit from relatively constraint-free state funding.

To conclude, the new measures introduced pursue a partial marketization of relations between the various actors that together run the social care system. From this point of view, it is therefore correct to state that a 'contract culture' is developing, a culture that intends to progressively replace the traditional system based on trust and wide margins of discretionality.

9.3. THE PARADOXES OF MARKETIZATION

The introduction of market mechanisms to the social care field in the countries considered has created two fundamental problems:

(i)   the scarcity of information available to purchasers (whether the state or individual beneficiaries) and the difficulty in monitoring the supply (connected with the specific nature of the services provided and the uncertainty of the context in which these services are provided) have made it difficult for public administrations who fund the individual beneficiaries to select the best provider;

(ii) the introduction of competitive mechanisms is often frustrated by the scarcity of the supply of social care services and the tendency of providers to avoid exposure to competition by forming alliances or strengthening relationships of trust with public administrations.

Both these problems require closer examination together with the counter-measures that are most frequently adopted.

Scarcity of information is typical of fields in which the characteristics of the goods exchanged are not easy to define *ex ante* due to the large degree of uncertainty concerning the technologies adopted and the relationship between expected and actual results (DeHoog, 1990). The nature of the problem and the relative solutions that have been tried nevertheless differ depending on whether the right of choice is assigned to public administration (as in the case of contracting-out) or to individual beneficiaries (as in the case of quasi-markets).

In the case of contracting-out, the crucial question concerns the lack of information in the hands of the state on the quality of the services purchased, not to mention the considerable uncertainty over whether expected results have actually been achieved, and over maintaining the priorities established as a condition of funding. In these cases, public administrations risk being at the mercy of the strong leverage of service providers, since continuity in the provision of these services must be guaranteed and private or non-profit providers cannot simply be abandoned.

The creation of quasi-markets was proposed by LeGrand (1990) with the precise aim of overcoming the problem of the information available to public administrations; according to LeGrand quasi-markets are set up to overcome the failure of contracts due to information asymmetry, by identifying consumer selection as the best guarantee of the quality of the services provided. Nevertheless, concrete application of the idea very quickly revealed the limits of the beneficiaries capacity to choose and the 'creaming off' of high-risk customers caused by the attempts of providers to minimize costs.

Quasi-markets, like contracting-out, have also run into considerable problems because of the poor capacity of purchasers to choose. On the whole, these difficulties indicate that market pricing mechanisms are insufficient for regulation of relations between providers, funders and beneficiaries in the social care field. According to Laville (1994), in these cases there is a need to mobilize complementary devices capable of producing a common picture that defines the services: procedures for making regulations, instruments to measure the quality of services, etc.

In the countries considered in this study, the most widespread response to the problem of exercising greater control over service providers was the development of regulatory devices and forms of coordination to codify, as well as possible, the content of the services funded so that they could be evaluated and compared by purchasers. Therefore, there was much regulatory codification of the content of services purchased and of the procedures for selecting providers (by defining very strict approval criteria for state funded providers, strict control over the terms of contracts, etc.), precise and detailed definition of professional standards and competence that must be guaranteed by providers and the setting of particularly stringent cost criteria to make detailed *ex post* control possible. The German case seems to provide a particularly clear example of what has been done: as Evers and Struenk show in their chapter, care is divided up into a hundred single tasks and these tasks get lumped together again into standardized packages of home care performances with an agreed price for reimbursement of the package and a clear rating of each and every element of the package. There is also much evidence from the UK to confirm strong pressure to formalize relations between the state and providers and to stipulate detailed service contracts.

Detailed *ex ante* specification of the contents and terms of contracts is aimed at guaranteeing minimum quality standards and encouraging efficient service provision. It thus contains a strong requirement for competence and standardization of services. Alternative strategies and solutions were employed based on close involvement of private or non-profit providers in the planning and specification of contents and contracts through forms of partnership and joint planning. The creation of local partnerships was often considered as a tool that allows services to be provided by organizations already involved in policy planning and that are already known to provide good quality services.

In Great Britain, the NHS and Community Care Act of 1990 required local authorities to draw up annual plans in consultation with providers from the third and private sectors, carers and users. In Italy, various legislative measures have established methods of involving non-profit organizations in the joint planning of services. Criteria for assessing services emerged from these forms of coordination that did not concern only cost, but also the quality of services.

The second obstacle in the path of market mechanisms is the scarcity of the supply. In this situation purchasers are highly dependent on the conditions imposed by service providers who hold an oligopoly, often supported by privileged relations with public officials and by alliances that prevent new service providers from entering the field.

The response that is generally made to this problem consists of employing enabling measures, such as the concession of incentives and tax advantages to organizations that intend to start up service provision in the public interest and the introduction of certification and accrediting systems for providers to make the requirements to be met to obtain state funding more transparent. Put simply, the problem of scarce supply has been attacked by developing the ability of the state to act as an enabler, providing support and incentives to providers. Much regulation has therefore been introduced that is designed, on the one hand, to prevent privileged treatment of particular organizations and, on the other, to increase the numbers of providers until a 'genuine' competitive arena is created.

On the whole, the introduction of marketization has involved the construction of a strongly regulated market for social services, in which the forms of service specification are much more highly structured than was the case in the traditional grant system, based on wide margins of discretion and mutual trust. Now these relationships are being subject to more stringent procedures, which do not necessarily involve, at least in principle, a relationship of trust with a few 'privileged' service providers. Marketization, therefore, has not coincided with the creation of a 'true' market, but has rather involved the construction of a new regulatory environment in which competition is not created spontaneously, but is encouraged, and is not given free reign but is subject to strict control and regulation.

The drive to introduce competitive mechanisms and the consequent demand to subject the field of relations between the state and private or non-profit providers to a new form of 'mixed' regime (in which elements of market and state control co-exist) have, nevertheless, created two fundamental paradoxes. The future destiny of the welfare mix depends on the solution of such paradoxes:

(i) *The paradox of quality regulation:* the attempt to specify the contents of services and operational standards has produced paradoxes in a field, that of social care, in which the specification of services cannot avoid being imprecise. Where costs have been determined mainly by tendering procedures based exclusively on cost criteria or through the application of MbO procedures, the effect produced has been a deterioration in quality because service providers motivated exclusively by opportunist interests (which led them to reduce both costs and quality at the same time) were allowed to operate. Where state intervention sought to safeguard the quality of services by setting increasingly more detailed standards for the content of service, the result has been both a strong reduction in competition and considerable limitation of the flexibility and capacity to innovate of the organizations that provide services. The cases of Italy, Germany and Norway give very good examples of the latter process.

(ii) *The paradox of enabling:* the attempt by public authorities to increase the numbers of service providers has often brought with it the need to provide incentives for (as the UK case shows) and to facilitate the operation of specialist service providers. Where it was decided to support more specialized providers, unequal treatment of service providers based more heavily on voluntary work and innovation occurred, as shown by the cases of Norway and Italy. This practice inevitably gave rise to privileged relations with certain actors and produced an environment with very little competition. Where, on the other hand, it was decided to weaken the corporativist ties with traditional service providers and introduce more universalist regulations in granting funding (as occurred in Germany), there was a risk of encouraging the entrance of opportunist providers that were unreliable as far as quality was concerned.

On the whole, the attempt to introduce regulatory mechanisms taken from the market to the field of social care has had unexpected effects: on the one hand, state regulation and the degree of standardization of services has increased, while, on the other, new privileged statuses and new alliances have been generated reducing the space for innovation and flexibility. A new regulatory environment has been constructed with characteristics that are very distant from those of a 'genuine' market. The cases analysed in this study, therefore, confirm that marketization has often generated effects that were largely unexpected and different from those of a replacement of the state by the market:

(i) Marketization should have increased competition and efficiency, while, in reality, many limits were placed on competition, through detailed specification of contents and definition of stringent minimum quality criteria.

(ii) The attempt to reduce the regulatory role of the state in favour of 'spontaneous' regulation by the market led several countries to increase, and not to reduce, state intervention; in fact, the state found itself in the situation of having to select and provide incentives for the most suitable service providers: to modify their behaviour to take account of efficiency and effectiveness criteria; to change the statutes of their organizations in order to facilitate service provision; to renegotiate the conditions for government funding. Rather than a return to the market, there was more an introduction of administrative system based on new rules;

(iii) Finally, marketization has not freed private or non-profit providers from state controls but it has often subjected them to stricter control; new instruments have been introduced, which have paradoxically increased capacity for control by public administrations; for example, the introduction of contracting-out required the development of new skills inside the public administration: drawing up guidelines for welfare programmes making more accurate controls of costs and results, etc.

So far, marketization of social care has been more an exercise in restructuring rather than reducing the role of the state.

9.4. THE IMPACT ON THE WELFARE MIX STRUCTURE

The process of marketization has assumed very different meanings in different political and institutional contexts, and has determined outcomes that are equally different. It can be claimed that marketization has not been so much a 'revolution in social policy' (Bartlett et al., 1998) as a strongly path dependent process of policy transformation, which, at times has increased the differences between the various models of social care provision. On the other hand, as will be seen, some elements that are common to the different processes were observed and this makes it possible to bring the tendencies identified under the same label.

We will begin by considering the specific impact of marketization on the individual models of provision identified in the second chapter, and then go on, in the following section, to some more general considerations.

In the countries that developed a *market dominant model* (such as Great Britain), the starting point was a residual state intervention that hinged on means tested programmes, an already large private market partially supported by state funding and a 'buffer' area occupied by the third sector, which operated thanks to state support provided by a generous grant system. In this situation, marketization coincided, above all, with the penetration of market mechanisms into the relations between the state and non-profit organizations. These became increasingly more codified by resort to contracting-out. The expansion of 'contracting-out' implied a serious weakening of the network of relationships based on reciprocal trust between state and the third sector, which had previously been established, as well as greater formality in the funding relationships and in the services provided by non-profit organizations (Lewis, 1996). The most obvious consequences were the further penetration of for-profit agencies into areas occupied by the third sector and the gain of competition led by the more professional non-profit organizations, accompanied by greater financial weakness of the more pioneering organizations or those committed to advocacy.

In the *subsidiary models* (such as Germany), the third sector had a dominant role as a privileged partner in public policies, while there was no significant dimension of the private market. Here, marketization coincided with the introduction of contracts between the state and private or non-profit service providers and with the introduction of competitive mechanisms (in the form of a quasi-market) based on detailed *ex ante* specification of prices and service content. The main outcome of this process was the heavy codification to which state funding mechanisms were subject. The tightening up of state regulation weakened the corporative pact between public authorities and the main centres of the third sector on which the subsidiary model was traditionally founded, exposing non-profit organizations to greater competition, including that from private for-profit agencies (Zimmer, 1999). A tradition of heavy centralization of public policies contributed to making the state regulation of the market mechanisms even stronger.

In the *state dominant models* (Norway and, partially, France), there was practically no private provision in the social care field before marketization came along, except in specific and marginal sectors. Here marketization took the form of introducing much more stringent criteria for assessing costs and results of state funded service provision (by introducing MbO) and of a still timid contracting-out of services. This, nevertheless, translated into a considerable loss of autonomy for non-profit organizations and to greater subjection to administrative procedures of assessment and control. What seems to have happened is, above all, a transformation of non-profit organizations into service providers with a weakening of their voluntary and associative nature, as well as of their political influence. There is, nevertheless, no clear trend towards the introduction of competitive elements in state and social care provider relations.

In *third sector dominant models* (Italy and Spain), a double barrelled system predominated, in which the state funded a largely autonomous third sector in a dominating and privileged position. Here marketization coincided with an increase in state regulation and with a strong structuring of relations between public authorities and the third sector, which at least partially, attenuated their particularistic nature. The third sector obtained institutional legitimation and public funding support, which has gradually become more stable. Nevertheless, the formalization of relations left ample room for local and privatist negotiation. What came into being was a negotiation model which has stabilized relations between funders and providers and made them more transparent.

To summarize, it is not possible to attribute any uniform meaning to marketization. The ways in which marketization was introduced into different institutional contexts were, in fact, extremely different. In the market dominant and the subsidiary models, it coincided with the introduction of competition to an arena previously dominated by relationships of trust or corporativist compromises. Here, marketization indicated a change in the rules of state funding which allowed levels of state funding to be maintained, if not expanded, and also the mobilization of new financial and professional resources from the world of private enterprise. Nevertheless, in these contexts too, the overall impact modified only partially the previously existing model: both in Great Britain and in Germany the diffusion of competition was in fact fought and attacked for a long time and in the end was applied partially.

In the state and the third sector dominant models, marketization did not mean replacing state regulation with market mechanisms so much as an increase and further structuring of the coordinating and controlling role of public authorities. As opposed to what is claimed by the epigones of privatization, the introduction of contracting-out or quasi-markets did not create competitive arenas so much as greater dependence of non-profit organizations on the criteria for assessing costs adopted by public administrations. If there has been an increase in efficiency and the more parasitic positions have been abandoned, this is not due to market action so much as to an increase in state regulation. In southern European countries (Italy and Spain), the increase in state regulation has, nevertheless, had only a partial effect on the traditional relationships of trust, and sometimes of clientelism, on which funding relations between state and third sector were based.

9.5. MARKETIZATION: A REVOLUTION BETRAYED

Ten years ago, those who indicated privatization and competition as the keys to solving the financial problems of welfare policies and expanding the provision of social care in order to meet the challenge of the profound social changes in progress, were far from few. Privatization was long considered the right means for preventing social policies from finding themselves without resources and prospects for development, just at the time when social care needs were exploding.

Today, the results of these policies can be observed and we can ask whether they came up to the initial expectations. As we have seen, all the countries considered in this study adopted the dominating ideas in the 1990s and in different ways set reforms in motion. The forms of the relations between state, third and private sectors were critically considered and subjected to different transformations. After a decade, it can be stated that these relationships have changed considerably. The sense of the transformations, however, only partially reflects the initial expectations.

On the whole, the introduction of marketization to European social care systems has not translated into true and genuine privatization, neither in the sense of introducing a pure market philosophy, nor in the sense of a strong devolution in state regulation. What has, in fact, happened is that some rules taken from market mechanisms have been introduced to the organization of the system of service provision: there has been a clear split between funding and provision, an increase in services contracted-out to non-profit and for-profit organizations, greater competition to obtain state funding, and stringent criteria have been introduced in calculating costs and assessing results. *Taken together, these measures have required new state regulatory activity and institution building aimed at guaranteeing effective pursuit of policy objectives as well as the maintenance of service quality standards.*

The main outcomes of this tendency are much more formal relations between public and private sectors, the third and the accentuated professionalization and specialization in non-profit service providers, and a reallocation of decision making to a more technical-procedural rather than a general political level. These three aspects are considered separately in the conclusion.

Marketization has coincided, first and foremost, with relations between public and private actors becoming generally more formal. This consequently determined a reduction in the elements of trust intrinsic to these relationships. In Germany and Great Britain, the weakening of the privileged alliance between state and third sector meant that non-profit organizations were placed on a par with private for-profit agencies. In Italy and Norway, the funding relationship with public administrations did not determine an increase in competition so much as subject it more to 'objective' criteria: control of costs and results, assessment of effectiveness, verification of approval requirements for contracting-out and accrediting procedures.

On the other hand, formalization has sacrificed flexibility and the innovative capacities of non-profit organizations, paradoxically reducing the advantages of resorting to these organizations for public provision of social care services. The most obvious effects have been the standardization of services, the suppression of diversity and disincentives for the traditional innovative role of voluntary organizations. Put simply, non-profit organizations have gradually ceased to constitute an 'independent alternative' to state intervention and have changed into new hybrid organizations, a mix of a voluntary organization, a service agency and a government bureaucracy.

On the other hand, the detailed specification of services has also encouraged the professionalization and specialization of services, allowing space for a wide diversification of services and skills. Rather than standardizing, then, formalization has recognized the expertise of many private or non-profit providers even when they did not enjoy privileged relations with public administrations. The weakening of parasitic positions has therefore determined further diversification of the provision system, which has become more flexible and sensitive to the variable and diversified needs of beneficiaries.

It is nevertheless true that specialization has generally involved a loss of organizational flexibility and a severe reduction in opportunities to innovate. On the whole, the new regulation had coincided with a general process of structuring of a public policy field that is traditionally residual and often dominated by neo-corporative alliances.

Another consequence of marketization is that it set in motion profound transformations in the organization and characteristics of the third sector. In all the countries considered, there has been a strong polarization in the third sector between very professional organizations with strong management skills on the one hand, and organizations based on voluntary work and strong ties with membership, on the other.

Non-profit organizations were called upon in the last decade to adjust to the new institutional climate in which they operated. In all the countries considered they faced a paradoxical situation: on the one hand, the new measures allowed non-profit organizations to play a more important role and to obtain more resources than ever before; however, this went with a profound change in the identity of the organizations themselves. The third sector was profoundly affected by the changes that occurred and ended up changing its structure considerably.

The paradox that non-profit organizations were faced with had a side to it that was above all economic: given the generalized increase in state funding, a renewed financial fragility of many non-profit organizations was observed. They had to come to terms with a competitive climate and accountability requirements, which were much more stringent than in the past. As is clearly shown in the chapter on Great Britain, many organizations found themselves doing more for less; furthermore, the tendency to tie funding to results generally shortened the length of contracts, making many organizations less financially secure in the medium to long term. Finally, in some fields the introduction of efficiency parameters in tendering made less specialized organizations less competitive.

The paradox did not only involve the financial sustainability of non-profit organizations, but also their identity. Professionalization did, in fact, weaken their ability to mobilize volunteers and reorganization of internal powers weakened the position of traditional leaders in favour of professionals. Then, there were changes in objectives, towards the provision of services and away from advocacy and political pressure activity. In many countries there was a 'devoluntarization' of non-profit organizations and a weakening of their membership. While on the one hand these processes were necessary if non-profit organizations were to survive in a more difficult context, on the other hand it weakened their intermediary role and their social legitimation. As stated in the chapter on Germany, the gradual transformation into a modern enterprise was quite inevitable, but it only concerned one dimension of the organizational identity. A frequent solution to the problem of the requirement for professionalism was to separate the different aspects of the multiple identity of non-profit organizations, distinguishing between service provision and the internal life of the association. Nevertheless, this separation occurred in a context of strong pressure to take responsibility for service provision; faced with external pressures and the need to guarantee economic survival, many organizations simply forgot to keep their social and democratic functions of mobilizing civic society.

Finally, a third general consequence of marketization was the reallocation of political discretionary powers concerning welfare policies to a technical-procedural level and the progressive reduction in the capacity to draw up general policy guidelines.

The introduction of new measures and new competitive mechanisms coincided with the dominance assumed by 'technical' forms of government, sensitive to managerial financial planning criteria and the assessment of costs and results. The crisis of public planning based on rational parameters was replaced by a 'contextual' regulation, which renounced dictation of general policy objectives and focused instead on negotiation and coordination of the growing plurality of actors involved in welfare policies.

The social care field saw an increase in its mixed and plural character. Behind this plurality there was, nevertheless, a profound change in the previous power arrangement. While the main demand for changes came from governments increasingly worried about the growing costs of social care services, specific interests within the third and private sectors were constituted to support marketization trends. From this point of view, marketization coincided with the growth of a new coalition of interests between funders and producers who saw that considerable advantages were to be gained from the change to a contract culture.

Note

1. The financial crisis was made even more evident in some countries—such as Italy and Spain—by budget constraints imposed by the process of European integration; in other countries, such as Great Britain and Germany, it was mainly due to the growing costs of public programmes in place and due to an increase in the numbers of beneficiaries.

References

6, P. (1993). The Co-ordination Problem and Institutions in Non-profit Studies: A Research Agenda. Paper presented at the conference *Well-being in Europe by Strengthening the Third Sector*. Barcelona, May 27–29.

6, P. (1997). The new politics of welfare contracting. In 6, P. and J. Kendall (Eds.), *The contract culture in public services: studies from Britain, Europe and the USA*, Aldershot: Arena.

6, P. and Kendall, J. (1997). Introduction. In 6, P. and J. Kendall (Eds.), *The contract culture in public services: studies from Britain, Europe and the USA*, Aldershot: Arena.

6, P. and Vidal, I. (eds.) (1994). *Delivering welfare: nonprofit and cooperative action in Western European countries*. Barcelona: CIES.

Afchain, J. (1997). *Les associations d'action sociale—Outils d'analyse et d'intervention*. Paris: Dunod.

Aguiar, F. and Pérez-Yruela, M. (1995). Aproximación al sector voluntario andaluz en el ámbito de los servicios sociales. In S. Sarasa and L. Moreno (Eds.), *El Estado del Bienestar en la Europa del Sur*. Madrid: Consejo Superior de Investigaciones Científicas-IESA.

Aguilar, M., Gaviria, M. and Laparra, M. (1995). *La caña y el pez. Estudio sobre los salarios sociales en las Comunidades Autónomas*. Madrid: Fundación FOESSA.

Alber, J. (1995). A framework for the comparative study of social services. *Journal of European Social Policy*, 5/2, 131–149.

Alber, J. (1996). The debate about long-term care reform in Germany. In: OECD, *Caring for frail elderly people. Policies in evolution* (Social Policy Studies 19). Paris: OECD

Alexander, J., Stivers, C. and Nank R. (1998). *Implication of welfare reform: Do nonprofit survival strategies threaten civil society?* Paper presented at the Arnova Conference, Washington.

Alix, N. (1993). Associations sanitaires et sociales et pouvoirs publics: l'impact de la construction communautaure sur leurs relations en matière de gestion d'établissements et services sociaux. *Revue des études coopératives, mutualistes et associatives*, 47.

Ambrosini, M. (1999). *Tra altruismo e professionalità*. Milano: FrancoAngeli.

Anheier H. K. (1992) 'An elaborate network: profiling the third sector in Germany', in Gidron B., Kramer R. M. and Salamon L. S., (eds.), *Government and the third sector. Emerging relationships in welfare states*, Jossey-Bass, S. Francisco.

Angerhausen, S., Backhaus-Maul, H. and Schiebel, M. (1995). Nachwirkende Traditionen und besondere Herausforderungen: Strukturentwicklung und Leistungsverständnis von Wohlfahrtsverbänden in den neuen Bundesländern. In T. Rauschenbach C., Sachße and T. Olk (Eds.), *Von der Wertgemeinschaft zum Dienstleistungsunternehmen. Jugend- und Wohlfahrtsverbände im Umbruch*. Frankfurt am Main: Suhrkamp.

Anheier, H. (1997). Der Dritte Sector in Zahlen: Ein sozial-oekonomisches Portraet. In H. Anheier, H. Priller, W. Seibel and A. Zimmer (Eds.), *Der Dritte Sektor in Deutschland*. Berlin: WZB.

Anheier, H. and Seibel, W. (Eds.) (1990). *The Third Sector: comparative studies of nonprofit organisations*. Berlin, New York: de Gruyter.

Anttonen A. and Sipilä, J. (1996). European social care services: is it possible to identify models? *Journal of European Social Policy, 6(2)* 87–100.

Anttonen, A. and Sipilä, J. (1997). Cinco regímenes de servicios sociales de atención. In L. Moreno (Ed.), *Unión Europea y Estado del Bienestar*. Madrid: Consejo Superior de Investigaciones Científicas-IESA.

APO (1997). *Nye trender nye utfordringer. En rapport om utkontraktering av offentlige tjenester innen eldreomsorgen*. Apo-rapport, 1/97.

Archambault, E. (1990). Public authorities and the nonprofit sector in France. In H. K. Anheier and W. Seibel (Eds.), *The Third sector: comparative studies of nonprofit organizations*. Berlin: De Gruyter.

Archambault, E. (1994). La gestion privée des services sociaux: production publique déguisée ou partenariat innovant. *Colloque de l'association d'economie politique, Repenser l'économie: de la redistribution à la réciprocité*, Montréal.

Archambault, E. (1997). *The nonprofit sector in France*. Manchester: Manchester University Press.

Archambault, E. and Boumendil, J. (1997). *Les dons et le bénévolat en France* Paris: Laboratoire d'économie sociale, Fondation de France.

Arrow, K. J. (1975). Gifts and Exchanges. In Edmund S. Phelps (Ed.), *Altruism, Morality and Economic Theory* (pp. 13–28). New York: Rusell Sage Foundation.

Ascoli U. (1987) 'The Italian welfare state: between incrementalism and rationalism', in Friedman R., Gilbert N. and Sherer M., (eds.), *Modern welfare states. A comparative view of trends and prospects*, New York University Press, New York; 110-150.

Ascoli, U. (1993). Introduzione. In U. Ascoli and S. Pasquinelli (Eds.).

Ascoli, U. and Pasquinelli, S. (Eds.) (1993). *Il Welfare mix. Stato sociale e Terzo settore*. Milano: Angeli.

Ascoli, U., Ranci, C. and Pavolini, E. (1998). The New Welfare Mix in Italy. Paper presented at the II ISTR Conference, Geneva.

Bagguley, P. (1994). Prisoners of the Beveridge dream? The political mobilisation of the poor against contemporary welfare regimes. In R. Burrows and B. Loader (Eds.), *Towards a post-Fordist welfare state*, London: Routledge.

Baldwin, S. and Lunt, N. (1996). *Charging Ahead: charging policies for community care*. Bristol: The Policy Press.

Barbetta, P. (ed.) (1996). *Senza scopo di lucro*. Bologna: Il Mulino.

Barbetta, P. (ed.) (1997). *The nonprofit sector in Italy*, Manchester, Manchester University Press.

Bartlett, W., Roberts, J. A. and Le Grand J. (Eds.) (1998). *A revolution in social policy. Quasi-market reforms in the 1990s*. Bristol: Policy Press.

Bassanini, M. and Ranci, P. (1990) (eds.), *Non per profitto. Il settore dei soggetti che erogano servizi di interesse collettivo senza fine di lucro*, Quaderni della Fondazione Olivetti, 23.

Batley, R. and Stoker, G. (eds.), *Local government in Europe: Trends and developments*, London: Macmillan.

Batsleer, J. and Paton, R. (1997). Managing voluntary organisations in the contract culture: continuity or change? In 6, P. and J. Kendall (Eds.), *The Contract Culture in Public Services: Studies from Britain, Europe and the USA*. Aldershot: Arena.

Bemrose, C. and MacKeith, J. (1996). *Partnerships for Progress: Good practice in the relationship between local government and voluntary organisations*. Bristol: The Policy Press.

Billis, D. (1998). Policy Contexts and Voluntary Organizations: The Case of Social Exclusion. Paper presented at the Arnova Conference, Washington.

Bjerke, P. and Eilertsen, R. (1998). *Konkurranse i eldreomsorgen*. Oslo: DEFACTO rapport.

Blackmore, M., Bradshaw, Y., Jenkinson, S., Johnson, N. and Kendall, I. (1995). The voluntary sector and quality assurance. Paper presented to ESRC seminar *Challenges for Voluntary Agencies in a Changing Social Policy Environment*. London: London School of Economics.

Bloch-Lainé, F. (1994). Identifier les associations de Service social. *Revue des études cooperatives, mutualistes et associatives, n.251.*

Blom, I. (1998). *Feberens ville rose: tre omsorgssystemer i tuberkulosearbeidet 1900–1960.* Fagbokforlaget. Bergen.

Bogen, H. and Nyen, T. (1998). *Privatisering og konkurranseutsetting i norske kommuner.* Fafo—rapport 254.

Bönker, F. and Wollmann, H. (1996). Incrementalism and reform waves: The case of social service reform in the Federal Republic of Germany. *Journal of European Public Policy, 3,* 441–460.

Borzaga, C., Fiorentini, G. and Matacena, A. (1996). *Non profit e sistemi di welfare.* Roma: NIS.

Boumendil, J. and Triomphe, A. (1996). La place des associations dans la gestion des services sociaux. *Revue des études coopératives, mutualistes et associatives, 59.*

Bourdieu, P. et al. (1993), *La misére du monde*, Paris, le Seuil.

Brovelli, G. (1989). Les incidences de la décentralisation sur les associations: l'exemple du domaine sanitaire et social. *Revue française des Affaires sociales, 2,* Avril–Juin, 23–72.

BAGFW, Bundesarbeitsgemeinschaft der Freien Wohlfahrtspflege (1997). *Gesamtstatistik der Einrichtungen der Freien Wohlfahrtspflege.* Bonn.

Carbognin M. (1998). *Il campo di fragole. Reti di imprese e reti di persone nelle imprese sociali italiane.* Milano: FrancoAngeli.

Cawson, A. (1982). *Corporatism and welfare. Social policy and state intervention in Britain,* Heinemann, London.

CGM (1997). *Imprenditori Sociali. Secondo rapporto sulla cooperazione sociale in Italia.* Brescia: CGM.

Chapman, P., Pickford, R. and Greig, R. (1999). *The implications of Best Value for Social Services. Managing Community Care, 7.1,* 7–14.

Chauviere, M. (1997). Quand le marché hante le social. *Les cahiers de l'ACTIF.* La marchandisation du social, 254/255, pp. 5–18.

Chauviere, M. (1980). Enfance inadaptée, l'héritage de Vichy. *Economie et Humanisme,* Paris: Ed. Ouvrières.

Chéroutre, M. T. (1993). *Exercice et développement de la vie associative dans le cadre de la loi du 1er Juillet 1901.* Avis et rapport du conseil économique et social, Conseil économique et social, Paris.

Clegg, S. (1990). *Modern Organisations: organisational studies in the post-modern world,* London: Sage.

Commissione di indagine sulla povertà e sull'emarginazione (1997), *La spesa pubblica per l'assistenza in Italia,* Roma, Istituto Poligrafico di Stato.

Commission on the Future of the Voluntary Sector (1996). *Meeting the Challenge of Change: voluntary action into the 21st century,* London: NCVO Publications.

Conseil économique et social (1996). *Le développement des services de proximité.* Avis adopté par le Conseil économique et social le 10 Janvier 1996./Paris: Avis et rapports du Conseil économique et sociale.

Craig, G., Taylor, M., Szanto, C. and Wilkinson, M. (1999). *Developing Local Compacts: relationships between local public sector bodies and the voluntary and community sectors,* York: Joseph Rowntree Foundation.

Crespo, M. T. and Rimbau, C. (1998). Els serveis socials a Catalunya. In S. Giner (Ed.), *La societat catalana* (pp. 733–756). Barcelona: Institut d'Estadística de Catalunya.

Daly, M. and Lewis, J. (1998). *Introduction. Conceptualising Social care in the Context of Welfare State Restructuring,* in J. Lewis (ed.), *Gender, Social care and Welfare State. Restructuring in Europe,* Aldershot, Ashgate, pp. 1–24.

DARES (1994). L'insertion professionnelle des travailleurs handicapés dans les établissements assujettis à l'obligation d'emploi en 1995. *Premières synthèses, 17.1,* 4.

David, P. (1998). Governare il welfare a livello locale. *Prisma, 6,* 58–63.

Davis Smith, J. (1998). *Volunteering in the UK—some findings from a new national survey,* in Charities Aid Foundation, *Dimensions of the Voluntary Sector,* Tonbridge: Charities Aid Foundation.

Davis Smith, J. and Hedley, R. (1994). *Volunteers and the Contract Culture,* London: The National Institute for Volunteering.

Deakin, N. (1996a). 'What dies contracting do to users?' in Billis, D. and Harris, M. (eds.) *Voluntary Agencies: challenges of organization and management,* Basingstoke: Macmillan, pp. 113–129.

Deakin, N. (1996b) 'The devil's in the detail', *Social Policy and Administration,* 30:1.

Deakin, N. and Gaster, L. (1998). Local Government and the Voluntary sector: Who needs whom—why and what for? Paper presented at the III International Conference of the International Society for Third Sector Research, Geneva.

Deakin, N. and Walsh, K. (1996). 'The enabling state: the role of markets and contracts', *Public Administration,* 74, 1 (Spring 1996), pp 33–48.

DeHoog, R. (1990). Competition, Negotiation, or Cooperation. Three Models for Service Contracting. *Administration and Society,* vol. 22.

Department of Health/Price Waterhouse (1991). *Purchaser, Provider and Commissioner Roles,* London: Department of Health.

DETR Department of the Environment, Transport and the Regions (1998). *Improving Services through Best Value.* London.

DiMaggio, P and Powell, W. W. (1983). 'The iron cage revisited: institutional isomorphism and collective rationality in organizational fields', *American Sociological Review,* 48, pp. 147–160.

Dore, R. (1983). Goodwill and the spirit of capitalism. *British Journal of Sociology,* 34(4).

Douglas, J. (1987). Political theories of nonprofit organizations. In W. W. Powell (Ed.), *The nonprofit sector: A research handbook* (pp. 43–54). New Haven: Yale University Press.

Eikås, M. (2001). *Kommunal tenesteproduksjon på kontrakt? Om bruk av privat aktørar i helse–og sosialsektoren i norske kommunar,* Rapport nr.10/2001, Høgskulen i Sogn og Fjordane.

Eisen, R. and Sloan, F. A. (Eds.) (1996). *Alternatives for ensuring long-term care. Economic issues and policy solutions.* Amsterdam: Kluwer Academic Publications.

Enjolras, B. (1992). Services de proximité dans l'action sociale: l'apport de la théorie du choix institutionnel. *Revue des études coopératives, mutualistes et associatives,* 44–45.

Enjolras, B. (1995). *Le marché providence.* Paris: Editions Desclée de Brouwer.

Erichsen, V. (1996). Den særegne norske tannpleien. In V. Erichsen (Ed.), *Profesjonsmakt. På sporet av en norsk helsepolitisk tradisjon.* Tano Aschehoug.

Esping-Andersen, G. (1990). *The three worlds of welfare capitalism.* Cambridge: Polity Press.

Esping-Andersen, G. (1999). *Social Foundations of Postindustrial Economies.* Oxford: Oxford University Press.

Essex, T. (1998). Trust in the market-place: The value of relationships in community care contracting. Paper presented at NCVO Research conference, Loughborough, September 1998.

Etzioni, A. (1973). The Third Sector and Domestic Missions. *Public Administration Review,* n. 33, 314–323.

Evers, A. (1995). Part of the welfare mix: The third sector as an intermediate area between market economy, state and community. *Voluntas. International Journal of Voluntary and Nonprofit Organisations,* 6/2, 159–183.

Evers, A. (1997). Tipi diversi di welfare pluralism. Il nuovo scenario delle politiche sociali in Europa. In G. Rossi (Ed.), *Terzo Settore, Stato e Mercato nella Trasformazione delle Politiche Sociali in Europa.* Milano: FrancoAngeli.

Evers, A. (1998). The new long-term-care insurance program in Germany. *Journal of Aging & Social Policy*, 10(1), 77–98.

Fazzi, L. (1998). *Il welfare mix in Italia: primi passi*. Milano: FrancoAngeli.

Fazzi, L. (Ed.) (1999). *Modelli di welfare mix*. Milano: FrancoAngeli.

Fenet, F. (1988). *L'aide sociale à l'enfance: exemple de régulation d'un système économique non-marchand*. Thesis. University of Paris I.

Fenet, F. and Sagot-Duvauroux, D. (1988). Histoire de la protection sociale de l'enfance: une lecture économique. *Ensemble*, XLV, 4.

Fenet, F. and Sagot-Duvauroux, D. (1989). *Analyse économique des associations gestionnaires d'établissements sociaux*, CRESGE.

Ferrera, M. (1993). *Modelli di solidarietà*. Bologna: Il Mulino.

Ferrera, M. (1996). 'The "southern model" of welfare in social Europe', in *Journal of European Social Policy*, 6, 1, 17–37.

Fimreite, A. and Stenvoll, D. (1998). *Organisering av kommunalt tjenestetilbud*. Unpublished article.

France, G. and Arcangeli, L. (1996). 'La concorrenza amministrata nel nuovo sistema di Welfare', *L'Assistenza Sociale*, n. 1.

Franz, H.-J. (1991). 'Interorganizational policy coordination: arrangements of shared government', in Kaufmann F.-X., (ed.), *The public sector. Challenge for coordination and learning*, De Gruyter, Berlin.

Frisanco, R. and Ranci, C. (1999) (eds.). *Le dimensioni della solidarietà. Secondo rapporto sul volontariato italiano*, Roma, Fondazione Italiana per il Volontariato.

Garms-Homolová, V. (1994). Comprehensive health for the aged and initiatives for an insurance in Germany. *Zeitschrift fuer Gesundheitswissenschaften*, 1, 26–38.

Garvia, R. (1992). Mutual dependence between government and private service monopoly: the case of Spanish blind. In S. Kuhnle and P. Selle (Eds.), *Governments and voluntary organizations* (pp. 108–135). Aldershot: Avebury.

Gaster, L. (1995). *Quality in Public Services: managers' choices*, Buckinghamshire: Open University Press.

Gaster, L., Deakin, N., Riseborough, M., McCabe, A., Wainwright, S. and Rogers, H. (1999). *History, strategy or lottery? The realities of local government/voluntary sector relationships*. London: IDEA.

Giddens, A. (1998). *The Third Way: the renewal of social democracy*, Cambridge: Polity Press.

Gidron, B., Kramer, R. and Salamon, L. (1992). *Government and the Third Sector: emerging relationships in welfare states*. San Francisco: Jossey Bass.

Glennerster, H. and Le Grand, J. (1995). Le développement des quasi-marchés dans la protection sociale. *Revue française d'économie*, X-3, 111–135.

Goetting, U., Haug, K. and Hinrichs, K. (1994). The long road to long-term care insurance in Germany. *Journal of Public Policy*, 14, 285–309.

Goll, E. (1991). *Die freie Wohlfahrtspflege als eigener Wirtschaftssektor*. Baden-Baden: Nomos Verlagsgesellschaft.

Gornick, J., Meyers, M. and Ross, K. E. (1996). 'Supporting the Employment of Mothers', in *Journal of European Social Policy*, 7, pp. 45–70.

Groth, A. M. (1999). *Bistandsorganisasjonene—mellom tradisjonell frivillighet og moderne kontraktskultur*. Los-notat. Bergen.

Gutch, R. (1992). *Contracting: lessons from the United States*. London: NCVO.

Hallenstvedt, A. and Trollvik, J. (Eds.) (1993). *Norske organisasjoner*. Oslo: Fabritius Forlag 1993.

Hansmann, H. (1980). 'The role of nonprofit enterprise', *Yale Law Journal*, 89, 835–901.

Hansmann, H. (1986). The role of nonprofit enterprises. In S. Rose-Ackerman (Ed.) *The economics of nonprofit institutions; studies in structure and policy*. Oxford: Oxford University Press.

Hansmann, H. (1987). Economic theories of nonprofit organisations. In W. W. Powell (Ed.), *The nonprofit sector. A research handbook*. New Haven: Yale University Press.

Harding, T. and Beresford, P. (1996). *The Standards We Expect: what service users and carers want from social services workers*, London: National Institute for Social Work.

Harris, M. E. (1998). Federal devolution and national policy reform: Does the independent sector have the capacity to be effective? Paper presented at the Arnova Conference, Washington.

Hastings, A., McArthur, A. and McGregor, A. (1996). *Less than equal: community organisations and estate regeneration partnerships*. Bristol: The Policy Press.

Haugland, B. (1992). *Det profesjonelle medmenneske. En analyse av frivillig arbeid i Kirkens SOS*. Hovedoppgave i Sosiologi. University of Oslo.

Heinze, R. G., Schmid, J. and Strünck, C. (1997). Zur Politischen Ökonomie der sozialen Dienstleistungsproduktion. Der Wandel der Wohlfahrtsverbände und die Konjunkturen der Theoriebildung. *Kölner Zeitschrift für Soziologie und Sozialpsychologie*, 2, 242–271.

Hems, L. and Passey, A. (1998). *The Voluntary Sector Almanac*, London: National Council for Voluntary Organisations.

Heitman, J. and Selle, P. (1999). *Frivillige organisasjoner. Fornyelse, vekst og utvikling*. Kristiansand: Høyskoleforlaget, Nordic Academic Press.

Hermange, C. and Triomphe, A. (1996). *Personnes handicapées—droits et démarches*. Ctnerhi-Nserm- Ministère du travail et des affaires sociales.

Hirschman, A. O. (1970). *Exit, Voice and Loyalty*. Cambridge, Massachusetts: Harvard University Press.

Hirschman, A. (1982). *Shifting Involvements, Private Interest and Public Action*. Martin Robertson.

Home Office (1998). *Getting It Right Together*, London: Home Office.

Hoyes, L., Lart, R., Means, R. and Taylor, M. (1994). *Community Care in Transition*, York: Joseph Rowntree Foundation.

Hood, C. (1991). A public management for all seasons? *Public Administration*, 69, 3–19.

Hood, C. (1995). The new public management in the 1980's: Variation on a theme. *Accounting, Organizations and Society*, 20, (2/3) 93–109.

INSERSO, (1995). *Guia-directorio de centros para personas meyores*. Madrid: Instituto Nacional de Servicios Sociales.

Inspection générale des affaires sociales, (1984). *La politique sociale et les associations*. Rapport annuel.

Inspection générale des affaires sociales, (1993). *Rapport annuel*.

IRS, Istituto per la Ricerca Sociale (1992). *La spesa pubblica per l'assistenza in Italia*, Milano. Istituto per la Ricerca Sociale.

James, E. (1989). *The nonprofit sector in international perspective. Studies in comparative culture and policy*. Oxford: Oxford University Press.

Johnson, N., Jenkinson, S., Kendall, I., Bradshaw, Y. and Blackmore, M. (1998). Regulating for quality in the voluntary sector. *Journal of Social Policy*, 27:3, 307–328.

Kaiser, J. C. (1993). Freie Wohlfahrtsverbände im Kaiserreich und in der Weimarer Republik. In Teppe, Karl (Hg.). *Jahrbuch Westfälische Forschungen*, Bd. 43. Münster: Lit Verlag.

Kendall, J. and Almond, S. (1998). *The UK voluntary (third) sector in comparative perspective: Exceptional growth and transformation*. Canterbury: Personal Social Services Research Unit.

Kendall, J. and Knapp, M. (1996). *The voluntary sector in the UK*. Manchester: Manchester University Press.

Kjerstad, E. and Kristiansen, F. (1996). *Erfaringer med konkurranseutsetting av kommunal ten-esteproduksjon*. Rapport 87/96. SNF. Bergen.

Klausen, K. and Selle, P. (1996). The third sector in Scandinavia. *Voluntas*, 7:2, 99–122.

Knapp, M. and Wistow, G. (1994). Welfare pluralism and community care development: The role of local government and the non-statutory sectors in social welfare services in England. In

OECD, *Private sector involvement in the delivery of social welfare services: Mixed models from six OECD countries*. Paris: OECD.

Knight, B. (1993). *Voluntary Action*. London: The Home Office.

Kramer, R. M. (1981). *Voluntary Agencies in the Welfare State*, Berkeley: University of California Press.

Kramer, R. M. (1989). The use of government funds by voluntary social service agencies in four Welfare states. In E. James (Ed.), *The Nonprofit sector in international perspective: Studies in comparative culture and policy*. Oxford: Oxford University Press.

Kramer, R. M. (1992). The roles of voluntary social service organisations in four European states: policies and trends in England, The Netherlands, Italy and Norway. In S. Kuhnle and P. Selle (Eds.), *Government and voluntary organisations* (pp. 34–53). Bristol: Avebury.

Kramer, R. M. (1994). Voluntary agencies and the contract culture: 'Dream or nightmare?'. *Social Service Review*, March, 33–59.

Kramer, R. M. (1998). Non profit organizations in the twentieth century: Will sector matter? Paper presented at the Arnova Conference, Washington.

Kramer, R. M., Lorentzen, H., Melief, W. B. and Pasquinelli, S. (1995). *Privatization in four European countries. Comparative studies in Government–Third Sector relationships*, New York: M.E. Sharpe.

Kuhnle, S. and Selle, P. (Ed.) (1990). *Frivillig organisert velferd—alternativ til offentlig?* Bergen: Alma Mater.

Kuhnle, S. and Selle, P. (1992). Government and voluntary organizations: a relational perspective. In S. Kuhnle and P. Selle (Eds.), *Government and voluntary organizations*. Bristol: Avebury.

Kumar, S. (1997). *Accountability relationships between voluntary sector 'providers', local government 'purchasers' and service users in the Contracting State*, York: York Publishing Services.

Lægreid, P. (1999). *Administrative reforms in Scandinavia—testing the cooperative model*. Los—senter Notat 9903. Bergen.

Laville, J. L. (1992). *Les services de proximité en Europe*. Paris: Collection TEN, SYROS-Alternatives.

Laville, J. L. (Ed.) (1994). *L' économie solidaire*. Paris: Desclée de Brouwer.

Laville, J. L. and Bernard E. (1994). *Cohésion sociale et emplois*. Collecion sociologie économique, Aout/Septembre. Paris: Desclée de Brouwer.

Leat, D. (1995). *Challenging management: An exploratory study of perceptions of managers who have moved from for-profit to voluntary organisations*. London: Volprof.

Le Grand, J. (1990). Quasi-markets and Social Policy. *Studies in decentralization and Quasi-markets*. Working paper I, Bristol: SAUS Publications.

Le Grand, J. and Robinson, R. (Eds.) (1984). *Privatisation and the welfare state*. London: Allen and Unwin.

Leibfried, S. (1992). 'Towards a European Welfare State?' in Ferge, Z. and Kalbery, J.E. (eds.), *Social Policy in a Changing Europe*, Westview Press, Boulder.

Les cahiers de l'ACTIF. *La marchandisation du social*. 254/255, 1997.

Lewis, J. (1993). Developing the mixed economy of care: Emerging issues for voluntary organisations. *Journal of Social Policy*, 22.2, 173–192.

Lewis, J. (1995). Welfare state or mixed economy of welfare? *History Today*, 45.2, 4–6.

Lewis, J. (1996). Contracting and voluntary agencies. In D. Billis and M. Harris (Eds.), *Voluntary agencies. Challenges of organisation and management*. London: Macmillan Press.

Lewis, J. and Glennerster, H. (1996). *Implementing the New Community Care*. Buckingham: Open University Press.

Lipsky, M. and Smith, S. (1993). *Nonprofits for hire. The Welfare State in the age of contracting*. Cambridge, Massachusetts: Harvard University Press.

Lorentzen, H. (1988). *Mellom byråkrati og bevegelse. De frivillige organisasjonenes rolle i sosialsektoren*. INAS—rapport nr. 3/88. Oslo.

Lundstrøm, T. and Wijkstrøm, F. (1997). *The nonprofit sector in Sweden*. Manchester and New York: Manchester University Press.

Lyons, M. (1997). Contracting for care: What is it and what is at issue. *Third Sector Review*, 3, 5–22.

Meyer, J. (1997). Probleme der Pflegeleistungsbemessung in der ambulanten Pflege. Alternativen zum Leistungskomplexsystem. *Pflege und Gesellschaft*, 2, 13–18.

Mocroft, I. (1998). *The survey of local authority payments to voluntary and charitable organisations of 1996–7*, in Charities Aid Foundation, *Dimensions of the Voluntary Sector*, Tonbridge: Charities Aid Foundation.

Moore, B. jr. (1966). *The social origins of dictatorship nad emocracy. Lord and peasant in the making of the modern world*, Boston, Beacon Press.

Mietle, C. B. (1999). *A comparative study of contracting-out nursing homes*. Thesis in Comparative Politics. University of Bergen.

Montraveta, Mª. I. and Vilà, A. (1995). Corresponsabilidad, subsidiariedad y autonomía municipal. Ejes de las interrelaciones administrativas. At the *Congress of Municipal Social Services. Conferences and Papers. Sitges, 2–4 March 1995*.

Moreno, L. and Sarasa, S. (1993). Génesis y desarrollo del Estado de Bienestar en España. *Revista Internacional de Sociologia*, 6, 27–69.

Munday, B. and Ely, P. (Eds.) (1996). *Social Care in Europe*. Hemel Hempstead: Prentice Hall.

Nagel, A.-H. (1991). *Velferdskommunen*. Bergen: Alma Mater.

NCVO (1998). *The Government's Proposals for Best Value*. NCVO Members' Briefing, June.

NOU (1984). *Produktivitetsfremmende reformer i statens budsjettsystem*.

NOU (1988). *Frivillige organisasjoner*.

NOU (1995). *Statlige tilskuddsordninger til barne-og ungdomsorganisasjoner*.

Nylehn, B. and Støkken, A. (1996). *Kommunalt samspill med private. Analyser og eksempler fra tre kommuner*. HBO rapport 6/1996. Bodø.

Offe, C. (1981). 'The attribution of public status to interest groups: observations on the West Germany case', in Berger, S. (ed.), *Organizing interests in Western Europe: pluralism, corporatism, and the transformation of politics*, Cambridge, Cambridge University Press, pp.125–158.

Oliver, M. (1996). 'User involvement in the voluntary sector—a view from the disability movement', in Commission on the Future of the Voluntary Sector, *op. cit.*

Olsen, J. P. (1993). Et statsvitenskaplig perspektiv på offentlig sektor. In Lægreid and Olsen (Eds.), *Organisering av offentlig sektor*. Oslo: Tano.

Olsen, J. P. (1996). Norway: Slow learner—or another triumph of the tortoise? In J. P. Olsen and B. G. Peters (Eds.), *Lessons from experience*. Oslo: Scandinavian University Press.

Onarheim, G. (1990). Organisasjonar for funksjonshemma og tilhøvet til det offentlege. In S. Kuhnle and P. Selle (Eds.), *Frivillig organisert velferd—alternativ offentlig?* Bergen: Alma Mater.

Paci, M. (1987). Long waves in the development of welfare systems. In C. S. Meier (Ed.), *Changing boundaries of the political: Essays on the evolving balance between the state and society, public and private in Europe* (pp. 179–197). Cambridge: Cambridge University Press.

Paci, M. (1989). *Pubblico e privato nei moderni sistemi di welfare*, Napoli, Liguori.

Pasquinelli, S. (1993). Italy: Toward an unplanned partnership. In R. Kramer (Ed.), *Privatization in four European countries*. New York: M.E. Sharpe.

Paton, R. and Batsleer, J. (1997). Managing voluntary organisations in the contract culture: Continuity or change?. In 6, P. and J. Kendall. (Eds.), *The contract culture in public services: Studies from Britain, Europe and the USA*. Aldershot: Arena.

Pavolini, E. (2000). *Politiche pubbliche e terzo settore*. Doctoral Dissertation.

Powell, W. W. and diMaggio, P. J. (Eds.) (1991). *The new institutionalism in organizational analysis*. Chicago/London: The University of Chicago Press.

Powell, W. W. and Friedkin, R. (1987). Organizational Change in Nonprofit Organizations. In W. W. Powell (Ed.), *The nonprofit sector. A research handbook*. New Haven: Yale University Press.

Prins, M. C. (1995). Organisational change in small voluntary organisations: a study of twelve day centres and luncheon clubs for elderly people. Paper presented to *Researching the Voluntary Sector*. National Council for Voluntary Organisations, 7–8 September.

Public Management Service (PUMA), (1995). *Governance in transition: Public management reform in OECD countries*. Paris: OECD.

Putnam, R, Leonardi, R. and Nanetti, R. (1993). *Making democracy work*. Princeton: Princeton University Press.

Raaum, J. (1988). De frivillige organisasjoners framvekst og utvikling i Norge. In NOU 1988: 17, *Frivillige organisasjoner*. Oslo.

Ramar, A. (1996). L'insertion professionnelle des personnes handicapées: les enjeux d'une loi. *Données sociales*. INSEE, 480–486.

Ranci, C. (1994). Il terzo settore nelle politiche di welfare in Italia: le contraddizioni di un mercato protetto. *Stato e Mercato*, 42.

Ranci, C. (1999). *Oltre il Welfare State*. Bologna: Il Mulino.

Ranci, C. and Ascoli, U. (Eds.) (1997). *La solidarietà organizzata*. Roma: FIVOL.

Ranci, C. and Costa, G. (1999). *Dimensioni e caratteristiche delle IPAB. Un quadro nazionale*. Dipartimento Affari Sociali, Roma.

Ranci, C. and Frisanco, R. (eds.) (1999). *Le dimensioni della solidarietà*. Roma: FIVOL.

Ranci, C., Pasquinelli, S. and De Ambrogio, U. (1991). *Identità e servizio. Il volontariato nella crisi del welfare*. Bologna: Il Mulino.

Ranci, C. and Vanoli, A. (1994). *L'evoluzione dei rapporti contrattuali tra operatore pubblico ed imprese senza fine di lucro*. Rapporto ricerca Irs, Fondazione Olivetti.

Ranci, P. and Barbetta, P. (1996). *Fondazioni bancarie italiane verso l'attività grant-making*, Torino, Fondazione Agnelli.

Ravaud, J. F. and Fardeau, M. (Eds.) (1994). *Insertion sociale des personnes handicapées: méthodologies d'évaluation*. CTNERHI–INSERM.

Ravneberg, B. and Solvang, P. (1995). Funksjonshemmedes organisasjoner og personlig assistanse: Skandinaviske utviklingstrekk. In K. Klausen and P. Selle (Eds.), *Frivillig organisering i Norden*. Tano.

Repstad, P. (ed.) (1998). *Den lokale velferdsblanding. Når offentlige og frivillige skal samarbeide*. Oslo: Universitetsforlaget.

Rhodes, R. A. W. (1997). *Understanding Governance. Policy Networks, Governance, Reflexivity and Accountability*. Buchingham: Open University Press.

Richardson, J. (1995). *Purchase-of-Service contracting: Some evidence on UK implementation*. London: National Council for Voluntary Organisations.

Ring, P. S. and van de Ven, A. H. (1992). 'Structuring co-operative relationships between organisations', *Strategic Management Journal*, 13, 483–498.

Robson, P., Locke, M. and Dawson, J. (1997). *Consumerism or Democracy? User involvement in the control of voluntary organisations*. Bristol: The Policy Press.

Rodriguez Cabrero, G. (1990). *El gasto público en Servicios Sociales en España (1972–1988)*. Madrid: Ministerio de Asuntos Sociales.

Rodriguez Cabrero, G. (1993). *Realidad y tendencias del tercer sector en España*. Seminar on State, Altruism and Civil Society organized by the Sociology Department of the Pompeu Fabra University. Barcelona.

Rodriguez Cabrero, G. and Montserrat, J. (1996). *Las entidades voluntarias en España*. Madrid: Ministerio de Asuntos Sociales.

Room, G. (ed.) (1991). *Towards a European welfare state?*. Bristol, SAUS.

Rostgaard, T. and Fridberg, T. (1998). *Caring for children and older people. A comparison of European policies and practises*, The Danish National Institute of Social Research, Copenhagen.

Røvik, K. (1998). *Moderne organisasjoner: trender i organisasjonstenkningen ved tusenårskiftet*. Bergen: Fagbokforlaget.

Russell, J. and Scott, D. (1997). *Very Active Citizens? The impact of the contract culture on volunteers*. University of Manchester: Department of Social Policy and Social Work.

Russell, J., Scott, D. and Wilding, P. (1995). *Mixed Fortunes: the Funding of the Voluntary Sector*. Manchester: University of Manchester.

Sabatier, P. A. (1993). Policy change over a decade or more. In P. A. Sabatier and H. C. Jenkins Smith (Eds.), *Policy change and learning: An advocacy coalition approach*. Westview Press.

Sachsse, C. (1993). Frühformen der Leistungsverwaltung: die kommunale Armenfürsorge im deutschen Kaiserreich. *Jahrbuch für europäische Verwaltungsgeschichte, 5*, 1–20.

Sachsse, C. (1995). Verein, Verband und Wohlfahrtsstaat: Entstehung und Entwicklung der "dualen" Wohlfahrtspflege. In T. Rauschenbach, C. Sachße and T. Olk (Eds.), *Von der Wertgemeinschaft zum Dienstleistungsunternehmen. Jugend- und Wohlfahrtsverbände im Umbruch* (pp. 123–149). Frankfurt am Main: Suhrkamp.

Sainsbury, D. (1994). 'Women's and Men's Social Rights: Gendering Dimensions of Welfare States' in D. Sainsbury (ed.), *Gendering welfare states*, London, Sage, 150–169.

Salamon, L. M. (1987a). Of market failure, voluntary failure, and third-party government: Toward a theory of government–nonprofit relations in the modern Welfare State. In Ostrander and Langton (Eds.), *Shifting the debate. Public/Private Sector relations in the modern Welfare State*. New Brunswick (USA) and Oxford (UK): Transaction Books.

Salamon, L. M. (1987b). Partners in public services: The scope and the theory of government–nonprofit relations. In W. W. Powell (Ed.), *The nonprofit sector. A research handbook* (pp. 99–116). New Haven: Yale University Press.

Salamon, L. M. (1993). The marketization of welfare: Changing nonprofit and for-profit roles in American Welfare State. *Social Service Review*, March, 16–39.

Salamon, L. M. (1995). *Partners in public service. Government–nonprofit relations in the modern Welfare State*. Baltimore and London: The Johns Hopkins University Press.

Salamon, L. M. and Anheier, H. (1994a). *The Emerging Sector; the nonprofit sector in comparative perspective—an overview*. Baltimore: The Johns Hopkins University.

Salamon, L. M. and Anheier, H. (1994b). The Third Route: subsidiarity, Third Party Government and the provision of social services in the United States and Germany. In OECD, *Local Economic and Employment Development, 19, Private sector involvement in the delivery of social welfare services* (pp. 14–34). Paris: OECD.

Salamon, L. M., Anheier, H. and Sokolowski, W. (1995). *The Emerging Sector; a statistical supplement*, Baltimore: Johns Hopkins University.

Salamon, L. M. and Anheier, H. K. (Eds.) (1997). *Defining the nonprofit sector. A cross-national analysis*. Manchester: Manchester University Press.

Salamon, L. M. and Anheier, H. (1998). 'Social Origins of Civil Society: Explaining the Nonprofit Sector Cross-Nationally', in *Voluntas. International Journal of Voluntary and Nonprofit Organisations*, vol.9, no.3, 213-248.

Salamon, L. M., Anheier, H., List, R., Toepler S., Sokolowski S. W. and Associates (1999). *Global Civil Society. Dimensions of the nonprofit sector*, The Johns Hopkins Center for Civil Society Studies, Baltimore.

Sandvin, J. and Søder, M. (1998). Fullt og helt eller stykkevis og delt? En sammenligning av HVPU- reformen og nedbyggingen av institusjonsplasser i psykiatrien. *Tidsskrift for Velferdsforskning*, Årgang 1, *1*, 35–49.

Sarasa, S. (1993). *El servicio de lo social*. Madrid: Ministerio de Asuntos Sociales.

Sarasa, S. (1995). La sociedad civil en la Europa del Sur. In S. Sarasa and L. Moreno (Eds.), *El estado del Bienestar en la Europa del Sur*. Madrid: Consejo Superior de Investigaciones Sociales—IESA.

Sarasa, S. and Martinez, N. (1996). *Informe sobre les necessitats dels disminuïts psiquics a Barcelona*. Barcelona: Instituto de Estudios Sociales Avanzados.

Savas, E. S. (1987). *Privatization. The key to better government*. Chatham: Chatham House.

Schmid, H. (1997). *For-profit and nonprofit human services: A comparative analysis*. Paper presented at the Arnova Conference, Washington.

Schulin, B. (1994). Verträge mit den Leistungserbringern im Pflegeversicherungsrecht (SGB XI). *Vierteljahresschrift für Sozialrecht*, 4, 285–307.

Scott, R. and Meyer, J. (1993). 'The organization of societal sectors: propositions and early evidence', in Powell, W. and DiMaggio, P. (eds) *The New Institutionalism in Organizational Analysis*, Chicago: The University of Chicago Press.

Scott, D. and Russell, J. (2001). 'Contracting: the experience of service delivery agencies' in Harris, M. and Rochester, C. (eds.) *Voluntary Organizations and Social Policy in Britain: perspectives on change and choice*, Basingstoke: Palgrave, pp. 49–63.

Seibel, W. (1989). The function of mellow weakness. Nonprofit organizations as problem nonsolvers in Germany. In E. James (Ed.), *The nonprofit sector in international perspective. Studies in comparative culture and policy*. Oxford: Oxford University Press.

Seibel, W. (1990). Government/third sector relationship in a comparative perspective: The case of France and West-Germany. *Voluntas*, 1/1, May, 42–60.

Seibel W. (1992). Government-nonprofit relationship: styles and linkage patterns in France and Germany, in Kuhnle, S. e Selle, P., (eds.) *Government and voluntary organizations*, Avebury Publ, Aldeshot.

Seip, A.-L. (1984). *Sosialhjelpstaten blir til. Norsk sosialpolitikk 1740–1920*. Oslo: Gyldendal Norsk Forlag.

Selle, P. (1998). Organisasjonssamfunnet—ein statsreiskap? In T. Grønlie and P. Selle (Eds.), *Ein stat?—Fristillingas fire ansikt*. Det Norske Samlaget.

Selle, P. and Øymyr, B. (1995). *Frivillig organisering og demokrati*. Samlaget.

SESI (1995). *L'accueil des jeunes enfants. Informations rapides*, 63.

SESI (1997a). *Les établissements et services en faveur des adultes handicapés au 1er janvier 1994*, 281.

SESI (1997b). *Les établissements et services en faveur des enfants et adolescents handicapés au 1er janvier 1994*, 280.

SEU, Social Exclusion Unit (2001) *A New Commitment to Neighbourhood Regeneration: the action plan*, London: The Stationery Office.

Skov Henriksen, L. (1996). *Lokal frivillig organisering i nye omgivelser*. ALFUFF. Aalborg: Aalborg Universitet.

Smith, R. S. and Lipsky, M. (1993). *Nonprofits for hire. The Welfare State in the age of contracting*, Cambridge: Harvard University Press.

St meld nr 27 (1996–1997). *Om statens forhold til frivillige organisasjoner*.

St meld nr 27 (1996–1997). *Om statens forhold til frivillige organisasjoner*. Kulturdepartementet. Oslo.

Starr, P. (1989). The meaning of Privatization. In S. Kamerman and A. Kahn (Eds.), *Privatization and the Welfare State*. Princeton: Princeton University Press.

Statham, D. (1996). *The future of social and personal care: The role of social services organisations in the public, private and voluntary sectors*. London: National Institute for Social Work.

Statskonsult (1995). *Statlige overføringer til frivillige organisasjoner*. Rapport 1995, 3.

Statskonsult (1996). *Statlig støttepolitikk og endringer i det frivillige organisasjonslivet*. Rapport 1996, 4.

Stiker, H. (1996). Politiques sociales et personnes handicapées. In S. Aymé (Ed.), *Handicap et vieillissement*, INSERM.

Stiker, H. (1998). *Corps infirmes et sociétés*, Dunod.

Streek, W. and Schmitter, P. C. (1985). *Private Interest Government. Beyond Market and State.* London: Sage.

Taylor, M. (1990). *New Times, New Challenges: Voluntary Organisations Facing 1990*, London: National Council for Voluntary Organisations.

Taylor, M. (1992). The changing role of the nonprofit sector in britain: Moving toward the market. In Gidron et al. (Eds.), *Government and the third sector. Emerging relationships in Welfare States.* San Francisco: Jossey-Bass Publishers.

Taylor, M. (1995). *Unleashing the potential: Bringing residents to the centre of estate regeneration.* York: Joseph Rowntree Foundation.

Taylor, M. (1997). Il terzo settore nel Regno Unito. In Rossi (Ed.), *Terzo Settore, Stato e Mercato nella Trasformazione delle Politiche Sociali in Europa.* Milano: FrancoAngeli.

Taylor, M. and Bassi, A. (1996). Changing relationships between national and local government in two European countries: what are the implications for third sector organisations in social care? *Voluntas*, 9:2, 113–136.

Taylor, M. and Hoggett, P. (1993). Quasi markets and the transformation of the independent sector. Paper delivered to the conference *Quasi markets in public sector service delivery.* University of Bristol.

Taylor, M., Langan, J. and Hoggett, P. (1995). *Encouraging diversity: Voluntary and private organisations in community care.* Aldershot: Arena.

Taylor, M. and Lansley, J. (1992). 'Ideology and welfare in the UK: the implications for the voluntary sector', *Voluntas*, 3.2, pp. 153–74.

Tchernonog, V. (1992). The role of the local authorities in the financing and delivery of social welfare services in France. *Innovation and Employment, 10*, Study series, Occasional papers, Paris: OECD.

Tchernonog, V. (1994). Decentralization and privatization of social services in France. In *Local Economic and Employment Development, 19, Private sector involvement in the delivery of social welfare services*, Paris: OECD.

Tennstedt, F. (1992). Die Spitzenverbände der Freien Wohlfahrtspflege im dualen Wohlfahrtsstaat. Ein historischer Rückblick auf die Entwicklung in Deutschland. *Soziale Arbeit, 10–11*, 342–356.

Thery, H. (1986). *La place et le rôle du secteur associatif dans le développement de la politique d'action éducative, sanitaire et sociale*, Conseil économique et social.

Thorsvik, J. (1991). Målstyring av offentlig virksomhet. *Norsk Statsvitenskaplig Tidsskrift*, 4/91 pp. 267–282.

Titmuss, R. (1974). *Social Policy.* London: Allen & Unwin.

Toharia, L. (1994). Empleo y paro. In VVAA. *V° Informe Sociológico sobre la situación social en España.* Madrid: Fundación FOESSA.

Triomphe, A. (Ed.) (1995). *Les personnes handicapées en France: données sociales.* INSERM–CTNERHI.

Try, H. (1985). *Assosiasjonsvekst og foreningsvekst I Norge.* øvre Ervik: Alvheim og Eide.

Turpin, P. (1995). Du coté des associations. *Informations sociales*, 42.

Ullman, C. F. (1992). *Nonprofit organizations, Public funding, and the boundaries of the Welfare State: The politics of public funding of nonprofit social services in France.* Annual Conference of Arnova.

Ullman, C. F. (1993). *New social partners: Nonprofit organizations and the Welfare State in France.* Annual meeting of the American Science Association, Washington.

Ulstein, K. (1998). *Organisasjon og ledelse i frivillig arbeid.* Oslo: Universitetsforlaget.

Unwin, J. and Westland, P. (1996). *Trends, myths and realities: Funding policies and the local voluntary sector*. London: Association of Charitable Foundations/Charities Aid Foundation.

Velche, D. (1995). L'emploi des personnes handicapées. In A. Triomphe (Ed.), *Les personnes handicapées en France: données sociales*. INSERM–CTNERHI.

Vidal, I. (1992). *Les inisictives socials a Catalunya en l'ambit dels serveis socials*. Barcelona: Centre d'Iniciatives de l'Economia Social.

Vilà, A. (1997). *Informe del ámbito autonòmico*. Mimeo. Barcelona.

Walker, A. (1984). The political economy of privatisation. In J. Le Grand and R. Robinson (Eds.), *Privatisation and the welfare state*, London: Allen and Unwin.

Walsh, K., Deakin, N., Smith, P., Spurgeon, P. and Thomas, N. (1997). *Contracting for Change: contracts in health, social care and other local government services*. Oxford: Oxford University Press.

Ware, A. (1990). *Between profit and State: Intermediate organizations in Britain and the United States*. Cambridge: Polity Press.

Weisbrod, B. A. (1988). *The nonprofit economy*. Cambridge, Massachusetts: Harvard University Press.

Wistow, G., Knapp, M., Hardy, B. and Allen, C. (1994). *Social care in a mixed economy*. Buckingham: Open University Press.

Wistow, G., Knapp, M., Hardy, B., Forder, J., Kendall, J. and Manning, R. (1996). *Social care markets: Progress and prospects*. Buckingham: Open University Press.

Woitrain, E. and Ruault, M. (1997). En dix ans, l'accueil en établissement pour adultes handicapés a augmenté de 63%. *Informations rapides—premiers résultats*, SESI, 3, Juillet.

Wolch, J. (1990). *The Shadow State: government and the voluntary sector in transition*. New York: The Foundations Center.

Wollmann, H. (1997). Modernization of the public sector and public administration in the Federal Republic of Germany—(mostly) a story of fragmented incrementalism. In M. Muramatsu and F. Naschold (Eds.), *State and administration in Japan and Germany*. Berlin/New York: de Gruyter.

Wuthnow, R. (1991). *Between States and Markets*. New Jersey: Princeton University Press.

Younghusband, E. (1978). *Social work in Britain: 1950–75, Vol. 1*. London: Allen and Unwin.

Zimmer, A. (1999). 'Corporatis Revisited. The Legacy of Hostory and the German Nonprofit Sector', in *Voluntas. International Journal of Voluntary and Nonprofit Organisations*, vol.10, n.1, pp.37–49.

Zipfel, T. (1994). *On Target: extending partnership to tackle problems on estates*, London: PEP.

Index